GENDER DIFFERENCES IN HUMAN COGNITION

COUNTERPOINTS: *Cognition, Memory, and Language*
SERIES EDITOR: Marc Marschark

Rochester Institute of Technology
National Technical Institute for the Deaf

ADVISORY BOARD

Martin Conway
University of Bristol

Margaret Jean Intons-Peterson
Indiana University

Giovanni Flores d'Arcais
Max-Planck Institute and
University of Padua

Douglas L. Nelson
University of South Florida

Robert S. Siegler
Carnegie Mellon University

STRETCHING THE IMAGINATION
Representation and Transformation in Mental Imagery
C. Cornoldi, R. Logie, M. Brandimonte, G. Kaufmann, D. Reisberg

MODELS OF VISUOSPATIAL COGNITION
M. de Vega, M. J. Intons-Peterson, P. N. Johnson-Laird,
M. Denis, M. Marschark

WORKING MEMORY AND HUMAN COGNITION
J. T. E. Richardson, R. W. Engle, L. Hasher,
R. H. Logie, E. R. Stoltzfus, R. T. Zacks

RELATIONS OF LANGUAGE AND THOUGHT
The View from Sign Language and Deaf Children
M. Marschark, P. Siple, D. Lillo-Martin,
R. Campbell, V. Everhart

GENDER DIFFERENCES IN HUMAN COGNITION
P. J. Caplan, M. Crawford, J. S. Hyde,
J. T. E. Richardson

GENDER DIFFERENCES IN HUMAN COGNITION

PAULA J. CAPLAN
MARY CRAWFORD
JANET SHIBLEY HYDE
JOHN T. E. RICHARDSON

New York   Oxford
OXFORD UNIVERSITY PRESS
1997

Oxford University Press

Oxford   New York
Athens   Auckland   Bangkok   Bogota   Bombay   Buenos Aires
Calcutta   Cape Town   Dar es Salaam   Delhi   Florence   Hong Kong
Istanbul   Karachi   Kuala Lumpur   Madras   Madrid   Melbourne
Mexico City   Nairobi   Paris   Singapore   Taipei   Tokyo   Toronto   Warsaw

and associated companies in
Berlin   Ibadan

Library of Congress Cataloging-in-Publication Data
Gender differences in human cognition / Paula J. Caplan . . . [et al.].
    p.   cm. — (Counterpoints)
Includes bibliographical references and indexes.
ISBN 0-19-511290-3; — ISBN 0-19-511291-1 (pbk.)
1. Cognition.   2. Sex differences (Psychology)   3. Sex role.
I. Caplan, Paula J.   II. Series: Counterpoints (Oxford University Press)
BF311.G445   1997
155.3'3—dc21   96-44115

1 3 5 7 9 8 6 4 2

Printed in the United States of America
on acid-free paper

Preface

This contribution to the Counterpoints series is concerned with the issue of whether women and men differ in terms of their intellectual abilities. Women are sometimes said to outperform men in verbal ability, and men are sometimes said to outperform women in mathematical and spatial ability. Are these assertions true? If so, where should one look for the origins of these differences? In the biological makeup of women and men? In influences during childhood? Or in cultural stereotypes? Yet, if these assertions are not true, why do people continue to make them?

In Chapter 1, I set the scene by providing a brief review of the historical development of research into differences between women and men insofar as it is relevant to contemporary discussions regarding actual or potential differences in intellectual abilities. I then describe the various issues that are involved in conducting and evaluating research on differences between men and women, as well as the broad range of theoretical explanations of the findings obtained in such research.

In Chapter 2, Janet Shibley Hyde and Nita McKinley introduce the techniques of meta-analysis, which have been used to integrate the results of studies on the existence and magnitude of differences in the cognitive performance of men and women. Hyde and McKinley review research on verbal, mathematical, spatial, and scientific abilities, and they examine findings from the Study of Mathematically Precocious Youth. They also describe results that suggest that gender differences have been growing smaller over recent decades.

In Chapter 3, Paula Caplan and Jeremy Caplan maintain that much research on gender differences in cognition has been poorly conceived and executed, and that its findings have been quite irresponsibly interpreted in order to keep women "in their place." They suggest that profound conceptual and methodological problems undermine the validity of research on gender differences in mathematical, spatial, and verbal abilities, and they raise the more basic question of why the search for gender differences in cognition has been, and continues to be, so intense.

In Chapter 4, Mary Crawford and Roger Chaffin illustrate some of the negative consequences of a focus on *differences*. As an alternative, they locate the subject of differences between men and women within a framework that regards gender as a social system that organizes relations of power and status. By referring to research on mathematical and spatial abilities, they use this framework to demonstrate how situational and contextual variables can give rise to systematic gender-related effects on cognitive performance.

Finally, in Chapter 5, I integrate the main conclusions from the various contributors into a single statement regarding the nature and origins of gender differences in human cognition.

The idea for this volume was originally proposed by the series editor, Marc Marschark, and the Executive Editor at Oxford University Press, Joan Bossert. In editing the volume, I have been most grateful for their kind support, for the cooperation and input of the other contributors, and for technical assistance from Mark Mower and his colleagues in the Department of Human Sciences at Brunel University.

Brunel University   *J. T. E. R.*
June 1996

Contents

Contributors

Jeremy B. Caplan, Department of Physics, Brandeis University, Waltham, Massachusetts

Paula J. Caplan, Pembroke Center for Research and Teaching on Women, Brown University, Providence, Rhode Island

Roger Chaffin, Department of Psychology, The College of New Jersey, Trenton, New Jersey

Mary Crawford, Department of Psychology, West Chester University, West Chester, Pennsylvania

Janet Shibley Hyde, Department of Psychology, University of Wisconsin, Madison, Wisconsin

Nita M. McKinley, Department of Psychology, University of Wisconsin, Madison, Wisconsin

John T. E. Richardson, Department of Human Sciences, Brunel University, Uxbridge, Middlesex

GENDER DIFFERENCES IN HUMAN COGNITION

CHAPTER 1

Introduction to the Study of Gender Differences in Cognition

John T. E. Richardson

Men and women have probably been alleged to differ from each other in every area of psychological functioning at some time or another. This book is concerned with the specific hypothesis that women and men differ in terms of their cognitive abilities and, by implication, in terms of the underlying cognitive representations and processes. In his *Dictionary of Psychology,* Drever (1952) explained that "cognition" was "a general term covering all the various modes of knowing—perceiving, imagining, conceiving, judging, reasoning" (p. 42). However, the psychological research exploring gender differences has focused on particular domains of cognitive functioning: mathematical, spatial, and verbal abilities. It is typically claimed that men outperform women in mathematical and spatial abilities, and that women outperform men in verbal abilities. Accordingly, these specific aspects of human cognition are the ones that receive the most attention in this volume.

In this chapter, I briefly review the historical development of research into differences between women and men as it relates to contemporary discussions concerning actual or potential differences in cognition. I then consider methodological issues that are involved in research on differences between men and women and the broad variety of theoretical accounts that tend to be put forward in order to explain the findings obtained in such research. I illustrate some of these issues by discussing the research findings obtained in the case of one particular measure of spatial ability, the Rod and Frame Test. Finally, I summarize the main points to be presented in each of the substantive contributions to this volume and trace the evolving thread of argument that runs through the book as a whole.

HISTORICAL BACKGROUND

The origins of contemporary research on differences between women and men lie in traditional concerns either to support or to refute assumptions and expectations about the appropriate social roles for men and women (see Mosedale, 1978; Shields, 1975). When conventional explanations based upon religious doctrine ceased to command general assent in the early 19th century, scientists and other thinkers began to look for differences that could account for men's supposedly greater intellect, because this, in turn, was assumed to explain the subordinate social position of women and their consequent confinement to the roles of wife and mother.

Because the seat of the intellect was believed to be situated in the brain, researchers focused upon differences between the brains of men and women. The discipline of phrenology was based on the assumption that the structure of the brain would be manifest in the structure of the cranium; consequently, the expected differences in women's and men's brains should be evident in studying the cranium. Phrenologists believed that they had found such differences: The frontal lobe was less developed in women than in men; women's brains were more developed for nurturing traits, but men's were more developed for aggressiveness and constructiveness; and the brain tissue itself was softer in the female brain, they claimed (Walker, 1850).

As more sophisticated techniques were developed for investigating the brain, phrenology fell into disuse, but the search for gender differences favoring men persisted. It was frequently assumed that the female brain was smaller than the male brain, supposedly reflecting inferior reasoning ability. Traditionally, the size of the brain was estimated at autopsy by weighing the excised brain or by measuring the volume of the cranium. In living subjects, the volume of the brain can be estimated indirectly from external measurements of the skull. Today, the volume of the brain can be estimated from X-ray photographs or from magnetic resonance images.

By the mid 1800s, considerable evidence had accumulated that the male brain was indeed both larger and heavier in absolute terms than the female brain. It was usually assumed that the "missing five ounces of the female brain" accounted both for women's alleged intellectual inferiority and for their restricted social position (see Mosedale, 1978). Nevertheless, the use of the absolute size of the brain as an index of intellectual ability was problematic, because it entailed that animals with larger brains were more intelligent than humans were. The hypothesis that the male brain was larger than the female brain was consequently revised to refer to a gender difference in the size of the brain relative to the size of the body.

In fact, the evidence suggested that the weight of the brain relative to the weight of the body was actually greater in women than in men. This led to the development of other measures that might once again confirm the presumed intellectual superiority of men, including comparisons with body height or the weight of the thigh bone (Haller & Haller, 1974, pp. 50–51). It was argued that the surface area of the brain relative to the surface area of the body was greater in men than in women, and more specifically that the cortex of the female brain contained fewer convolutions than its male counterpart. However, one critic pointed out that, on this basis, men ought to be inferior to "certain animals which are regarded as stupid and dull, such as sheep" (see Mosedale, 1978, p. 47).

More recently, adjusting or scaling physiological measurements by the use of simple ratios has been criticized on the grounds that it assumes that the relevant measurement varies *isometrically* with body size: in this case, that absolute brain size is just a direct proportion of body size, so that relative brain size is constant for each sex. Packard and Boardman (1988) showed that these adjustments could give rise to misleading conclusions if the variable in question varied *allometrically* with body size (i.e., if it was not a direct linear function of body size). Jerison (1982) noted that the function that provided the best fit to the relation between brain size and body size, both within the human species and across different species, was a negatively accelerating curve and not a straight line. This implies that relative brain size varies inversely with absolute body size, a point that was demonstrated empirically by Ankney (1992).

During the 19th century, some writers postulated that the average weight of the brain was greater for men than for women of the same height (see Haller & Haller, 1974, p. 51). This seems to have been demonstrated first by Gould (1981, p. 106), but Ankney (1992) confirmed that, for any given body size, the average size of the brain was larger in males than in females. Although some have tried to link this finding to putative gender differences in intelligence (e.g., Lynn, 1994), the difference between men and women in the overall size of their brains does not seem to correspond to any difference in the number of cortical neurons (Haug, 1987). Indeed, Ankney recognized that the difference in brain size might be determined by variables that had little to do with cognitive functioning, such as muscularity or metabolic rate.

The logic of this kind of argument can indeed be reversed. This was first noted by Mosedale (1978), who reported the observation by one 19th-century writer that "the male brain can not fall below 37 ounces without involving idiocy; while the female may fall to 32 ounces without such a result." As Mosedale pointed out, this "seems to imply that the feminine brain surpasses the masculine in 'productive capacity' per ounce of brain tissue, if males require more brain matter to be normal" (p. 32). Since women achieve similar test performance to men across a wide range of abilities despite having smaller brains, Ankney (1992) noted that women's brains might actually be regarded as more efficient than those of men, in that men apparently require more brain tissue to achieve the same level of ability at processing information. This interpretation is consistent with the finding that men and women possess the same number of cortical neurons in spite of the difference in their overall brain size or, in other words, that women have a higher density of neurons than men have (see Haug, 1987; Witelson, Glezer, & Kigar, 1995).

Other researchers examined specific areas of the brain in attempts to prove the alleged superiority of men. Until the end of the 19th century, it was believed that men had more developed frontal lobes but that women had more developed parietal lobes. Some scientists then proposed that the parietal lobes, not the frontal lobes, were the seat of the intellect, and evidence was soon forthcoming to show that in fact it was men who had more developed parietal lobes, but that women had more developed frontal lobes (Mosedale, 1978). More recently, researchers have continued to look for evidence that men and women differ in terms of the anatomical structure of their brains. However, they have tended to move away from making general statements concerning the gross anatomy of the brain to putting forward specific hypotheses about circumscribed neural structures.

One structure of interest is the corpus callosum, the band of fibers that transfers information between the cerebral hemispheres (cf. Gould, 1981, pp. 77–81). In one study, it was claimed that the posterior portion of the corpus callosum was larger and more bulbous in women than in men (de Lacoste-Utamsing & Holloway, 1982), in spite of the fact that women's brains as a whole tend to be smaller than those of men. However, another study based upon a larger sample of cases found no evidence for such a pattern; indeed, in those individuals who had not been consistently right handed, the posterior portion of the corpus callosum tended to be larger in males than in females, even when differences in the total weight of the brain had been taken into account (Witelson, 1985; see also Bleier, 1988).

Recently, other researchers have adopted a different strategy in light of more general developments in understanding the physiology and organization of the brain. They have proposed that women and men differ in the anatomical localization of particular psychological functions in the brain, especially with regard to the lateralization of those functions between the two cerebral hemispheres (see Tavris, 1992). For instance, it has been claimed that women are less likely than men to exhibit asymmetries favoring structures within the left hemisphere that are thought to be involved in language function (Kulynych, Vladar, Jones, & Weinberger, 1994). Speculations of this kind constitute one type of explanation for apparent differences in the cognitive performance of men and women, and I examine them in more detail later in this chapter. Before doing so, however, I need to discuss several methodological and definitional issues that arise in this kind of research.

RESEARCH ISSUES

First, it is very important to clarify the distinction between *sex differences* and *gender differences*. "Sex" marks an essentially biological distinction between women and men that may be based upon their anatomical, physiological, or chromosomal properties. "Gender" marks a sociocultural distinction between men and women on the basis of the traits and behavior that are conventionally regarded as characteristic of and appropriate to the two groups of people. Feminist theorists and others have classically argued that gender is a social construction that is linked by society to each sex in a wholly arbitrary way and learned quite independently of the underlying biological information (see Humm, 1989, pp. 84, 203; Tresemer, 1975; Unger, 1979). In most psychological research (but not all), it is appropriate to talk of "gender differences" rather than "sex differences," because the participants are categorized on the basis of their outward appearance and behavior, not on the basis of biological characteristics. This is reflected in the title that we have chosen for this volume.

The idea that "gender" is constructed, created, and acquired through social interactions is often contrasted uncritically with the notion that "sex" is given, innate, and based upon objective biological reality. For instance, in introducing a recent volume concerned with the psychology of gender (Beall & Sternberg, 1993), Sternberg (1993) asserted that "everyone agrees that sex is biologically determined" (p. 2), and, indeed, all the contributors to that volume appear to concur with this idea without exception. Recently, however, radical feminist theorists have pointed out that the biological notion of sex is itself socially constructed: More precisely, it is constituted in those cultural practices according to which specific biological characteristics or markers are taken to "underlie" the assumed dichotomy between male and female.

This can be illustrated by the fate of those children born in Western societies who do not fit neatly into one of the two available categories. Children with congenital adrenal hyperplasia, for example, receive surgery and hormonal treatment in order to reconcile their external appearance and sexual functioning with their gonadal structures and chromosomal status. On the other hand, children with Turner's syndrome are invariably labeled as "female" on the basis of their genital anatomy, even though they are in other respects essentially neuter. Either way, society chooses to alter the children in question rather than to expand the available categories. Nevertheless, other societies may construe the distinction between "male" and "female" in quite different ways (see, e.g., Porter Poole, 1981).

Although borderline examples arise in both cases, "sex" and "gender" relate to distinctions that are constructed as rigorous dichotomies. In contrast, most actual or alleged differences between females and males in their physical characteristics and their behavior constitute overlapping distributions on a continuous dimension rather than any strict dimorphism (see Morgan, 1980; Nyborg, 1983). Height and weight are obvious examples of this. Moreover, to talk of a "difference" tends to stress the contrast between these two groups at the expense of the within-group variation. A number of authors have noted that, in the case of psychological variables, gender differences often do not occur at all and that, when they do occur, their magnitude (in other words, the degree of separation between the two distributions) is often very small relative to the overall variation (see Anderson, 1987; Caplan, MacPherson, & Tobin, 1985; Hyde, 1981; Jacklin, 1981; Plomin & Foch, 1981; see also Chapter 2, this volume).

Some researchers have noted that even modest gender differences in ability could have major practical consequences (Eagly, 1995; Rosenthal & Rubin, 1982), especially if the effects are cumulative across individuals, or if people are being sampled from one end of a distribution, as in selection for education, training, or employment (Burnett, 1986; Johnson & Meade, 1987). However, such comments in themselves already assume that there are differences between women and men in terms of their underlying cognitive abilities and not simply in terms of observable behavior. To predicate social policies and action upon such assumptions runs the risk of reinforcing and perpetuating differential patterns of behavior in men and women, when these may in fact originate not in differences in ability but in social or cultural influences (see Chapter 3, this volume).

Sex and gender are also classification variables that are determined in advance of a research project rather than treatment variables that are under experimental control. In other words, in making comparisons between men and women, it is not possible to assign the participants at random to two different groups or conditions. It follows that the findings will be purely correlational in nature, and that any differences may well be due to the effects of other variables that are confounded with sex or gender (Ferguson & Takane, 1989, pp. 238, 246). These will presumably include the participants' socialization experiences and educational background, although precisely which variables will need to be taken into account may be far from clear (Anderson, 1987; Crawford, 1989; Hult & Brous, 1986).

The difficulty of constructing matched samples of women and men is often compounded, because for convenience most researchers obtain their participants from within particular institutions that recruit, select, or otherwise accept candidates according to criteria that are biased toward one gender or the other. As with most other areas of psychological research, the majority of research into gender differences is conducted using students in higher education and especially students taking introductory courses in psychology. However, men and women do not have the same opportunities to enter higher education or the same reasons and motives to pursue particular academic disciplines, and in some situations they may even be subject to different admission requirements (Grady, 1981; Hyde, Geiringer, & Yen, 1975).

A different problem in evaluating research on gender differences is that of publication bias (see Caplan, 1979). Jacklin (1981) expressed this point as follows: "If a positive instance is found, it is much easier to publish; it is more likely to be reprinted; it gets into the abstracts. In short, it becomes a part of the literature" (p. 267). In contrast, research studies that reveal no significant difference between males and females might be less likely to be accepted for publication. Rosenthal (1979) referred to this as the "file drawer problem," since the studies in question would be unpublished and would remain in the author's file drawer. Janet Shibley Hyde and Nita McKinley comment on this phenomenon in Chapter 2. As Grady (1981) commented, there is, as a consequence, no research literature of gender similarities, but only a research literature of gender differences. Moreover, any genuine differences in performance that do arise are likely to be exaggerated in their significance, and any spurious findings are likely to remain in the literature, even when they have proved impossible to replicate (Caplan et al., 1985; Eichler, 1988; Maccoby & Jacklin, 1974, pp. 3–5).

Nevertheless, most researchers totally ignore gender as an important social variable (see Peeck, 1973). Gender may be omitted from the design of the original experiment, overlooked in the data analysis, or eliminated from the final report; Maccoby and Jacklin (1974, p. 5) cited a case where findings of significant gender differences had been removed from a paper before publication under editorial instructions. Eichler (1988, chap. 4) declaimed against such "gender insensitivity" as a profound methodological problem that was inherently sexist in its probable consequences. However, other feminist writers have criticized the practice of routinely testing for gender differences without a coherent theoretical justification, thus generating a literature that is replete with "inconsequential, accidental, and incidental findings" (Grady, 1981, p. 632; see also Chapter 3, this volume).

BIOLOGICAL THEORIES

Human cognition is situated at the interface between biology and culture. On the one hand, the normal functioning of human intellectual capabilities is causally dependent upon the biological integrity of the human brain and ultimately upon that of the entire human organism. The same intellectual capabilities, in turn, represent the causal substrate that makes all forms of social behavior possible and, in particular, underpins the complex system of rule-governed institutions and interactions that constitutes a culture. On the other hand, the contents and the strategies of human cognition are acquired through experience with the social and physical world, and they are organized by means of a rich network of generic knowledge structures that are constituted and transmitted by means of sociocultural practices. In principle, then, individual differences in human cognitive functioning could originate in either biological or sociocultural processes.

Apparent differences between men and women in terms of psychological variables have traditionally been described as "sex differences," but one consequence of this is that the attention of researchers is drawn toward biological processes in endeavoring to explain these apparent differences (see Chapter 3, this volume). Indeed, the very use of the term "sex" often reflects the uncritical assumption that a biological mechanism is involved, and some critics (e.g., Grady, 1981; Unger, 1979) have pointed out that a vague reference to unspecified biological factors is sometimes offered as if it were a wholly sufficient explanation of the findings obtained. This device is often, in turn, an occasion for wild speculation concerning the evolutionary pressures that might have led to such findings. For example, the apparent tendency for men to excel in some spatial tests has been related to their exploratory and hunting behavior within subsistence environments (Buss, 1995; Dawson, 1972). This conveniently ignores the importance of spatial abilities for women in gathering food and keeping track of their children's whereabouts in the same environments.

Of course, explaining how some particular aspect of human performance might be prescribed for each individual as a portion of their genetic code is a major problem that has yet to be resolved in any domain of behavior. Genetic accounts of differences in the performance of women and men have been thought to be supported indirectly by findings of population studies and research on twins (e.g., Eliot & Fralley, 1976; McGee, 1979), as well as work on individuals with chromosomal abnormalities or endocrinological disturbances (Dawson, 1972; Temple & Carney, 1993). However, the detailed performance profiles of these latter individuals do not represent a simple exaggeration of normal gender differences (see Temple & Carney, 1995).

The normal chromosomal genotype is XY in males and XX in females. A particular explanation that is associated with the work of Stafford (1961), but that is at least 20 years older, postulates that spatial abilities are enhanced by a recessive gene that is linked to the X chromosome, so that in females the action of this gene may be countered by its allele on the second chromosome. This predicts a specific pattern of intercorrelations among different family members in terms of their spatial performance. However, these predictions have not been confirmed in empirical research (Bouchard & McGee, 1977; see also Caplan et al., 1985).

The theory that differences in the spatial abilities of men and women have a biological origin has been employed to argue for a biological basis for sexual orientation, too. Sanders and Ross-Field (1986) found that the performance of gay men on certain visuospatial tasks was similar to that of lesbians and poorer than that of heterosexual men. They postulated that perinatal exposure to "feminizing" hormones had influenced the development of both sexual orientation and cognitive ability. Gladue, Beatty, Larson, and Staton (1990) remarked that, on the analogous argument that lesbianism was associated with perinatal exposure to "masculinizing" hormones, lesbians should be expected to outperform heterosexual women on visuospatial tasks. In fact, they found no such difference in a test of mental rotation and significantly poorer performance in lesbians than in heterosexual women on a water-jar test. Even so, Gladue et al. continued to insist that their findings were "more compatible with a biological than with a psychosocial explanation of gender and sexual orientation differences in certain aspects of spatial ability" (p. 107).

As Caplan and Caplan remark in Chapter 3, biological accounts serve to reify the notion that there do exist reliable and consistent differences in terms of the cognitive abilities of men and women. However, such accounts have the problem of explaining how genetic, physiological, or hormonal differences between women and men come to be implicated in the mechanisms controlling human cognition. One solution is to appeal to the apparent representation of linguistic and spatial skills within the brain. Buffery and Gray (1972) claimed that the lateralization of language function within the left cerebral hemisphere (in other words, cerebral "dominance") occurred at an earlier stage in girls than in boys. They suggested that this constrained the development of spatial skills to the residual cortical regions within the right cerebral hemisphere, whereas these skills were able to develop in a bilateral manner among boys. Buffery and Gray then hypothesized that a bilateral representation of spatial skills would be more efficient than a unilateral one, and they concluded that this would explain the supposed superiority of men in tests of spatial ability.

An alternative theory was put forward by Levy (1972), who suggested that in many individuals spatial skills were represented within the right cerebral hemisphere but that women and left-handed men were somewhat more likely than right-handed men to have bilateral representation of language function. Consequently, she argued, the encroachment of verbal processes into the right cerebral hemisphere would lead to poorer spatial abilities. However, both this theory and that of Buffery and Gray were subjected to considerable criticism, and neither is well supported by the available empirical data (see Bleier, 1988; Fairweather, 1976; Fausto-Sterling, 1992; Marshall, 1973; Sherman, 1978, pp. 112–118; Tavris, 1992). Indeed, it can be doubted whether the existing evidence is sufficiently sound or coherent to motivate any particular theory concerning differences between women and men in the representation of cognitive faculties in the brain (see Bryden, 1982; McGlone, 1980).

One category of task that typically generates statistically reliable gender differences in performance is that involving the mental rotation of representations of two- or three-dimensional objects (see Chapter 2, this volume). However, in this kind of task, normal individuals usually exhibit either no difference in their speed or accuracy between stimuli presented in the left and right hemifields (Cohen & Polich, 1989; Corballis, 1982) or a right visual-field (left hemisphere) advantage that shows little difference between males and females (Masters, 1989; Ronsaville, 1986). Some writers have postulated that the efficient performance of complex cognitive tasks depends upon an active cooperation between the two hemispheres in all individuals (Caplan et al., 1985; McGuinness, 1980) or that variations in the organization of brain function may lead to differences in the use of cognitive strategies rather than to differences in abilities (Sherman, 1980; Wolff, 1980).

Another problem for biological accounts is to explain why it is that apparent differences between men and women in significant domains such as language, mathematics, or spatial thinking are often not manifested until adolescence or early adulthood (Unger, 1979) and, even then, are often not manifested in a consistent or reliable manner. Although such observations could be readily ascribed to the normal processes of socialization during childhood and adolescence, researchers who are biologically inclined have endeavored to link the development of these functions with puberty and the consequent increase in the circulating levels of reproductive hormones. A theoretical paper by Broverman, Klaiber, Kobayashi, and Vogel (1968) cited the effects of gonadal steroids in order to explain the "well-established differences between males and females in cognitive abilities" (p. 24).

On the basis of current neurophysiological thinking, Broverman et al. (1968) speculated that performance in simple (or "automatized") perceptual-motor tasks depended upon the activating influence of the central adrenergic nervous system, whereas performance in abstract perceptual-restructuring tasks depended upon the inhibitory influence of the central cholinergic nervous system. They then argued that women tended to be more activated and less inhibited than men were because of differences in the levels of circulating estrogen and androgen. In women, these differences would obviously be modulated by the normal cyclical processes of ovulation and menstruation (see Broverman, Vogel, Klaiber, Majcher, Shea, & Paul, 1981).

Broverman et al. (1968) claimed that available psychopharmacological research broadly supported their theory, but Parlee (1973) suggested that there was little or no direct evidence to support a number of fundamental assumptions in the theory. Moreover, both Parlee (1972) and Maccoby and Jacklin (1974, pp. 99–102) claimed that the putative findings which their theory was supposed to explain were simply unreliable; and, in subsequent research, variations in women's cognitive performance across the menstrual cycle have proved very hard to replicate (see Sommer, 1992, for a recent review). Nevertheless, the theory that was put forward by Broverman et al. (1968) remains the only fully articulated analysis of the effects of reproductive hormones on human cognitive processing.

SOCIOCULTURAL THEORIES

In contrast, one consequence of talking about "gender differences" (rather than "sex differences") is that researchers' attention is directed toward sociocultural factors in seeking to explain observed differences between the cognitive performance of women and men (Unger, 1979). Indeed, the magnitude of these differences is influenced by a number of nonbiological variables (Fairweather, 1976). For example, cognitive ability can depend upon the gender of rearing as much as upon biological sex when these are differentiated as the result of chromosomal abnormalities (Dawson, 1972; Unger, 1979). There is evidence of variation across cultures in the magnitude of differences in performance between men and women (Maccoby & Jacklin, 1974, pp. 129–133, 362), and in all cultures there are major differences in the socialization of boys and girls. Other researchers have suggested that apparent differences in the abilities of women and men may actually be artifacts arising from the use of materials or procedures that elicit stereotypical behavior among the participants (see Chapter 3, this volume).

A different possibility is that participants' expectations, beliefs, and attitudes induce them to perceive the tasks in question as being more congenial or more appropriate to men rather than to women, or vice versa. For instance, within Western cultures, spatial tasks tend to be perceived as being masculine in nature (Newcombe, Bandura, & Taylor, 1983; Stein & Smithells, 1969), a phenomenon that Markus and Oyserman (1989) related to the development of the self concept. Older women in particular appear to find these tasks both difficult and stressful (Wilson, DeFries, McClearn, Vandenberg, Johnson, & Rashad, 1975). There is evidence that the tendency for men to perform better than women on these tasks can be eliminated or even reversed when the participants are given instructions that disguise or deemphasize their spatial nature and render them more appropriate to women rather than to men (Birkett, 1976; Naditch, 1976, abstracted in Sherman, 1978, pp. 229–230; Sharps, Welton, & Price, 1993; however, cf. Richardson, 1994). Analogous results with regard to verbal memory are described in Chapter 4 of this volume.

In any field of experimental research, the possibility has to be considered that the findings may result from the participants' being subtly cued by the researcher or being influenced by unintended aspects of the researcher's behavior. In experiments in which the participants had to rate personal characteristics of people whose faces were presented as photographs, Rosenthal (1976, pp. 47–51) found that both male and female experimenters smiled at female participants more than at male participants before and during the administration of the instructions, and they glanced at female participants more than at male participants during the intervals between the presentation of successive faces to be rated. Moreover, both male and female experimenters exchanged fewer glances with participants of the other gender while reading the formal instructions and also tended to prolong the intervals between successive faces if testing participants of the other gender. Rosenthal concluded that an experimenter's behavior was related sometimes to the gender of the participants, sometimes to their own gender, and sometimes to both of these variables. As a result, "male and female subjects may, psychologically, simply not be in the same experiment at all" (p. 56; see also Caplan, 1979).

However, "passive" experimenter effects that seem to result from the mere presence of an experimenter of one gender or the other have also been found. For example, participants tend to report more irrelevant thoughts and images when they are tested by an experimenter of the other gender (see

Algom & Singer, 1984–85; Giambra, 1988–89). Nevertheless, several experiments have found that participants tend to achieve higher levels of performance under these circumstances (Archer, Cejka, & Thompson, 1961; Littig & Waddell, 1967; Stevenson & Allen, 1964). Stevenson and Allen hypothesized that being tested by an experimenter of the other gender "may result in increased competitiveness, higher anxiety, a greater desire to please, or a change in some other psychological process" (p. 216). These effects will presumably be contingent on the participants' personality and sexual orientation. For instance, Gralton, Hayes, and Richardson (1979) found that being tested by experimenters of the other gender gave rise to better performance in extraverts but to poorer performance in introverts.

Richardson (1982) pointed out that research on pupillary dilation had suggested that being tested by an experimenter of the other gender induced an increased level of arousal in heterosexual participants. He also noted that effects of individual differences in introversion-extraversion were typically attributed to variations in arousal or emotional responsiveness. He then pointed out that the results of Gralton et al. (1979) were wholly consistent with the view that introverts naturally approach optimal levels of arousal (and so would be impaired by any further increase in arousal), but that extraverts are naturally at suboptimal levels of arousal (and so would benefit from any increase in arousal). Certain manipulations would compound these effects of being tested by an experimenter of the other gender. For instance, in eye-blink conditioning experiments, subjects are typically tested in a horizontal position in an isolated dark room that contains elaborate technical equipment. It is known that female subjects tend to condition more readily than males, but also that anxiety produces faster conditioning. It seems likely that the apparent gender difference is largely the result of female subjects' greater anxiety when tested by male researchers in such a setting (Jacklin, 1981; Sherman, 1978, p. 25).

If differences between men and women in terms of their performance in cognitive tasks result from differential life experience, then it would be anticipated that such differences could be modified or eliminated by means of extended practice or training on the relevant tasks. There is evidence in accordance with this prediction at least in the case of spatial ability (Caplan et al., 1985; Sherman, 1978, pp. 168–169; although cf. Baenninger & Newcombe, 1989). Moreover, Burnett and Lane (1980) found that scores on the Guilford-Zimmerman Spatial Visualization Test tended to improve during a program of study in higher education. This improvement was greater in students majoring in mathematics and the physical sciences than in those majoring in the humanities and the social sciences. In all courses, men produced better performance than women when tested soon after admission to college, but in the physics majors the magnitude of this difference was significantly reduced when they were retested at the end of their fourth semester. Richardson (1994) obtained similar results in some aspects of spatial ability but not in others.

A different sort of evidence comes from the study of changes in the magnitude of differences between the performance of men and women over the course of time. According to Kogan (1978), Jacklin and Maccoby (1972) made an informal observation that differences in the intellectual ability of women and men appeared to have diminished in magnitude or even to have disappeared entirely in the findings of more recent investigations. This trend was confirmed by means of a formal meta-analysis that was conducted by Rosenthal and Rubin (1982) and also in a number of subsequent reports (Emanuelsson & Svensson, 1986; Feingold, 1988; Hilton, 1985; Hyde & Linn, 1988; Linn & Hyde, 1989; Stumpf & Klieme, 1989; but cf. Masters & Sanders, 1993; Voyer, Voyer, & Bryden, 1995). Hyde and McKinley discuss this issue in detail in Chapter 2 of this volume.

Rosenthal and Rubin (1982) commented that it was not at all clear how biological accounts of differences in the cognitive performance of men and women could be reconciled with shifts in the magnitude of such differences within a single generation. They concluded that this should make one "reluctant to make strong biogenic interpretations of such differences" (p. 711). Proponents of sociocultural accounts would have little or no difficulty in accommodating these findings, however, because the last 30 years have seen many changes in cultural attitudes and in educational and employment opportunities. In particular, as Kogan (1978) noted, there has been a "progressive reduction in sex-typed socialization practices in the home and school" (p. 103). It is notable too that a trend for differences between females and males to disappear has been most apparent in countries such as Sweden or the United States where more vigorous statutory measures have been adopted in order to secure equal opportunities in both education and employment (see, e.g., Emanuelsson & Svensson, 1986).

A CASE STUDY: THE ROD AND FRAME TEST

Many of the methodological issues mentioned above can be illustrated by the Rod and Frame Test (RFT), which was originally devised as a test of spatial orientation by Witkin and Asch (1948). In this procedure, the participant is presented with a movable luminous rod surrounded by a square luminous frame in an otherwise dark room. The rod and the frame are presented in an orientation that is rotated 28° to the left or the right from the true (i.e., gravitational) vertical. On 16 of the 24 trials, the chair on which the participant is seated is also tilted 28° either to the same side or to the opposite side as the frame. The participant's task is to instruct the experimenter to rotate the rod until it lies at the true vertical, and the final deviation of the rod from the vertical is taken as the measure of performance. The typical finding, the rod and frame effect (RFE), is that the participant places the rod tilted in the direction of the frame, which indicates that spatial orientation is influenced by the position of the prevailing visual field. The magnitude of the RFE is enhanced when the participant's body is itself tilted from the true vertical, and it is greatest when the body is tilted in the opposite direction to the frame (Witkin, Lewis, Hertzman, Machover, Meissner, & Wapner, 1954, pp. 25–27, 34, 42–44).

Witkin et al. (1954, chap. 6) found that performance on the RFT was correlated with performance on other tests that required the separation of a stimulus from the field in which it was incorporated but did not involve orientation toward the upright. An example is the Embedded Figures Test (EFT), which requires participants to find a simple figure within a larger complex figure. This suggested that these tests were measuring a single trait constituting a person's degree of independence from the structure of the prevailing visual field (p. 119). Subsequent research indicated that performance on the RFT was related to other cognitive dimensions that involved spatial restructuring, and it was concluded that tests such as the RFT and the EFT were primary indicators of *field independence* as a fundamental cognitive style (Witkin & Goodenough, 1981). Today, field independence is often characterized as a major determinant of cognitive and social functioning, although in practice it is rarely measured using the RFT (see Jonassen & Grabowski, 1993, pp. 87–98).

Nevertheless, more recent research suggests that the RFE may depend upon more basic forms of visual processing that have little or nothing to do with high-level cognition. Cian, Esquivié, Barraud, and Raphel (1995) showed that, when the participant's body was upright, the size of the RFE increased with the visual angle subtended by the display; this indicated that it was enhanced by mechanisms in peripheral vision. They also found that the size of the RFE was predicted independently by the tilt illusion (obtained when adjusting a rod to the vertical in the presence of a tilted inducing line) and by the self-tilt illusion (obtained when adjusting the body to the vertical in the presence of just a tilted frame). They argued that the RFE resulted from two components: an orientation-contrast effect that was mainly responsible for the RFE under parafoveal stimulation; and a visuovestibular or vection effect upon perceived posture that was mainly responsible for the RFE under peripheral stimulation. This conclusion was confirmed in a separate study by Cian and Raphel (1995), in which the RFE was attenuated (but not eliminated) when the visuovestibular component was removed by presenting the rod-and-frame displays tachistoscopically.

Witkin et al. (1954, p. 44) noted that errors in all the conditions of the RFT were significantly greater among women than among men. They concluded that "women, on the average, tend more than men to perceive the upright in accordance with the position of the visual field, and also are less able to utilize the position of their own bodies in perceiving the rod independently of its background" (p. 155). Gender differences were obtained on the EFT and some other tasks, and this led to the more global proposition that, "in perceptual situations where an item must be kept 'separate' from the surrounding field, women generally prove more field dependent or less analytical than men, in the sense of being more affected by the context in which the item occurs" (p. 170). There are, however, a number of fundamental problems with this account:

- Some other investigators have found that males are more field independent than females from early adolescence on, but others have failed to show this. It would appear that the EFT is less likely to give rise to statistically significant differences than the RFT is (Maccoby & Jacklin, 1974, pp. 95–97; Voyer et al., 1995; see also Chatterjea & Paul, 1982; Petrakis, 1981).
- In his original account of the EFT, Witkin (1950) presented data that showed a substantial practice effect across the individual stimulus items. Witkin et al. (1954, p. 86) subsequently reported significant practice effects in a retest that was carried out 3 years after the initial administration of the EFT. Goldstein and Chance (1965) confirmed that practice on the EFT led to substantial improvements in performance, and they pointed out that this was inconsistent with the idea that it was measuring a relatively constant psychological trait. They found a significant gender difference on the initial test items, but there was no sign of a gender difference after extended practice. Goldstein and Chance suggested that the initial difference reflected motivational factors rather than differences in perceptual ability.
- Witkin et al. (1954, pp. 85–88, 164–165) found that performance on the EFT was significantly correlated with performance on the RFT in the case of 46 men ($r = 0.64$) but not in the case of 45 women ($r = 0.21$). This was interpreted to mean that specific variations in the structure of these orientation tasks were pertinent for women but not for men. Nevertheless, it clearly undermines the notion of a single underlying dimension of field independence measured jointly by the EFT and the RFT, along which men are generally superior to women.

In fact, although the account that was offered by Witkin et al. (1954) was meant to apply to "women generally" (p. 170), Witkin (1979) subsequently became far more tentative: "While this difference is a persistent one, it is small in magnitude. The range within each sex is vastly greater than the difference in means between the sexes" (p. 368).

In addition, Sherman (1978, pp. 25–26) argued that gender differences on the RFT might be purely artifactual. To begin with, she commented that women's performance on the test might be affected by their unease at being tested by a (typically male) experimenter under conditions of nearly total darkness. Indeed, she implied that there were anecdotal reports of actual sexual harassment in these circumstances. The testing procedure for the RFT is in fact even more bizarre than Sherman suggested: The participant is brought into the test room blindfolded, is helped into the chair, and remains blindfolded for 4 minutes while the experimenter adjusts the headrest and administers the experimental instructions. Even after removal of the blindfold, the participant is required to sit with eyes closed for periods of up to 1 minute between successive trials (Witkin et al., 1954, pp. 26–27). Witkin et al. also reported that some of their own participants had become so disorientated that they felt unable to continue with the test (p. 47).

As in the case of eye-blink conditioning (see previous section), it is possible that the apparent gender difference in performance is the result of female subjects' greater anxiety when tested by male researchers in this setting. Indeed, Witkin et al. (1954, p. 191) had found that performance on the RFT was much worse in participants who were judged as "anxious" rather than as "self-assured" in a clinical interview, particularly in the most difficult condition (where they were tilted in the opposite direction to the frame). As Sherman (1978) noted, this problem could be alleviated by the use of the portable, table-top version of the RFT, which is intended to be used in normal lighting conditions. Oltman (1968), who devised this apparatus, found gender differences of similar magnitude on the standard and portable versions of the RFT, but in neither case was the difference statistically significant. However, Bogo, Winget, and Gleser (1970) found that men were significantly more field independent than women on the portable RFT.

Sherman (1978) also noted that, in the administration of the standard RFT, the rod was adjusted by the experimenter in small steps until stopped by the participant, and that as a consequence accurate responding demanded assertive social behavior. As she commented, those participants who were either not assertive in their character or not used to being assertive as part of their social role might be less likely to bother the experimenter to ensure that the rod was accurately adjusted. She noted that Witkin et al. (1954, p. 191) had found that performance on the RFT was worse in the participants who were judged as "passive" in the clinical interview. This problem appears not to arise in the tachistoscopic procedure employed by Cian and Raphel (1995). In this version of the RFT, the participants were presented with a

TABLE 1-1. Mean Errors (in Degrees) in Standard and Tachoscopic Versions of the Rod and Frame Test (RFT) by Size of Display (28° vs. 7°) and Gender of Participants

	Standard RFT		Tachistoscopic RFT	
	28°	7°	28°	7°
Men	2.36	0.11	0.73	0.54
Women	4.76	1.10	1.43	0.46
Overall	3.50	0.58	1.06	0.50

Source: Unpublished data from Cian and Raphel (1995).

random sequence of stimuli, each showing a frame tilted 28° to the left or the right and a rod at one possible orientation between 10° to the left and 10° to the right in steps of 1°. The entire procedure was computer-controlled, and on each trial the task was to respond whether or not the rod was in an upright position by pressing one of two keys.

Cian and Raphel had recorded the gender of 19 of the 24 participants in their Experiment 3, which involved large displays subtending 28° and small displays subtending 7° of visual angle. The standard RFT with free time adjustment of the rod was compared with a tachistoscopic RFT using a presentation time of 2,000 msec. The mean errors are shown in Table 1-1. Because of heterogeneous variances over the various groups and conditions, a square-root transformation was applied to the data before an analysis of variance was carried out, using the between-subjects factor of gender and the within-subjects factors of task and visual angle. The main effects of both task and visual angle were highly significant, as was the interaction between these factors. As in the original data, the use of tachistoscopic presentation reduced (but did not eliminate) the RFE. The main effect of gender was not significant, but it did generate a significant interaction with the effect of task. The effect of gender was significant for both large and small displays in the standard RFT but was not significant for large or small displays in the tachistoscopic RFT. This suggests that any gender differences that are obtained using the standard RFT are dependent on procedural variables (especially the need to instruct the experimenter) and do not reflect any intrinsic characteristics of women and men.

THE STRUCTURE OF THIS BOOK

This brief account has covered the range of theoretical options that have been exploited in endeavoring to explain observed differences between men and women in terms of their cognitive performance. In many cases, I have indicated the sorts of empirical evidence that would be taken either to confirm such accounts or to create difficulties for such accounts, although it is in the nature of scientific explanations that it is usually difficult if not impossible to refute them in any conclusive manner, since they can typically be elaborated to accommodate apparent counterevidence. Moreover, I have tried not to take a position as to the truth or falsehood of any specific account, because this would prejudge the arguments and the evidence that are to be presented in the following chapters. In any case, it may turn out that different accounts are needed to explain differences between women and men in different domains of cognitive functioning (such as mathematical abilities, spatial abilities, and verbal abilities).

In Chapter 2, Janet Shibley Hyde and Nita McKinley introduce the statistical technique of meta-analysis. This constitutes a quantitative method for evaluating what different research studies, taken together, have to say about the existence and magnitude of differences in cognitive performance between men and women. They review the results of meta-analyses concerning differences in verbal, mathematical, spatial, and scientific abilities, and they examine the evidence obtained from the much-publicized Study of Mathematically Precocious Youth. They then examine evidence that gender differences have been growing smaller in terms of their absolute magnitude over recent decades. Finally, they discuss the idea that men as a group exhibit greater variability in their cognitive performance than women and the possibility that this difference, too, has been growing smaller over the course of time.

Paula Caplan and Jeremy Caplan begin Chapter 3 by remarking that so-called scientific research concerning differences between men and women in cognitive abilities and performance has been used historically to "keep women in their place," despite the fact that this research has often been poorly conceived and executed and its findings irresponsibly interpreted. They then discuss some of the major conceptual and methodological problems in research concerning differences in mathematical, spatial, and verbal abilities, under the headings of definitional dilemmas, problems in specific studies, problems in reviews of the literature, and problems with the construction of theories. Finally, they raise the underlying question of why the search for differences between women and men in terms of their cognitive performance has been and continues to be so intense.

In Chapter 4, Mary Crawford and Roger Chaffin illustrate some of the consequences of this focus upon difference. They argue that it leads to a proliferation of studies that treat the sex of the participants as a decontextualized variable, that it encourages a dichotomization of the sexes, and that it fosters individual explanations for behavior at the expense of sociocultural or situational explanations. As an alternative, they locate the subject of differences between men and women within a framework that conceives of gender as being a social system that organizes relationships of power and status. This gender system can be analyzed at three different levels: sociocultural, interactional, and individual.

Crawford and Chaffin argue that the gender system operates so as to sustain a social system of inequality at each level. They go on to provide a selective review of the research into mathematical and spatial abilities to try to demonstrate how gender-related effects on cognitive performance can be systematically produced, particularly at the interactional level. Crawford and Chaffin point out that the gender system framework connects with recent models of "situated cognition," and that it helps in examining issues of sex differences and the social order. They conclude that it is a means of expanding one's understanding of how situation and context give rise to "sex differences in ability."

The subject of differences between men and women in their cognitive abilities and performance is certainly a classic topic for a contribution to the *Counterpoints* series. There are current disputes about what the relevant phenomena actually are, about how they can most appropriately be investigated, and whether in developing theoretical explanations of these differences it is more useful to appeal to biological or to sociocultural mechanisms and processes. In the concluding chapter, I identify the main conclusions that will have emerged from the substantive contributions to this volume, and I try to integrate them into a single statement regarding the nature and origins of gender differences in human cognition.

ACKNOWLEDGMENTS

I have developed many of the ideas in this chapter from a previous article cited in the References section as Richardson (1991). I am grateful to Janet Shibley Hyde and Nita McKinley for their contribution on the historical background to ideas concerning gender differences in human cognition; to Jeremy Caplan, Paula Caplan, Roger Chaffin, Mary Crawford, and Michael Wright for their advice, comments, criticisms, and suggestions; and to Corinne Cian for kindly providing the raw data that are summarized in Table 1-1.

REFERENCES

Algom, D., & Singer, J. L. (1984–85). Interpersonal influences on task-irrelevant thought and imagery in a signal detection experiment. *Imagination, Cognition, and Personality, 4,* 69–83.

Anderson, N. S. (1987). Cognition, learning, and memory. In M. A. Baker (Ed.), *Sex differences in human performance* (pp. 37–54). Chichester, U.K.: Wiley.

Ankney, C. D. (1992). Sex differences in relative brain size: The mismeasure of woman, too? *Intelligence, 16,* 329–336.

Archer, E. J., Cejka, J. A., & Thompson, C. P. (1961). Serial-trigram learning as a function of differential meaningfulness and sex of subjects and experimenters. *Canadian Journal of Psychology, 15,* 148–153.

Baenninger, M., & Newcombe, N. (1989). The role of experience in spatial test performance: A meta-analysis. *Sex Roles, 20,* 327–344.

Beall, A. E., & Sternberg, R. J. (Eds.). (1993). *The psychology of gender.* New York: Guilford Press.

Birkett, P. (1976). Sex differences and reasoning vs. imagery strategies in the solution of visually and auditorily presented family relationship problems. *Bulletin of the Psychonomic Society, 8,* 139–142.

Bleier, R. (1988). *Science* and the construction of meanings in the neurosciences. In S. V. Rosser (Ed.), *Feminism within the science and health care professions: Overcoming resistance* (pp. 91–104). Oxford, U.K.: Pergamon.

Bogo, N., Winget, C., & Gleser, G. C. (1970). Ego defenses and perceptual styles. *Perceptual and Motor Skills, 30,* 599–605.

Bouchard, T. J., Jr., & McGee, M. G. (1977). Sex differences in human spatial ability: Not an X-linked recessive gene effect. *Social Biology, 24,* 332–335.

Broverman, D. M., Klaiber, E. L., Kobayashi, Y., & Vogel, W. (1968). Roles of activation and inhibition in sex differences in cognitive abilities. *Psychological Review, 75,* 23–50.

Broverman, D. M., Vogel, W., Klaiber, E. L., Majcher, D., Shea, D., & Paul, V. (1981). Changes in cognitive task performance across the menstrual cycle. *Journal of Comparative and Physiological Psychology, 95,* 646–654.

Bryden, M. P. (1982). *Laterality: Function asymmetry in the intact brain.* New York: Academic Press.

Buffery, A. W. H., & Gray, J. A. (1972). Sex differences in the development of spatial and linguistic skills. In C. Ousted & D. C. Taylor (Eds.), *Gender differences: Their ontogeny and significance* (pp. 123–157). Edinburgh, U.K.: Churchill Livingstone.

Burnett, S. A. (1986). Sex-related differences in spatial ability: Are they trivial? *American Psychologist, 41,* 1012–1014.

Burnett, S. A., & Lane, D. M. (1980). Effects of academic instruction on spatial visualization. *Intelligence, 4,* 233–242.

Buss, D. M. (1995). Psychological sex differences: Origins through sexual selection. *American Psychologist, 50,* 164–168.

Caplan, P. J. (1979). Beyond the box score: A boundary condition for sex differences in aggression and achievement striving. In B. A. Maher (Ed.), *Progress in experimental personality research* (Vol. 9, pp. 41–87). New York: Academic Press.

Caplan, P. J., MacPherson, G. M., & Tobin, P. (1985). Do sex-related differences in spatial abilities exist? A multilevel critique with new data. *American Psychologist, 40,* 786–799.

Chatterjea, R. G., & Paul, B. (1982). Cognitive style, social environment, sex and recognition capacity. *Psycho-lingua, 12,* 37–45.

Cian, C., Esquivié, D., Barraud, P. A., & Raphel, C. (1995). Respective contributions of orientation contrast and illusion of self-tilt to the rod-and-frame effect. *Perception, 24,* 623–630.

Cian, C., & Raphel, C. (1995). The role of limited time exposure on the rod and frame illusion: Vection or orientation contrast effect? *Cahiers de Psychologie Cognitive, 14,* 367–386.

Cohen, W., & Polich, J. (1989). No hemispheric differences for mental rotation of letters or polygons. *Bulletin of the Psychonomic Society, 27,* 25–28.

Corballis, M. C. (1982). Mental rotation: Anatomy of a paradigm. In M. Potegal (Ed.), *Spatial abilities: Developmental and physiological foundations* (pp. 173–198). New York: Academic Press.

Crawford, M. (1989). Agreeing to differ: Feminist epistemologies and women's ways of knowing. In M. Crawford & M. Gentry (Eds.), *Gender and thought: Psychological perspectives* (pp. 128–145). New York: Springer-Verlag.

Dawson, J.L.M. (1972). Effects of sex hormones on cognitive style in rats and men. *Behavior Genetics, 2,* 21–42.

De Lacoste-Utamsing, C., & Holloway, R. L. (1982). Sexual dimorphism in the human corpus callosum. *Science, 216,* 1431–1432.

Drever, J. (1952). *A dictionary of psychology* (rev. H. Wallerstein, 1964). Harmondsworth, U.K.: Penguin Books.

Eagly, A. H. (1995). The science and politics of comparing women and men. *American Psychologist, 50,* 145–158.

Eichler, M. (1988). *Nonsexist research methods.* Boston: Allen & Unwin.

Eliot, J., & Fralley, J. S. (1976). Sex differences in spatial abilities. *Young Children, 31,* 487–498.

Emanuelsson, I., & Svensson, A. (1986). Does the level of intelligence decrease? A comparison between thirteen-year-olds tested in 1961, 1966 and 1980. *Scandinavian Journal of Educational Research, 30,* 25–37.

Fairweather, H. (1976). Sex differences in cognition. *Cognition, 4,* 231–280.

Fausto-Sterling, A. (1992). *Myths of gender: Biological theories about women and men* (2nd ed.). New York: Basic Books.

Feingold, A. (1988). Cognitive gender differences are disappearing. *American Psychologist, 43,* 95–103.

Ferguson, G. A., & Takane, Y. (1989). *Statistical analysis in psychology and education* (6th ed.). New York: McGraw-Hill.

Giambra, L. M. (1988–89). The influence of subject-experimenter sexual congruence on the frequency of task-unrelated imagery and thought: Further evidence. *Imagination, Cognition, and Personality, 8,* 249–260.

Gladue, B. A., Beatty, W. W., Larson, J., & Staton, R. D. (1990). Sexual orientation and spatial ability in men and women. *Psychobiology, 18,* 101–108.

Goldstein, A. G., & Chance, J. E. (1965). Effects of practice on sex-related differences in performance on Embedded Figures. *Psychonomic Science, 3,* 361–362.

Gould, S. J. (1981). *The mismeasure of man.* New York: Norton.

Grady, K. E. (1981). Sex bias in research design. *Psychology of Women Quarterly, 5,* 628–636.

Gralton, M. A., Hayes, Y. A., & Richardson, J. T. E. (1979). Introversion-extraversion and mental imagery. *Journal of Mental Imagery, 3,* 1–10.

Haller, J. S., Jr., & Haller, R. M. (1974). *The physician and sexuality in Victorian America.* Urbana, IL: University of Illinois Press.

Haug, H. (1987). Brain sizes, surfaces, and neuronal sizes of the cortex cerebri: A stereological investigation of man and his variability and a comparison with some species of mammals (primates, whales, marsupials, insectivores, and one elephant). *American Journal of Anatomy, 180,* 126–142.

Hilton, T. L. (1985). *National changes in spatial-visual ability from 1960 to 1980* (ETS Report No. RR-85-27). Princeton, NJ: Educational Testing Service.

Hult, R. E., Jr., & Brous, C. W. (1986). Spatial visualization: Athletics skills and sex differences. *Perceptual and Motor Skills, 63,* 163–168.

Humm, M. (1989). *The dictionary of feminist theory.* New York: Harvester Wheatsheaf.

Hyde, J. S. (1981). How large are cognitive gender differences? A meta-analysis using ω^2 and d. *American Psychologist, 36,* 892–901.

Hyde, J. S., Geiringer, E. R., & Yen, W. M. (1975). On the empirical relation between spatial ability and sex differences in other aspects of cognitive performance. *Multivariate Behavioral Research, 10,* 289–309.

Hyde, J. S., & Linn, M. C. (1988). Gender differences in verbal ability: A meta-analysis. *Psychological Bulletin, 104,* 53–69.

Jacklin, C. N. (1981). Methodological issues in the study of sex-related differences. *Developmental Review, 1,* 266–273.

Jacklin, C. N., & Maccoby, E. E. (1972). *Sex differences in intellectual abilities: A reassessment and a look at some new explanations.* Paper presented at the annual meeting of the American Educational Research Association, Chicago.

Jerison, H. J. (1982). The evolution of biological intelligence. In R. J. Sternberg (Ed.), *Handbook of human intelligence* (pp. 723–791). Cambridge, U.K.: Cambridge University Press.

Johnson, E. S., & Meade, A. C. (1987). Developmental patterns of spatial ability. *Child Development, 58,* 725–740.

Jonassen, D. H., & Grabowski, B. L. (1993). *Handbook of individual differences, learning, and instruction.* Hillsdale, NJ: Erlbaum.

Kogan, N. (1978). Sex differences in creativity and cognitive styles. In S. Messick & Associates, *Individuality in learning: Implications of cognitive styles and creativity for human development* (pp. 93–119). San Francisco: Jossey-Bass.

Kulynych, J. J., Vladar, K., Jones, D. W., & Weinberger, D. R. (1994). Gender differences in the normal lateralization of the supratemporal cortex: MRI surface-rendering morphometry of Heschl's gyrus and the planum temporale. *Cerebral Cortex, 4,* 107–118.

Levy, J. (1972). Lateral specialization of the human brain: Behavioral manifestations and possible evolutionary basis. In J. A. Kiger, Jr. (Ed.), *The biology of behavior* (pp. 159–180). Corvallis, OR: Oregon State University Press.

Linn, M. C., & Hyde, J. S. (1989). Gender, mathematics, and science. *Educational Researcher, 18*(8), 17–19, 22–27.

Littig, L. W., & Waddell, C. M. (1967). Sex and experimenter interaction in serial learning. *Journal of Verbal Learning and Verbal Behavior, 6,* 676–678.

Lynn, R. (1994). Sex differences in intelligence and brain size: A paradox resolved. *Personality and Individual Differences, 17,* 257–271.

Maccoby, E. E., & Jacklin, C. N. (1974). *The psychology of sex differences.* Stanford, CA: Stanford University Press.

Markus, H., & Oyserman, D. (1989). Gender and thought: The role of the self-concept. In M. Crawford & M. Gentry (Eds.), *Gender and thought: Psychological perspectives* (pp. 100–127). New York: Springer-Verlag.

Marshall, J. C. (1973). Some problems and paradoxes associated with recent accounts of hemispheric specialization. *Neuropsychologia, 11,* 463–470.

Masters, M. P. (1989). Visual half field studies of mental rotation. *Dissertation Abstracts International, 50,* 2179B.

Masters, M. S., & Sanders, B. (1993). Is the gender difference in mental rotation disappearing? *Behavior Genetics, 23,* 337–341.

McGee, M. G. (1979). Human spatial abilities: Psychometric studies and environmental, genetic, hormonal, and neurological influences. *Psychological Bulletin, 86,* 889–918.

McGlone, J. (1980). Sex differences in human brain asymmetry: A critical survey. *Behavioral and Brain Sciences, 3,* 215–263.

McGuinness, D. (1980). Strategies, demands, and lateralized sex differences. *Behavioral and Brain Sciences, 3,* 244.

Morgan, M. J. (1980). Influences of sex on variation in human brain asymmetry. *Behavioral and Brain Sciences, 3,* 244–245.

Mosedale, S. S. (1978). Science corrupted: Victorian biologists consider "the woman question." *Journal of the History of Biology, 11,* 1–55.

Naditch, S. F. (1976). *Sex differences in field dependence: The role of social influence.* Paper presented at the convention of the American Psychological Association, Washington, DC.

Newcombe, N., Bandura, M. M., & Taylor, D. G. (1983). Sex differences in spatial ability and spatial activities. *Sex Roles, 9,* 277–286.

Nyborg, H. (1983). Spatial ability in men and women: Review and new theory. *Advances in Behaviour Research and Therapy, 5,* 89–140.

Oltman, P. K. (1968). A portable rod-and-frame apparatus. *Perceptual and Motor Skills, 26,* 503–506.

Packard, G. C., & Boardman, T. J. (1988). The misuse of ratios, indices, and percentages in ecophysiological research. *Physiological Zoology, 61,* 1–9.

Parlee, M. B. (1972). Comments on "Roles of activation and inhibition in sex differences in cognitive abilities" by D. M. Broverman, E. L. Klaiber, Y. Kobayashi, and W. Vogel. *Psychological Review, 79,* 180–184.

Parlee, M. B. (1973). The premenstrual syndrome. *Psychological Bulletin, 80,* 454–465.

Peeck, J. (1973). Sexeverschillen in leerprocessen met plaatjes. *Nederlands Tijdschrift voor de Psychologie, 28,* 343–349.

Petrakis, E. (1981). Cognitive styles of physical education majors. *Perceptual and Motor Skills, 53,* 574.

Plomin, R., & Foch, T. T. (1981). Sex differences and individual differences. *Child Development, 52,* 383–385.

Porter Poole, F. J. (1981). Transforming "natural" woman: Female ritual leaders and gender ideology among Bimin-Kuskusmin. In S. B. Ortner & H. Whitehead (Eds.), *Sexual meanings: The cultural construction of gender and sexuality* (pp. 116–165). Cambridge, U.K.: Cambridge University Press.

Richardson, J.T.E. (1982). Introversion-extraversion and experimenter effects in memory tasks. *Personality and Individual Differences, 3,* 327–328.

Richardson, J.T.E. (1991). Gender differences in imagery, cognition, and memory. In R. H. Logie & M. Denis (Eds.), *Mental images in human cognition* (pp. 271–303). Amsterdam: Elsevier.

Richardson, J.T.E. (1994). Gender differences in mental rotation. *Perceptual and Motor Skills, 78,* 435–448.

Ronsaville, D.L.S. (1986). Sex differences in processing spatial rotations as related to brain organization and strategy. *Dissertation Abstracts International, 47,* 1764B.

Rosenthal, R. (1976). *Experimenter effects in behavioral research* (enlarged ed.). New York: Irvington.

Rosenthal, R. (1979). The "file drawer problem" and tolerance for null results. *Psychological Bulletin, 86,* 638–640.

Rosenthal, R., & Rubin, D. B. (1982). Further meta-analytic procedures for assessing cognitive gender differences. *Journal of Educational Psychology, 74,* 708–712.

Sanders, G., & Ross-Field, L. (1986). Sexual orientation and visuo-spatial ability. *Brain and Cognition, 5,* 280–290.

Sharps, M. J., Welton, A. L., & Price, J. L. (1993). Gender and task in the determination of spatial cognitive performance. *Psychology of Women Quarterly, 17,* 71–83.

Sherman, J. A. (1978). *Sex-related cognitive differences: An essay on theory and evidence.* Springfield, IL: Thomas.

Sherman, J. A. (1980). Sex-related differences in functional human brain asymmetry: Verbal function—no; spatial function—maybe. *Behavioral and Brain Sciences, 3,* 248–249.

Shields, S. A. (1975). Functionalism, Darwinism, and the psychology of women: A study in social myth. *American Psychologist, 30,* 739–754.

Sommer, B. (1992). Cognitive performance and the menstrual cycle. In J. T. E. Richardson (Ed.), *Cognition and the menstrual cycle* (pp. 39–66). New York: Springer-Verlag.

Stafford, R. E. (1961). Sex differences in spatial visualization as evidence of sex-linked inheritance. *Perceptual and Motor Skills, 13,* 428.

Stein, A. H., & Smithells, J. (1969). Age and sex differences in children's sex-role standards about achievement. *Developmental Psychology, 1,* 252–259.

Sternberg, R. J. (1993). What is the relation of gender to biology and environment? An evolutionary model of how what you answer depends on just what you ask. In A. E. Beall & R. J. Sternberg (Eds.), *The psychology of gender* (pp. 1–6). New York: Guildford Press.

Stevenson, H. W., & Allen, S. (1964). Adult performance as a function of sex of experimenter and sex of subject. *Journal of Abnormal and Social Psychology, 68,* 214–216.

Stumpf, H., & Klieme, E. (1989). Sex-related differences in spatial ability: More evidence for convergence. *Perceptual and Motor Skills, 69,* 915–921.

Tavris, C. (1992). *Mismeasure of woman.* New York: Simon & Schuster.

Temple, C. M., & Carney, R. A. (1993). Intellectual functioning of children with Turner syndrome: A comparison of behavioural phenotypes. *Developmental Medicine and Child Neurology, 35,* 691–698.

Temple, C. M., & Carney, R. A. (1995). Patterns of spatial functioning in Turner's Syndrome. *Cortex, 31,* 109–119.

Tresemer, D. (1975). Assumptions made about gender roles. In M. Millman & R. M. Kanter (Eds.), *Another voice: Feminist perspectives on social life and social science* (pp. 308–339). Garden City, NY: Anchor Books.

Unger, R. K. (1979). Toward a redefinition of sex and gender. *American Psychologist, 34,* 1085–1094.

Voyer, D., Voyer, S., & Bryden, M. P. (1995). Magnitude of sex differences in spatial abilities: A meta-analysis and consideration of critical variables. *Psychological Bulletin, 117,* 250–270.

Walker, A. (1850). *Woman physiologically considered.* New York: Langley.

Wilson, J. R., DeFries, J. C., McClearn, G. E., Vandenberg, S. G., Johnson, R. C., & Rashad, M. N. (1975). Cognitive abilities: Use of family data as a control to assess sex and age differences in two ethnic groups. *International Journal of Aging and Human Development, 6,* 261–276.

Witelson, S. F. (1985). The brain connection: The corpus callosum is larger in left-handers. *Science, 229,* 665–668.

Witelson, S. F., Glezer, I. I., & Kigar, D. L. (1995). Women have greater density of neurons in posterior temporal cortex. *Journal of Neuroscience, 15,* 3418–3428.

Witkin, H. A. (1950). Individual differences in ease of perception of embedded figures. *Journal of Personality, 19,* 1–15.

Witkin, H. A. (1979). Socialization, culture and ecology in the development of group and sex differences in cognitive style. *Human Development, 22,* 358–372.

Witkin, H. A., & Asch, S. E. (1948). Studies in space orientation: IV. Further experiments on perception of the upright with displaced visual fields. *Journal of Experimental Psychology, 38,* 762–782.

Witkin, H. A., & Goodenough, D. R. (1981). *Cognitive styles: Essence and origins.* New York: International Universities Press.

Witkin, H. A., Lewis, H. B., Hertzman, M., Machover, K., Meissner, P. B., & Wapner, S. (1954). *Personality through perception: An experimental and clinical study.* New York: Harper & Brothers.

Wolff, P. H. (1980). A difference that may make no difference. *Behavioral and Brain Sciences, 3,* 250–251.

CHAPTER 2

Gender Differences in Cognition

Results from Meta-Analyses

Janet Shibley Hyde and Nita M. McKinley

For more than 100 years, psychologists and the general public have been fascinated with the notion that there are gender differences in cognitive abilities. The interest continues unabated today, as evidenced in flashy cover stories in major news magazines. In this chapter we first introduce the statistical technique of meta-analysis, which provides a quantitative method for assessing what many different research studies, taken together, say about the existence and magnitude of gender differences in abilities. We review the results of meta-analyses of gender differences in verbal, mathematical, spatial, and scientific abilities. We critically examine the evidence on gender differences from the much-publicized Study of Mathematically Precocious Youth. Next we examine the evidence on whether gender differences in cognition have been growing smaller over the course of time. Finally, we consider the hypothesis of greater male variability and evaluate the current evidence relating to this hypothesis.

As John Richardson pointed out in Chapter 1, research into gender differences in cognition has historically been driven by the attempt to support or refute societal beliefs about the appropriate roles for women and men (see also Shields, 1975). Replacing older religious explanations for these roles, scientists began in the early 19th century to search for differences that could account for men's supposed greater intellect, which was assumed to explain women's subordinate social position and confinement to the roles of wife and mother. The debate over gender differences in the brain subsided when psychologists developed tests of mental functioning. Alfred Binet in France and Lewis Terman in the United States based their IQ tests on the conceptualization of intelligence as a single dimension. The data indicate that there are no reliable gender differences in general intelligence, although this may be the result of deliberate efforts by the early test constructors to create tests that showed no gender differences (see Maccoby & Jacklin, 1974, p. 68).

Thurstone (1938) believed that there were several different types of intellectual ability, and he developed the Primary Mental Abilities scale to measure verbal comprehension; word fluency; numerical computation; spatial visualization; memory; speed and accuracy on clerical tasks; and reasoning. Once this multidimensional view of intelligence had become established, data on gender differences began to accumulate. From the 1930s on, reviewers agreed that females excelled in verbal ability and that males excelled in numerical reasoning and spatial ability (see Hyde, 1990). In 1974, Maccoby and Jacklin published a systematic review of the research on gender differences in cognitive abilities, personality, and social behaviors that had been conducted between 1966 and 1973. Although they were able to refute many popular beliefs about gender differences, they concluded that gender differences were evident in the social domain of aggression and the cognitive domains of verbal ability, visual-spatial ability, and mathematical ability (pp. 351–352). What Hyde (1990) called the "holy trinity" of gender differences in cognitive abilities had been reaffirmed.

META-ANALYSIS

As empirical research on gender differences in cognition has accumulated, how to integrate scientific knowledge has become an important question. Earlier reviewers, including Maccoby and Jacklin (1974), used narrative review and the systematic counting of available studies. This method is subjective, in that it is for the reviewer to decide when enough "votes" have accumulated to support an alleged difference. Also, simple counting, however systematic, can lead to false conclusions (see Hunter, Schmidt, & Jackson, 1982; Hyde, 1986). This may occur if many studies are based on small samples and therefore have poor statistical power to detect differences. The result may be that only a minority of studies detect a true (i.e., nonzero) effect in the population as a whole.

Meta-analysis is a systematic, quantitative technique for aggregating results across different studies, thus reducing some of the subjectivity involved in narrative review. Beginning in the early 1980s, researchers used meta-analysis to integrate the psychological literature on cognitive gender differences (for example, Hyde, 1981). As in the case of narrative review, the meta-analyst collects as many different studies as possible, and a measure of effect size is computed for each study. A commonly used index is d, the difference between the means of two groups expressed in terms of standard units by dividing by the pooled within-group standard deviation. In analyses of gender differences, the statistic d represents the ratio of the difference between the means obtained by the male and female participants to the within-gender variability. Whether the effect size is positive or negative indicates the direction of the difference: a positive value of d indicates higher scores for males, and a negative value of d indicates higher scores for females. Once the value of d is computed for each study, a weighted mean effect size is computed across all the studies. According to Cohen (1969, pp. 22–24), an effect size of ± 0.20 is small, an effect size of ± 0.50 is medium, and an effect size of ± 0.80 is large.

One of the advantages of meta-analysis is that the researcher can examine variations in effect sizes as a function of moderator variables. For instance, in a study of gender differences in mathematical ability, Hyde, Fennema, and Lamon (1990) examined the average effect size across studies as a function of the age of sample, the selectivity of the sample, and the year of publication. The meta-analyst computes a homogeneity statistic developed by Hedges and his colleagues (Hedges & Olkin, 1985) to verify whether the average effect size is likely to represent a single underlying effect size. If the effect sizes are heterogeneous, testing for moderator variables is warranted.

Meta-analysis has several advantages over narrative review. As noted, it reduces some of the subjectivity inherent in narrative review by providing a quantitative average of effect sizes across different studies. Rather than tallying the results of studies, meta-analysis utilizes other information, such as the size of the difference found and the size of the sample. Meta-analysis converts the results of a wide range of studies to standard units to allow meaningful comparison and allows the quantitative study of moderator variables. Moreover, in the context of research into gender differences, an important consideration is that meta-analysis takes into account within-gender variability (Hyde, 1990): If this variability is ignored, finding a mean gender difference in mathematical performance, for example, might lead readers to assume that most women perform less well in tests of mathematical ability than most men, when in fact there is a great deal of overlap between the distributions for women and men.

Meta-analysis does share several disadvantages with narrative review. Biases can enter through the behaviors and measures that the meta-analyst chooses to include and through the biases of researchers in the relevant field. Aggregating across studies can also minimize the importance of situational variables (Unger, 1990). This disadvantage can be turned into an advantage by the use of moderator variables that code for the situation and hence allow the meta-analyst to assess variations in results across the different situations. One final disadvantage for meta-analysts is that they must have access to the appropriate statistics for computing the effect size. Especially in the case of studies in which no significant difference has been found, these statistics are often not reported in the published literature, and, as a result, they have to be obtained by other methods, estimated, or omitted. Moreover, studies that fail to yield significant effects may simply not be published and therefore may be inaccessible to the reviewer. This point was termed the "file drawer problem" by Rosenthal (1978), and we discuss it in more detail later in this chapter.

GENDER DIFFERENCES IN COGNITIVE ABILITIES

Maccoby and Jacklin's (1974) conclusions that there were reliable gender differences in verbal, mathematical, and spatial abilities were refined considerably by subsequent meta-analytic research. An early meta-analysis by Hyde (1981) computed effect sizes for gender differences with regard to verbal, mathematical, and spatial abilities for the sample of studies that had been evaluated by Maccoby and Jacklin. Hyde showed that the average effect size was −0.24 for verbal ability, +0.43 for mathematical ability, and +0.45 for spatial ability. However, this early analysis has now been superseded by more recent meta-analyses based on larger samples of studies and more advanced statistical methods. The results of these meta-analyses will be reviewed in the following sections.

Verbal Ability

Hyde and Linn (1988) located 165 studies that had reported data on gender differences in verbal ability. Averaged across all of these samples, the mean effect size was −0.11. This indicated a slight female superiority in performance, but the authors argued that the difference was so small that it indicated that there were not (or were no longer) any gender differences in verbal ability. When separate meta-analyses were conducted for different types of verbal ability, the results indicated that the mean effect size was −0.02 for vocabulary, +0.16 for analogies (that is, males tended to perform better than females), −0.03 for reading comprehension, −0.09 for essay writing, −0.22 for anagrams, and −0.20 for tests of general verbal ability.

All of these gender differences are clearly small: The largest gender difference (-0.33) was obtained on measures of speech production.

A new meta-analysis of gender differences in abilities appeared more recently. Hedges and Nowell (1995) adopted a somewhat different strategy in
surveying only large, well-sampled studies of the general population of the
United States such as the National Longitudinal Study of Youth. All of the
samples consisted of high-school students. In the case of reading comprehension, the values of d ranged between -0.15 and $+0.002$ with a mean of
-0.09. In the case of vocabulary, the values of d ranged between -0.06
and $+0.25$ with a mean of $+0.06$. These estimates cluster around zero and
are quite similar to those obtained by Hyde and Linn (1988). Once again,
they confirm the finding of no gender difference in verbal ability.

With regard to developmental trends, Maccoby and Jacklin (1974) had
earlier concluded that there were no gender differences in verbal ability during the elementary-school years, but that gender differences began to appear
around the age of 11, with female superiority increasing through the high-
school years and possibly beyond. Results of the meta-analysis conducted
by Hyde and Linn (1988) provided no support for this assertion. The gender
differences were uniformly small but favored females at all age levels: The
average effect size was -0.13 in the case of children aged 5 years or less,
-0.06 in the case 6- to 10-year-olds, -0.11 in the case of 11- to 18-year-
olds, -0.06 in the case of 19- to 25-year-olds, and -0.20 in the case of
adults aged 26 or older.

These results relied mainly upon psychometrically developed tests of verbal ability, administered either to samples from the general population, such
as schoolchildren, or to selected samples, such as college students. In other
words, the estimates of effect size were based upon participants who were
functioning within the normal range. If one turns, instead, to various disturbances in verbal functioning, then a more dramatic pattern of gender differences emerges. For instance, as Halpern (1992, p. 65) noted, mild developmental dyslexia is five times more likely to occur in boys than in girls, and
severe developmental dyslexia is ten times more likely to occur in boys than
in girls; in addition, there are three to four times as many male stutterers as
there are female stutterers (but cf. Chapter 3, this volume).

In conclusion, based upon the meta-analyses reported by Hyde and Linn
(1988) and by Hedges and Nowell (1995), gender differences with regard to
general verbal ability appear to be so small that they are now essentially
nonexistent. There are, however, many distinct types of verbal ability, and
genuine differences may exist within particular areas such as speech production. Moreover, there are marked gender differences in disturbances of verbal functioning, where more boys exhibit difficulties than girls.

Mathematics Performance

Hyde et al. (1990) conducted a meta-analysis of gender differences with regard to performance in mathematics. This was based on 100 studies that provided effect sizes for 254 separate samples and represented the testing of over 3 million people. The findings were quite surprising, given the long-held belief in a male superiority in mathematics. The average effect size across all the samples was $d = +0.15$, indicating better performance in males than in females, but by only a small amount. When only samples from the general population were used, excluding any studies that involved highly selected samples such as mathematically precocious youth, then the average effect size was -0.05, indicating superior female performance, but by a negligible amount. In short, the much-touted male superiority in mathematics was not supported by this mcta-analysis. In the case of the meta-analysis reported by Hedges and Nowell (1995), which used only large, well-sampled studies of high-school students, the values of d ranged between $+0.03$ and $+0.26$ for mathematics performance with a mean of $+0.16$, a value that is remarkably close to the estimate obtained by Hyde et al.

However, the results of the meta-analysis carried out by Hyde et al. (1990) were more complex than might be suggested by a single mean estimate of effect size. Problems in mathematics can be designed to tap different cognitive levels: computation (involving simple memorized mathematical facts), concepts (involving the analysis or comprehension of mathematical ideas), or problem solving (involving the extension of knowledge or its application to new situations, such as in story problems). In addition, Hyde et al. felt that it was important to analyze the data for possible age trends. Accordingly, they carried out an analysis based on both age and cognitive level. The results are shown in Table 2-1. Notice that girls tend to be better than boys at computation, by a small amount, in both elementary school and middle school, but that there is no gender difference in high school. In terms of the understanding of mathematical concepts, there is no gender difference at any age. Finally, in terms of problem solving, there is no gender difference in elementary school or middle school, but there is a small-to-moderate difference favoring boys in high school and men during the college years. (In Chapter 3 in this volume, however, Caplan and Caplan discuss the heterogeneity of definitions, the sampling problems, and the methodological issues that are implicated in studies of gender differences in mathematical ability as well as in studies of gender differences in verbal and spatial abilities.)

This last finding gives some cause for concern, because mathematical problem-solving ability is critical to success in courses and careers in the

TABLE 2-1 Magnitude of Gender Differences in Mathematics Performance as a Function of Age and Cognitive Level of the Test[a]

Age (years)	Cognitive Level			
	Computation	Concepts	Problem Solving	All Studies
5–10	−0.20	−0.02	+0.00	−0.06
11–14	−0.22	−0.06	−0.02	−0.07
15–18	+0.00	+0.07	+0.29	+0.29[b]
19–25	NA	NA	+0.32	+0.41
26 and older	NA	NA	NA	+0.59

[a]Positive values indicate better performance by males, and negative values indicate better performance by females. The category "All studies" includes studies involving tests that contained a mixture of cognitive levels, as well as studies involving tests that could not be classified by cognitive level. NA = not available: There were two or fewer effect sizes, and so a mean could not be computed.

[b]Data for the Scholastic Aptitude Test were excluded in the computation of this effect size.

Source: Adapted from "Gender Differences in Mathematics Performance: A Meta-Analysis," by J. S. Hyde, E. Fennema, and S. J. Lamon, 1990, *Psychological Bulletin, 107,* p. 148. Copyright 1990 by the American Psychological Association. Reprinted by permission.

sciences, not to mention in mathematics. However, this difference is explained, in part, by the fact that girls in high school are less likely to take additional courses in mathematics when these become optional (Linn & Hyde, 1989). It is not surprising that girls do less well on tests that tap material in courses that they may not have taken. Moreover, science courses provide extensive additional experience with mathematical problem solving (such as balancing chemistry equations), and girls in high school also appear to be less likely to take science courses. For example, data from California high schools indicate that girls constitute only 38% of physics students and only 42% of chemistry students (Linn & Hyde, 1989). Girls' double disadvantage of taking fewer mathematics courses and fewer science courses is clearly a major factor in their lower performance on tests of mathematical problem solving in high school and beyond.

Spatial Ability

Linn and Petersen (1985) conducted a meta-analysis of gender differences in spatial ability. On the basis of a cognitive analysis and an analysis of effect size, they concluded that there were three distinct types of spatial ability. The first type, which they termed "spatial perception," is measured by procedures such as the Water-Level Test, which taps the participant's sense of horizontality or verticality. For these tests, the average effect size was +0.44. The second type, which they termed "mental rotation," is measured by procedures that involve mentally rotating a three-dimensional object that is depicted in two dimensions to see whether it matches one of a number of other illustrations. For these tests, the average effect size was +0.73. The third type, which they termed "spatial visualization," is measured by procedures such as the Embedded Figures Tests, which involve visually locating a simple figure within a complex one. For these tests, the average effect size was +0.13.

A more recent meta-analysis of gender differences in spatial ability was conducted by Voyer, Voyer, and Bryden (1995). Their results supported the distinction between mental rotation, spatial perception, and spatial visualization, and their estimates of effect size were similar to those that had been obtained by Linn and Petersen: +0.56 for mental rotation, +0.44 for spatial perception, and +0.19 for spatial visualization. (The results obtained by Voyer et al. are discussed in more detail in Chapter 4, this volume.) Based upon these findings, it makes no sense to make general statements concerning gender differences in spatial ability. Depending upon the nature of the test, the gender difference can range in magnitude from near zero (as in the Embedded Figures Tests) to large (in three-dimensional mental rotation). In addition, a meta-analysis of research on the efficacy of programs for improving spatial ability found that scores on spatial ability tests can be improved by training (Baenninger & Newcombe, 1989). It follows that even these gender differences are not necessarily immutable.

Science Achievement

Fleming and Malone (1983) conducted a meta-analysis of studies of science performance for students from kindergarten (5- to 6-year-olds) to twelfth grade (17- to 18-year-olds) that had been published between 1960 and 1981. Averaged over all ages, the effect size for gender differences in science achievement was +0.16. In other words, boys scored higher than girls, but the difference was small. When it was examined by grade level, the mean effect size was +0.04 for elementary school, +0.32 for middle school, and +0.15 for high school. It is interesting that the gender difference was largest in middle school (11- to 14-year-olds), which is precisely the time when gender-role issues and heterosexual popularity are so salient and unsettling. When it was examined by subject matter, the mean effect size was +0.02 for the life sciences, but +0.30 for the physical sciences: That is, there was no gender difference in achievement in the biological sciences, but there was a small-to-moderate gender difference in physics. Similar findings were obtained in the Study of Mathematically Precocious Youth, which will be discussed in the next section. It is clear that, when speaking of gender differences in science achievement, we should not aggregate across all areas of science.

Becker (1989) carried out another meta-analysis, based on 30 studies. The average effect size for gender differences in science achievement was +0.16. This result is remarkable, because it is identical to the overall effect size obtained in the meta-analysis reported by Fleming and Malone, despite the fact that the sets of studies reviewed in these meta-analyses were considerably different (Fleming and Malone included many unpublished dissertations that Becker did not include). Like Fleming and Malone, Becker found variations in the magnitude of the gender difference as a function of the subject matter, with the largest estimate of effect size, +0.35, obtained in physics. Unlike Fleming and Malone, however, Becker found no significant relationship between grade level and average effect size. It is difficult to reconcile this discrepancy in their findings.

The meta-analysis carried out by Hedges and Nowell (1995) on large, well-sampled studies of high school students found values of d for science achievement ranging between +0.11 and +0.50 with a mean of +0.32. This value is somewhat higher than those found in the other two meta-analyses. This discrepancy is probably due to the fact that Hedges and Nowell had included data only for high-school students. As mentioned above, science courses at high school are taken by fewer girls when they become optional, and this then creates a disadvantage for many girls when taking tests of science achievement.

In conclusion, the overall gender difference in science achievement is small, with a mean effect size of +0.16. The magnitude of this gender difference varies as a function of science content, and it appears to be largest for physics or the physical sciences, with a mean effect size of +0.30 according to Fleming and Malone (1983) or +0.35 according to Becker (1989). Whether the magnitude of the gender difference also changes with age is at present an open question, since the two available meta-analyses produced different results in this regard.

THE STUDY OF MATHEMATICALLY PRECOCIOUS YOUTH

Julian Stanley founded the Study of Mathematically Precocious Youth (SMPY) at Johns Hopkins University in 1971. More recently, the project has been carried on by Camilla Benbow (e.g., Benbow, 1988; Benbow & Stanley, 1980). These researchers have chosen to highlight findings of gender differences in their sample. Their results have been widely publicized in the popular press, and they are often discussed in textbooks. Because the SMPY is so widely known, it deserves to be reviewed here.

The SMPY sought to identify mathematically talented 12- and 13-year-olds. It is important to understand the search strategy in order to gain some understanding of the nature of the sample. Seventh graders (and, in the first 3 years of the project, eighth graders as well) were eligible to participate if they had scored in the upper 3% (with certain variations during the early years of the study) on national norms in the mathematics portion of standardized tests such as the Iowa Test of Basic Skills. All eligible middle-school children in the geographic region of the search (the Mid-Atlantic states) were informed by means of letters to their school's principal, guidance counselors, and mathematics department chair, who were to give an application form to the students in question. The students then applied to be in the talent search and took a national administration of the Scholastic Aptitude Test (SAT). In other words, a self-selection process intervened, and the nature of this self-selection process is not known. Neither is it known whether gender affected this self-selection process, but it is certainly a possibility. These talented students who participated obtained mean scores in the 400s on the SAT-M.

Gender differences favoring boys have consistently been found in this sample (Benbow, 1988). For example, in 1979, the mean score on the SAT-M for 2,046 boys was 436 with a standard deviation of 87, and the mean score for 1,628 girls was 404 with a standard deviation of 77. When this gender difference is expressed as an effect size, it appears to be moderate: $d = +0.39$. However, the authors chose instead to emphasize the very lopsided gender ratios found at the extremes of the distribution for this already extremely talented group. Across all of the 12-year-olds in the sample, there was a male:female ratio of 2:1 in the case of those scoring 600 or better on the SAT-M (based on 5,325 cases), and a ratio of 4:1 in the case of those scoring 700 or better (based on 806 cases) (Benbow, 1988).

There are a number of problematic aspects to these reports. First, although the sample was highly selected—in some ways that are known and others that are unknown—the popular press often reports these results as if they characterized the general population. The researchers themselves have sometimes been careful to specify the nature of their population but at other times have slipped into more casual language. For example, the title of their 1980 *Science* article was "Sex Differences in Mathematical Ability: Fact or Artifact?" A more accurate title would have been "Sex Differences in Mathematical Ability in a Highly Talented Sample." This extraordinary sample provides little or no information about gender and mathematics performance in the general population. Indeed, Becker and Hedges (1988) demonstrated that there could be a mean gender difference favoring *females* in the general population but a gender ratio favoring *males* in the upper tail of the distribution, created by greater variance in the males' scores than in the females' scores.

There is an additional cause for concern, because Jacobs and Eccles (1985) found that publicity about the SMPY had had negative effects on the beliefs of parents in the general population. In ongoing research, Jacobs and Eccles had been collecting parents' estimates of their own children's mathematical ability. Following the publicity over the article by Benbow and Stanley (1980), Jacobs and Eccles were able to retest the same parents to evaluate its effects. Those mothers who reported that they had been exposed to the media coverage gave lower ratings of their daughters' mathematical ability when compared both with their own "pretest" ratings and with the ratings given by mothers who reported no exposure to the relevant media coverage. This decline in mothers' ratings following the publicity is particularly worrying, because other research has demonstrated the importance of key socializers' beliefs in shaping children's own expectations with regard to their success in mathematics (e.g., Eccles, 1987).

What can be said in favor of the research by Benbow and Stanley? It could have many possible benefits, but among them, presumably, is the idea that the study is tracking the future leaders of the nation in mathematics and science. The project has now gathered sufficient longitudinal data to provide information on this matter, but the results in turn raise serious questions. Of those SMPY students who attended graduate school, only 41% of the men and 22% of the women were enrolled in mathematics and science programs (Benbow, 1988). One conclusion, then, is that the majority of these talented youth do *not* pursue graduate training in mathematics or the sciences, and therefore they cannot be expected to have brilliant careers in these areas. Furthermore, when those pursuing graduate training in mathematics and the sciences were subdivided by area, it turned out that there was no gender difference with regard to the percentage of students who were enrolled in graduate programs in either mathematics or biology: The difference arose in engineering, computer science, and the physical sciences. There is a troubling disjuncture here: If the girls had been less talented than the boys when they were in middle school, why were they successfully pursuing graduate degrees in mathematics in equal numbers?

In conclusion, the findings of the SMPY tell us nothing about gender differences in mathematics performance in the general population. Media coverage of the SMPY may, however, have had negative effects (for example, on mothers' estimates of their daughters' mathematical ability). Finally, there are serious questions relating to the issue of predictive validity.

ARE COGNITIVE GENDER DIFFERENCES DISAPPEARING?

A number of meta-analysts have addressed the question of whether gender differences in cognitive abilities have grown smaller over the past 30 years or so. For measures of verbal ability, Hyde and Linn (1988) found an average effect size of -0.23 for studies published in 1973 or earlier but an average effect size of -0.10 for the studies published after 1973. In their meta-analysis of gender differences in mathematics performance, Hyde et al. (1990) found an average effect size of $+0.31$ for studies that had been published in 1973 or earlier, compared with $+0.14$ for studies that had been published after 1973. In both cases, then, more recent studies produced gender differences that were less than half the size of the gender differences produced in the pre-1973 studies. In the case of spatial ability, Voyer et al. (1995) found a small positive relationship with year of publication resulting from the latter being confounded with the participants' ages. When age was partialed out, several tests showed a significant negative relationship between effect size and year of birth.

Feingold (1988) examined this question by using the norms from four standardizations of the Differential Aptitude Tests (DAT) between 1947 and 1980 and from four standardizations of the Preliminary Scholastic Aptitude Test (PSAT) and the SAT between 1960 and 1983. He concluded that gender differences had declined "precipitously," with the exception of the gender gap in mathematics performance on the SAT in high-school students, which had remained constant. For instance, on the DAT Space Relations scale, which is a measure of spatial ability, d was 0.37 in 1947 but was 0.15 in 1980. For mathematics performance on the PSAT, d was 0.34 in 1960 but was 0.12 by 1983. However, gender differences in mathematics performance on the SAT had remained constant: d was 0.37 in 1967 and 0.42 in 1983.

There is converging evidence from a number of sources, then, that gender differences in cognitive abilities have declined over the last 30 or more years, with smaller effect sizes for data collected in the 1970s and 1980s than in previous decades. How should this trend be interpreted? Several questions must be addressed in order to understand what the trend means: (1) Has there been a true trend toward smaller cognitive gender differences, or is the apparent trend a methodological artifact? (2) If the trend is a true one, what factor or factors caused it to occur? (3) If the trend is a true one, which gender is changing? For example, for mathematics, where there is a male advantage, does the narrowing gender difference represent an increase in female scores, a decline in male scores, or a shift in both?

First, has there been a true trend toward smaller gender differences, or is the apparent trend merely a methodological artifact? A number of methodological factors are possible candidates for explanation. One is the "file drawer effect" mentioned earlier (Rosenthal, 1978) and whether file-drawer tendencies have changed over time. The "file drawer effect" refers to the tendency of studies with null findings to wind up in the researcher's file drawer, unpublished, rather than finding their way into print. It might be that the Zeitgeist during the 1950s and 1960s made it fashionable to publish findings of gender differences, whereas findings of no significant gender differences were uninteresting or even unbelievable, leading them to languish unpublished in file drawers. A number of forces in the early 1970s may have acted to change that Zeitgeist. One was the feminist movement, with its emphasis on gender equity. Another was the publication of Maccoby and Jacklin's influential book *The Psychology of Sex Differences* (1974), which dismissed many claims of gender difference even while maintaining a firm belief in cognitive gender differences. As a result of these and other forces, it might be argued, researchers became willing and able to publish findings of no significant gender differences. Smaller effect sizes appeared in articles, creating an apparent reduction in the estimated magnitude of gender differences.

This argument cannot explain the decline in the magnitude of gender differences on the standardized tests examined by Feingold (1988), since publication was not an issue in that case. However, these findings bring us to another possible methodological artifact: Test publishers may have made efforts to decrease gender bias in their instruments, they may have succeeded at least to some extent, and as a result the magnitude of gender differences has declined. If this argument were true, it would be a very pleasing outcome. Moreover, it would also imply that the cognitive gender differences that were found several decades ago were largely artifacts of gender-biased test construction. Unfortunately, although we can raise these methodological possibilities, we cannot determine whether either or both has merit. Meta-analysis itself cannot differentiate these alternatives.

If we assume, instead, that the narrowing of gender differences in cognitive performance is not a methodological artifact, but rather is a real phenomenon, what factors might have caused it to occur? Parents' socialization practices may have changed over the last 25 years in the direction of gender equality. Parents may be more equitable in their treatment of their daughters and sons in many ways, ranging from engaging in similar play with boys and girls and providing them with similar toys, to encouraging girls in mathematics as much as boys. The schools may also have become more equitable environments for boys and girls: For example, girls are given more opportunities and encouragement in mathematics and science than they were previously. Moreover, experience with sports has been implicated in spatial performance; it therefore may be that, as girls participate more equally in both high-school sports and club sports, their spatial performance has improved.

Again, if we assume that there actually has been a narrowing of the gender difference in cognitive abilities, which gender has been changing? For instance, in the case of mathematics performance, is it the result of an increase in the performance of females, a decline in the performance of males, or perhaps both? Conversely, in the case of verbal ability, is it the result of an increase in the performance of males or a decline in the performance of females? Meta-analysis is not capable of distinguishing between these alternatives, because measures of effect size only look at the magnitude of the gender difference and ignore the absolute levels of performance achieved by males or females. It would in fact be difficult, if not impossible, to investigate these absolute levels of performance, because the relevant studies are based on many different tests that have no common metric. In conclusion, meta-analysis does not allow us to make definitive statements about the reality or the causes of any findings of declining gender differences in abilities. All the possible explanations raised here must be considered, and methods other than meta-analysis will be needed to address these issues.

GENDER DIFFERENCES IN VARIABILITY

Meta-analytic techniques can be used to study differences in dispersion as well as differences in central tendency. Indeed, researchers have looked for gender differences in variability for almost as long as they have been looking for gender differences in terms of absolute performance. Just as a greater intellectual ability was believed to account for men's superior social status compared with that of women, so greater male variability was also enlisted to try to account for these social differences. Updated and refined, the greater male variability hypothesis proposes that, although there may only be small gender differences or none at all in terms of the overall means in certain abilities, the greater number of high-achieving boys or men can be accounted for by gender differences in variability.

For instance, as mentioned earlier, Benbow (1988) found a male:female ratio of 4:1 in mathematically precocious youth. Although a small gender difference in means could account for more males lying in the upper end of the distribution for mathematical ability, such a large ratio could not be accounted for without assuming a gender difference in variability (Hedges & Friedman, 1993a). However, before looking at current research on gender differences in variability, we shall review the history of this research.

Historical Background

In order to study the history of the greater male variability hypothesis, it is necessary to place it within the historical context of the changing roles of women. The period when this hypothesis first gained popularity, the latter half of the 19th century and the early 20th century, was a time when women in many countries, including the United States, were agitating for and gaining expanded roles and were challenging popular and scientific beliefs concerning women's allegedly inferior abilities. The greater male variability hypothesis returned to popularity in the 1970s, once again at a time when women demanded an end to limited roles and when research began to accumulate challenging social beliefs about women's lower intelligence. As research continues to demonstrate that gender differences in abilities are diminishing or nonexistent, so the hypothesis of gender differences in variability is used to explain the finding that males are overrepresented among the mathematically gifted (Benbow, 1988).

In Chapter 1, John Richardson pointed out that neuroscientists have adjusted their conception of the relation between intelligence and various brain structures when their hypotheses of gender difference have not been supported. In a similar manner, hypotheses about variability have shifted to fit changing social theory and empirical observations that contradict the idea of male superiority. Indeed, commentators before Darwin proposed that women were more variable and consequently inferior to men (Shields, 1975). However, the theory of evolution held that biological variation was the basic mechanism through which evolution proceeded. For Darwinian theorists, this idea made greater variability more adaptive and hence more desirable. In addition, the assumption that men were more variable than women neatly explained a social reality in which women were confined to a limited role of wife and mother whereas men enjoyed more expansive roles.

By the 1890s, scientists were claiming that greater variability might account for men's greater intellect. This reasoning was supported by the finding that, although there were more men than women in institutions for the mentally deficient, there were also more eminent men than there were eminent women (Ellis, 1894). This interpretation ignored the possibility that social factors rather than biological factors could account for this finding: Mental disability was less problematic and thus less visible in women's limited roles (Hollingworth, 1914). Subsequent researchers such as Cattell (1903) and Thorndike (1910) continued to maintain that greater male variability still accounted for the greater number of eminent men, paying little attention to research that contradicted this view (Pearson, 1897; Thompson, 1903) and to social factors that could account for these gender differences (Hollingworth, 1914). Based on this theory, it was proposed that the education of women should be geared toward what were supposedly their special talents.

When mental testing became popular, researchers began to look for evidence of greater male variability in measures of intelligence, because these were assumed to be unbiased by social influences (Feingold, 1992). Although Terman (1925) found more boys with high IQs than girls with high IQs, his sample was in all likelihood biased, because the children to be tested had been nominated by their teachers (see Terman and Tyler, 1954). Indeed, McNemar and Terman (1936) published a review that argued that no conclusions concerning greater male variability could be drawn, given the inconsistent evidence that was available.

In the 1970s, however, several studies took up the question of gender differences in variability. Jensen (1971) computed the ratio between male and female variances in general intelligence and concluded that males had greater variance than females. Lehrke (1972, 1978) revived the argument that institutions for the mentally retarded contained more men than women. However, based upon IQ scores, there was no evidence that there were more mentally retarded males than females (Reschly & Jipson, 1976). The review of gender differences that was carried out by Maccoby and Jacklin (1974) found greater male variability in mathematical and spatial abilities but no gender difference in the variability in verbal ability (pp. 114–120). However, most of the studies that were included in their review failed to report measures of variability, and so these conclusions were based upon only a small number of samples (Feingold, 1992).

More systematic studies of gender differences in variability were conducted in the 1980s. Green (1987) examined the ratio between male and female variance in 110,000 children from kindergarten to grade 12 on the California Achievement Tests. He concluded that boys were more variable than girls on a majority of the tests. This was true for African American and Hispanic students as well as for Euro-American students. Martin and Hoover (1987) followed 9,372 students from the third to the eighth grade on the Iowa Basic Skills Test. Using the ratio between the male standard deviation and the female standard deviation, they reported variability to be approximately equal for girls and boys in the third grade for all the subtests except for Visual Materials, in which boys were more variable. Both sexes became more variable with time; however, by the eighth grade, the boys were more variable than the girls on all the subtests except for vocabulary. Jensen (1988) studied performance on the Stanford Achievement Tests from the fourth to the sixth grade. In the case of Euro-American children, he found greater male variability in arithmetic computation, arithmetic concepts, and arithmetic applications. In the case of African American students, there were no gender differences in variability.

Meta-Analyses of Gender Differences in Variability

Feingold (1992) conducted a meta-analysis of variance in several batteries of standardized tests (including the Differential Aptitude Tests and the California Achievement Test) that had been taken by boys and girls between grades 8 and 12 from 1947 to 1980. He computed the ratio between the male variance and the female variance, so that a ratio of 1.00 indicates equal variation, a ratio greater than 1.00 indicates greater male variation, and a ratio less than 1.00 indicates greater female variation. These ratios were calculated as a function of grade in school and year of test, and the median variance ratio was calculated by grade, year, and overall. Using the variance ratios and the effect size for gender differences on each of tests, Feingold estimated effect sizes for gender differences in the tails of the distribution.

Feingold's results showed gender differences in variability in terms of general knowledge, mechanical reasoning, quantitative ability, spatial visualization, and spelling, but no gender differences in terms of verbal ability, short-term memory, abstract reasoning, or perceptual speed. The differences in variance decreased from 1947 to 1980 on several tests: In particular, by 1980, gender differences no longer existed for high-school students on tests of mechanical reasoning and abstract reasoning. Based on his estimates, Feingold concluded that the girls' scores compared more favorably with the boys' scores in the left-hand tail (lower scores) than in the right-hand tail (higher scores) of these distributions.

However, several criticisms have been expressed concerning Feingold's study. First, calculating variance ratios using the male variance as the numerator and the female variance as the denominator will overestimate the average variance of males relative to that of females (Katzman & Alliger, 1992). This can be illustrated by comparing the variance ratios when the male variance is 125 and the female is 100 with the situation in which the variances are reversed. The variance ratio is 1.25 in the first case and 0.80 in the second. The mean of these two ratios is 1.025, rather than the expected 1.00. Although Feingold (1992) used medians rather than means, Shaffer (1992) demonstrated that this also would overestimate the average variance of males because, in the case of even numbers, the median is still a mean of the two center-most scores. Katzman and Alliger (1992) suggested the use of a log-transformed mean variance ratio, whereas Shaffer (1992) suggested the use of the geometric mean of the variance ratio to solve both the problem of overestimation and the problem of reporting the results in the same scale as the original ratio.

Another criticism was put forward by Hedges and Friedman (1993b), who argued that the subjective method used by Feingold to determine the effect sizes within the tails of the distribution would often overestimate gender differences. They used a quantitative method to recompute the tails and found that the effect sizes in the tails were usually smaller than the overall effect size. Of 56 tail effect sizes, none was large, and only one, the effect size within the right-hand 5% tail for the Mechanical Reasoning Scale, was medium. However, in comparing the *number* of boys and girls in the distributions, they found substantially more boys than girls in the right-hand tail (i.e., reflecting high scores) for the mechanical and mathematical tests. Boys outnumbered girls in the higher scores for all tests except spelling, language, and clerical ability.

Finally, Hedges and Nowell (1995) computed variance ratios for their meta-analysis of research involving large, well-constructed samples of high-school students. In the case of mathematics performance, they found variance ratios ranging between 1.05 and 1.25, with a mean of 1.15. In the case of vocabulary, the variance ratios ranged between 1.00 and 1.08, with a mean of 1.05.

Interpretation

Although there is some evidence that boys may be more variable than girls in certain cognitive abilities, it is important not to extrapolate these findings to infer that there is a generalized greater variability in males (Noddings, 1992). We can only draw conclusions about male variability on the types of test in which it has been studied. Greater male variability is not found on all types of tests, and gender differences in variability have also been shown to vary as a function of ethnicity (Jensen, 1988), age (Martin & Hoover, 1987), and year of testing (Feingold, 1992). These findings demonstrate that greater male variability is not universal.

Greater male variability is often ascribed to biological influences, but the finding of greater male variability in some domains does not imply that biological factors account for these differences: Cultural factors can as easily be implicated (Feingold, 1992). Findings of ethnic and age differences in male variability, as well as decreasing gender differences in variability across time, support the argument that cultural influences contribute to greater male variability where it is found. Noddings (1992) cautioned against interpreting gender differences in variability per se as an explanation; they are simply descriptive data and in themselves provide us with no explanation as to *why* these differences exist.

The greater male variability hypothesis has become important at the very times in history when women have challenged the limitations imposed on them by society. This pattern should sound a warning to be careful of arguments that there is a generalized greater male variability or that any gender difference is explained by the finding of greater male variability.

CONCLUSIONS

The history of research on gender differences in cognitive abilities is long and tortured, and is littered with claims of female inferiority and biological determinism. Modern meta-analyses indicate that there are no gender differences in verbal ability except for better female performance on measures of speech production. In the case of mathematics performance, there are no gender differences in computation or in the understanding of mathematical concepts; however, gender differences in problem solving do appear in high school, and these may be a result of the reduced enrollment of girls in optional mathematics and science courses. Gender differences in spatial ability vary markedly as a function of the type of ability that is assessed: They are moderately large on measures of three-dimensional mental rotation, but they are small or nonexistent on other measures such as the Embedded Figures Test. (However, see Chapter 3, this volume, for a different perspective.) Gender differences in science achievement are small and vary as a function of the area of science being tested. The findings of the Study of Mathematically Precocious Youth, although widely publicized, are uninformative concerning gender differences in mathematics performance in the general population.

There is some evidence that gender differences in terms of absolute performance have narrowed over the course of time, but it is not clear how this effect is to be interpreted. Although there is evidence of greater male variability in some tests of general knowledge, quantitative ability, spatial ability, and spelling, greater male variability does not extend to all cognitive abilities, and even less to other domains of behavior. In addition, some gender differences in variability—such as differences in mechanical and abstract reasoning—have decreased over time. When this finding is considered together with the effects of age and of ethnicity, greater male variability is clearly not a universal phenomenon.

Within the practical realm, the meta-analyses that we have reviewed here provide no evidence that deficits in abilities are responsible for the underrepresentation of women in the fields of mathematics, science, and engineering. If there is cause for concern, it is in the spatial domain of three-dimensional mental rotation, as well as in complex mathematical problem-solving in high school and beyond. The message here is addressed to schools: (1) The curriculum should provide training in spatial ability in order to equalize educational opportunities for boys and girls; and (2) high schools should either require 4 years of mathematics for graduation or else be sure to advise women students—and men as well—that a strong preparation in mathematics is essential for many occupations and careers. Our concern should lie not with gender differences in abilities, but with gender equity in education and employment.

REFERENCES

Baenninger, M., & Newcombe, N. (1989). The role of experience in spatial test performance: A meta-analysis. *Sex Roles, 20,* 327–344.

Becker, B. J. (1989). Gender and science achievement: A reanalysis of studies from two meta-analyses. *Journal of Research in Science Teaching, 26,* 141–169.

Becker, B. J., & Hedges, L. V. (1988). The effects of selection and variability in studies of gender differences. *Behavioral and Brain Sciences, 11,* 183–184.

Benbow, C. P. (1988). Sex differences in mathematical reasoning ability in intellectually talented preadolescents: Their nature, effects, and possible causes. *Behavioral and Brain Sciences, 11,* 169–183.

Benbow, C. P., & Stanley, J. C. (1980). Sex differences in mathematical ability: Fact or artifact? *Science, 210,* 1262–1264.

Cattell, J. M. (1903). A statistical study of eminent men. *Popular Science Monthly, 62,* 359–377.

Cohen, J. (1969). *Statistical power analysis for the behavioral sciences.* New York: Academic Press.

Eccles, J. S. (1987). Gender roles and women's achievement-related decisions. *Psychology of Women Quarterly, 11,* 135–172.

Ellis, H. (1894). *Man and woman: A study of human secondary sexual characters.* New York: Scribner's.

Feingold, A. (1988). Cognitive gender differences are disappearing. *American Psychologist, 43,* 95–103.

Feingold, A. (1992). Sex differences in variability in intellectual abilities: A new look at an old controversy. *Review of Educational Research, 62,* 61–84.

Fleming, M. L., & Malone, M. R. (1983). The relationship of student characteristics and student performance in science as viewed by meta-analysis research. *Journal of Research in Science Teaching, 20,* 481–495.

Green, D. R. (1987). *Sex differences in item performance on a standardized achievement battery.* Paper presented at the Annual Meeting of the American Psychological Association, New York. (ERIC Document Reproduction Service No. ED 291 806)

Halpern, D. F. (1992). *Sex differences in cognitive abilities* (2nd ed.). Hillsdale, NJ: Erlbaum.

Hedges, L. V., & Friedman, L. (1993a). Computing gender difference effects in tails of distributions: The consequences of differences in tail size, effect size, and variance ratio. *Review of Educational Research, 63,* 110–112.

Hedges, L. V., & Friedman, L. (1993b). Gender differences in variability in intellectual abilities: A reanalysis of Feingold's results. *Review of Educational Research, 63,* 94–105.

Hedges, L. V., & Nowell, A. (1995). Sex differences in mental test scores, variability, and numbers of high-scoring individuals. *Science, 269,* 41–45.

Hedges, L. V., & Olkin, I. (1985). *Statistical methods for meta-analysis.* New York: Academic Press.

Hollingworth, L. S. (1914). Variability as related to sex differences in achievement. *American Journal of Sociology, 19,* 510–530.

Hunter, J. E., Schmidt, F. L., & Jackson, G. B. (1982). *Meta-analysis: Cumulating research findings across studies.* Beverly Hills, CA: Sage.

Hyde, J. S. (1981). How large are cognitive gender differences? A meta-analysis using ω^2 and *d. American Psychologist, 36,* 892–901.

Hyde, J. S. (1986). Introduction: Meta-analysis and the psychology of gender. In J. S. Hyde & M. C. Linn (Eds.), *The psychology of gender: Advances through meta-analysis* (pp. 1–13). Baltimore, MD: Johns Hopkins University Press.

Hyde, J. S. (1990). Meta-analysis and the psychology of gender differences. *Signs, 16,* 55–73.

Hyde, J. S., Fennema, E., & Lamon, S. J. (1990). Gender differences in mathematics performance: A meta-analysis. *Psychological Bulletin, 107,* 139–155.

Hyde, J. S., & Linn, M. C. (1988). Gender differences in verbal ability: A meta-analysis. *Psychological Bulletin, 104,* 53–69.

Jacobs, J., & Eccles, J. S. (1985). Science and the media: Benbow and Stanley revisited. *Educational Researcher, 14,* 20–25.

Jensen, A. R. (1971). The race x sex x ability interaction. In R. Cancro (Ed.), *Intelligence: Genetic and environmental influences* (pp. 107–161). New York: Grune & Stratton.

Jensen, A. R. (1988). Sex differences in arithmetic computation and reasoning in prepubertal boys and girls. *Behavior and Brain Sciences, 11,* 198–199.

Katzman, S., & Alliger, G. M. (1992). Averaging untransformed variance ratios can be misleading: A comment on Feingold. *Review of Educational Research, 62,* 427–428.

Lehrke, R. G. (1972). A theory of X-linkage of major intellectual traits. *American Journal of Mental Deficiency, 76,* 611–619.

Lehrke, R. G. (1978). Sex linkage: A biological basis for greater male variability in intelligence. In R. T. Osborne, C. E. Noble, & N. Weyl (Eds.), *Human variation: The psychobiology of age, race, and sex* (pp. 171–198). New York: Academic Press.

Linn, M. C., & Hyde, J. S. (1989). Gender, mathematics, and science. *Educational Researcher, 18,* 17–19, 22–27.

Linn, M. C., & Petersen, A. C. (1985). Emergence and characterization of sex differences in spatial ability: A meta-analysis. *Child Development, 56,* 1479–1498.

Maccoby, E. E., & Jacklin, C. N. (1974). *The psychology of sex differences.* Stanford, CA: Stanford University Press.

Martin, J. D., & Hoover, H. D. (1987). Sex differences in educational achievement: A longitudinal study. *Journal of Early Adolescence, 7,* 65–83.

McNemar, Q., & Terman, L. M. (1936). Sex differences in variational tendency. *Genetic Psychology Monographs, 18,* 1–65.

Noddings, N. (1992). Variability: A pernicious hypothesis. *Review of Educational Research, 62,* 85–88.

Pearson, K. (1897). *The chances of death* (Vol. 1). London: Edward Arnold.

Reschly, D. J., & Jipson, F. J. (1976). Ethnicity, geographic locale, age, sex, and urban-rural residence as variables in the prevalence of mild retardation. *American Journal of Mental Deficiency, 81,* 154–161.

Rosenthal, R. (1978). The "file drawer problem" and tolerance for null results. *Psychological Bulletin, 86,* 638–641.

Shaffer, J. P. (1992). Caution on the use of variance ratios: A comment. *Review of Educational Research, 62,* 429–432.

Shields, S. A. (1975). Functionalism, Darwinism, and the psychology of women: A study in social myth. *American Psychologist, 30,* 739–754.

Terman, L. M. (1925). *Genetic studies of genius* (Vol. 1). Stanford, CA: Stanford University Press.

Terman, L. M., & Tyler, L. E. (1954). Psychological sex differences. In L. Carmichael (Ed.), *Manual of child psychology* (2nd ed., pp. 1064–1114). New York: Wiley.

Thompson, H. B. (1903). *The mental traits of sex.* Chicago: University of Chicago Press.

Thorndike, E. L. (1910). *Educational psychology* (2nd ed.). New York: Teachers College, Columbia University.

Thurstone, L. L. (1938). *Primary mental abilities.* Chicago: University of Chicago Press.

Unger, R. K. (1990). Imperfect reflections of reality. In R. T. Hare-Mustin & J. Maracek (Eds.), *Making a difference: Psychology and the construction of gender* (pp. 102–149). New Haven, CT: Yale University Press.

Voyer, D., Voyer, S., & Bryden, M. P. (1995). Magnitude of sex differences in spatial abilities: A meta-analysis and consideration of critical variables. *Psychological Bulletin, 117,* 250–270.

CHAPTER 3

Do Sex-Related Cognitive Differences Exist, and Why Do People Seek Them Out?

Paula J. Caplan and Jeremy B. Caplan

Most people currently living in the English-speaking world have been raised to expect that people of different races or different sexes think differently from each other. Social Darwinists in the 19th century had effectively done the work of convincing the populace that males were more intelligent than females, that "White" people were more intelligent than members of other "races," and that "non-White" women were, accordingly, the least intelligent of all humans (for example, Mobius, 1901; Romanes, 1887; see Gildiner, 1977). (We put quotation marks around these terms to draw attention to the fact that, while generally used as though they were clear-cut and indisputable categories, their meanings and boundaries are, in fact, fuzzy.) These politically motivated claims were widely accepted as true and thought to be backed up by well-conducted scientific research.

Then, even more than now, political, social, and economic power was disproportionately concentrated in the hands of White men, and almost all of the so-called scientific researchers came from that highly privileged group. In general, then as now, researchers tended to produce apparent evidence that White men were the most intelligent humans. This made it easier to justify keeping racialized people of both sexes, as well as White women, out of influential or highly paid positions, using such arguments as: "You can't let African Americans (or women) run the country, because they don't know how to think about intellectually demanding issues like foreign policy and governmental budgets." In this way shoddy science was used to justify the social, political, and economic mistreatment of women of all "races" and racialized people of both sexes.[1]

We have serious concerns about the motives behind the whole project of seeking to find sex differences in cognition, and we discuss these later. Furthermore, it is crucial to keep in mind that sex differences in cognition are not found consistently (but depend on the choice of tests to administer, the ages of the participants, the conditions in which testing is carried out, and so on, as we discuss later), and that, when sex differences are found, they tend to account for only a tiny proportion of the variance (e.g., Caplan, MacPherson, & Tobin, 1985; Kimball, 1981; see also Chapter 2 and Chapter 4, this volume). It is, however, untrue that research on sex differences cannot be carried out carefully, and that the results of well-conducted research on sex differences can never be useful for humane purposes. Before we turn to an analysis of the existing research, let us consider the various scenarios of what can happen in the relatively rare case when research on sex differences is carefully designed and executed.

PRINCIPLES AND PROBLEMS IN RESEARCH
ON SEX DIFFERENCES

Any study in which the possibility of a sex difference on some particular test is explored can yield one of two outcomes: Either a statistically significant difference is found, or it is not. If no difference is found, this may be important for people to know if the popular opinion is that a difference *does* exist, and particularly if the alleged difference has been used to justify mistreating the "inferior" group. Alternatively, such a finding may confirm popular opinion, if that opinion is that there is no such difference. In the converse situation, a finding that suggests the existence of such a difference may be important for dispelling a popular misconception that the difference does not exist or that the difference is in the opposite direction (in other words, the group that had previously been thought to be the stronger in that respect turns out to be the weaker). Alternatively, it could simply confirm a popular opinion that there is a sex difference in the observed direction.

Moreover, if a sex difference is shown fairly definitively to exist, then one of two things might happen in the realm of educational or social policy. First, the evidence of that difference might be used to support claims that the sex that is deficient in this regard should be treated in a discriminatory fashion; or, second, the same evidence might be used to support claims that measures were needed to correct the apparent imbalance or to compensate for the difference. For example, if it were found that men achieved higher scores on mathematics tests than women, then we might decide that women should not be guided educationally or in the workplace into areas for which mathematical skills were required; or we might decide that girls and women should be given more instruction in mathematics.

Nevertheless, the situation is more complex than simply knowing that a difference exists. In an ideal world, if differences related to sex (or race or age or some other characteristic) were found, they would not lead directly to the mistreatment of already devalued groups (see Chapter 4, this volume). Instead, the potential causes of these differences and the implications of those causes would be responsibly considered. For example, if a male superiority on mathematics test scores emerged, and if this sex difference were shown to result from differential treatment by mathematics teachers, then the kinds of measures that were appropriate to redressing such an imbalance would be considered. Perhaps simply giving women more hours of instruction would not help. It might be necessary, instead, to seek to build their confidence levels so that they matched those of men, to present the study material in ways that were more appealing to women, or to train teachers to be as supportive and helpful to girls as they were to boys in their mathematics classes.

Now, suppose that a difference was found on some test but the cause appeared to be almost completely biologically based, rather than socially based. The expression "biological cause" often conjures up assumptions of *immutability*—that is, the notion that what is biologically caused is predetermined and therefore unalterable. This is not usually the case: Even something as genetically based as a person's height can vary to some extent, depending on such controllable factors as their diet and physical habits. However, it is often tempting to conclude that the members of the "inferior" sex should be restricted from activities that require the skill that the test is thought to measure. This idea is completely unjustified unless the difference obtained is very large and the degree of overlap is very small (in other words, most of the members of one sex perform better than most of the members of the other sex), which virtually never happens. However, even if this did happen, it would be both nonsensical and immoral to try to restrict flat out the education, treatment, and opportunities of individuals simply on account of the phenomenon that the average member of one group scores higher than the average member of the other group.

Researchers who wished to be as responsible as possible in conducting research into sex differences in cognition would, first, try to find tests that were not blatantly easier for one sex than for the other (unlike ones based on football play formations, for example), next use them to examine whether or not any difference existed, and then, if it did, determine the nature and cause of the difference. In the 19th century, researchers pretty much skipped the first step and aimed to identify in precisely which ways and for which physiologically based reasons males were smarter. So intent were they on proving males' intellectual superiority that the history of their work reads today like a bad television comedy script in which people cling absurdly to a belief despite repeated demonstrations of its falsehood.

Beginning with the hypothesis that men were the smarter sex because their brains were larger than women's, researchers found that relative to men's body size their brains appeared to be smaller than women's. Unwilling to question their unsubstantiated belief in men's intellectual superiority, they soon decided that intelligence was located not in the whole brain but only in a specific part of it, and surely, they assumed, that part would be larger in men than in women. As their initial guesses failed to be borne out by their research, they jumped from claiming that intelligence was located in one brain location to asserting that it was located in another, and another, and still another (see Gildiner, 1977; see also Chapter 1, this volume).

We can smugly laugh at this, attributing the obviousness of their motives to their having lived more than 100 years before research sophisticates such as ourselves, or we can honestly assess the extent to which we have or have not progressed beyond both the motives and the sloppy science that characterized so much 19th-century research into sex differences. In this chapter, we examine the recent research concerning sex differences in intelligence in general as well as in the three more specific areas of mathematical, spatial, and verbal abilities. Not only are these abilities fundamental in the sense that, taken together, they probably underlie the majority of cognitive tasks, but they also happen to be the abilities that are most commonly claimed to be characterized by important and reliable sex differences: male superiority in the case of mathematical ability and spatial ability, female superiority in the case of verbal ability.

However, before looking at contemporary research about sex differences in cognition, it is helpful to run through some disturbing patterns that clearly characterized 19th-century research and that turn out to be not so outdated insofar as they characterize much current work as well. Elsewhere (Caplan & Caplan, 1994), we have summarized these patterns as follows:

1. *Beginning with a biased assumption*—e.g., that males are more intelligent than females.

2. *Failing to question the assumption(s) underlying the research*—e.g., the assumption that the predominance of males in high academic and political positions is in fact proof of males' greater intelligence.
3. *Asking research questions based on that assumption*—e.g., is men's greater intelligence due to their bigger brains?
4. *When results of a study do not support the assumption, continuing to avoid questioning the assumption*—e.g., if men's brains turn out not to be larger than women's, relative to their body sizes, then not questioning whether men are more intelligent.
5. *Misinterpreting research results that seem to contradict the assumption*—e.g., when the ability to read quickly (a desirable characteristic) is reported to be more typical of woman than of men, then portraying it as an undesirable one, or one that *leads* to trouble.
6. *Failing to question the evidence for, the logic of, and the damaging consequences of theories.* (pp. 16–17)

We have also identified two important but *wrong* assumptions that have long muddied our understanding of research on sex differences:

1. The assumption that, if we find a "sex difference" in some ability or kind of behavior, that means that all males do a particular thing and all females do some quite different thing (e.g., all males are aggressive, and all females are passive and peace-loving). . . .
2. The assumption that sex differences are biologically based and, therefore, inevitable and unchangeable. (pp. 2–3)

The first assumption is wrong, because findings of psychological sex differences are generally differences between the average score of men and the average score of women on a certain test or set of tests, and there is generally a great deal of overlap between the two groups. Furthermore, as noted above, when sex differences in cognition do appear, they tend to be extremely small (see Chapter 2, this volume). Thus, in judging an individual (or perhaps comparing two individuals, one of either sex), simply knowing about the average sex difference provides almost no useful information. This is not to say that knowing general trends cannot be helpful, nor that one should deny sex differences if they are genuinely found to exist: Rather, the point is that it is vital to infer only what follows directly from the results. The second assumption is wrong for two reasons: First, many sex differences are influenced by social factors, and, second, even those that are biologically based can often be reduced or eliminated by manipulations in the ways the two groups are treated or behave (see Chapter 4, this volume). Although both of these assumptions are wrong, it is nevertheless crucial to keep in mind throughout this chapter that both have pervaded the study of sex differences in cognition.

WHAT IS INTELLIGENCE ANYWAY?

A crucial part of background for this entire chapter is the recognition that *intelligence, mathematical abilities, spatial abilities,* and *verbal abilities* are all conceptual constructs and are ill-defined clusters of concepts. At the most scientifically conservative level, this means that each time a person makes a claim about a sex difference in intelligence or in some set of cognitive abilities, all that they should really be saying is that in their study or in their review of studies, they had found a sex difference in the tests or skills that one or more researchers had chosen to include under that category. It is worth remembering that there is no such thing as intelligence, in the way that there *is* such a thing as a table that we can all point to and agree to be what we call a "table" (see Caplan, 1995); rather, the term *intelligence* is used by different people to refer to different clusters of abilities, aptitudes, or achievements.

When we think of "intelligence," we are most probably thinking either of the kinds of materials tapped by what are nowadays called "intelligence tests" or of some form of achievement in higher education or scholarship. However, the fact that such images come to mind certainly does not make it true that intelligence really is one thing or another. Indeed, the history of debates about how to define and measure intelligence has been marked by major disagreements. One has been about whether, on the one hand, there is a unitary or unifying essence of intelligence, called *"g,"* that every "real" test of intelligence would or should measure or whether, on the other hand, intelligence is a combination of skills or aptitudes, some of which may not overlap with each other at all. Other debates have raged among proponents of the latter view and have mostly concerned what should be included in the definition (Gardner, 1983, 1993; Sattler, 1982): Should creativity be defined as part of intelligence? Should the ability to recognize or carry a tune? Should common sense? Should sports ability?

The tests that came to be known as "intelligence tests" originated when the French government asked Alfred Binet to develop an instrument to predict which children would be able to manage in regular school classes and which ones would find these too difficult. Such tests became widely used in the United States for military placement purposes, and of course nowadays they are used to make a variety of educational and occupational decisions. They have often been criticized for being sexist and racist, but here our focus is on the question of how to deal with sex in relation to intelligence tests. It would seem that there is no satisfactory way to address this question. If we are told to design and construct a test of intelligence, it would make sense to begin by defining "intelligence," with all of the subjectivity and value judgments that this entails. But let us skip to the stage at which we have supposedly found a definition with which we are comfortable. Our next task is to find test items that will measure the characteristics that we have listed in our definition. What do we do about the problem of sex and intelligence?

Imagine that we choose 20 items to include in a vocabulary subtest and then administer that subtest to 1,000 people. Either we may find a sex difference in their scores, or we may find no sex difference. We are stuck either way. If we find a sex difference, how do we find out whether that is because too many of our test items happened to be sex-differential (whereas, if we had presented all possible vocabulary items, the difference would have been eliminated or even reversed), or whether that is because there is a "real" sex difference in the ability to learn new vocabulary? Isn't the only way to explore the latter possibility to include every word in the language in the subtest—a theoretically desirable but practically impossible task? And if we find no sex difference on the 20-item subtest, we cannot conclude that there is no sex difference in vocabulary-learning ability, because the choice of items might inadvertently have been skewed toward those few vocabulary words that people of both sexes learn equally well. So, should we choose a number of items and then, if we obtain a sex difference, eliminate those that generated that difference, based on the theory that sex differences in cognition are learned rather than innate? Or should we retain the sex-differential items? And if the latter, how do we ensure that we have not included a disproportionately high number of sex-differential items so that the sex difference looks greater than it is (in other words, perhaps there is a small, genuine sex difference, but we have included a higher percentage of sex-differential items than of items on which the sexes would not differ)?

For the purposes of psychological testing, it would be desirable if all the concepts that made up a construct such as intelligence were well correlated: in other words, that a person who excelled in one aspect of intelligence would be very likely to excel to roughly the same extent in another aspect of intelligence. It would then be easier to design tests that measured the construct as a whole, rather than just one specific and isolated aspect. This indeed might be the case if the brain's control structures were understood, but, as we stand today, we lack such thorough knowledge. Thus, even the aspects of the definition of intelligence that are broadly agreed upon have been formed largely for historical reasons. How well they conform to the brain's organization, if at all, is unknown.

In summary, there is no practical way to deal definitively with the issue of sex differences in designing a test, and tests are the primary ways that we use to study sex differences in intelligence and cognitive abilities. Historically, the lack of consensus about how to define the constructs being studied has caused great confusion. As a result of the lack of definitional clarity,

Researcher A might choose one definition of ability X, administer a particular test, and claim to have found a male superiority in that ability. Researcher B might choose another definition of ability X, administer a different test or battery of tests, and claim on that basis to have found no sex difference. As we shall discuss in a moment, those who attempt to summarize the research about ability X often then combine the results from Researchers A and B because they both claim to have studied ability X, overlooking the fact that they used different tests, and that, as a result, they are adding apples and oranges. Word then gets around that there is a male superiority in ability X, and this belief both fits neatly into and strengthens the fabric of sexist beliefs.

In their widely read book, *The Psychology of Sex Differences,* Maccoby and Jacklin (1974, pp. 351–352) summarized decades of research about sex differences in cognition by writing that males had superior mathematical and spatial abilities, while females had superior verbal abilities. This conclusion was consistent with what was generally believed at the time and what, indeed, is still widely believed. Our plan here is to consider, in turn, each of these three domains at several different levels (see Caplan et al., 1985). These levels are the following:

- definitional problems
- problems in specific studies
- problems with reviews of the literature
- problems with the construction of theories

Because the literature in these areas is so vast, we do not attempt to describe, analyze, and critique it all. Instead, we have chosen major or typical illustrations of the kinds of work being done and of the problems that this work entails. Many of the kinds of problems that we raise with respect to the research about one set of abilities are also found in the research about the others, so for some research problems our decision about where to raise them is arbitrary. However, when reading about each problem, it is important to remember that either this specific problem or one very much like it will be found with regard to all of the families of abilities that we discuss.

DO MALES HAVE BETTER MATHEMATICAL ABILITIES THAN FEMALES?

Definitional Problems

As we mentioned above, *mathematical ability* is a construct. Accordingly, in an important sense there is no such thing as "mathematical ability"; rather, different people choose to apply this term to different kinds of things. Some people define mathematical abilities as the capacities to add, subtract, multiply, divide, and perform algebraic and geometric manipulations, and so on. Some people would say that true mathematical abilities involve the capacity to perform such calculations rapidly, whereas others would say that accuracy was the main criterion and that speed was either irrelevant or of little importance. Some would say that true mathematical ability was the capacity for "mathematical reasoning," meaning the capacity to recognize (and perhaps to recognize quickly) which kinds of mathematical processes or formulae should be applied in order to solve a particular problem. Some would say that mathematical abilities included some combination or indeed all of the above.

Then there is the question of the homogeneity of the construct: Is the reasoning that is used in geometry, for instance, anything like the reasoning used in algebra? Or is calculus anything like statistics? One might very well decide that the abilities necessary for the tasks that we cluster together under the heading "mathematical abilities" were really as different as arithmetic ability is from reading ability, for instance. So then we should ask for some convincing justification for grouping these abilities under the same heading. Finally, there is the question whether we should define "ability" as aptitude or as actual performance, because some people learn to perform better than tests of their basic aptitude for the relevant skill would predict, and, of course, many people for a host of reasons perform less well than tests of their aptitude would predict.

To clarify this sort of research, one would ideally persuade everyone in the world to agree upon a single definition of mathematical abilities, preferably (but not necessarily) in which the components of the definition were well correlated, so that if a person performed well in one component, they would be likely to perform well in a different component—which would suggest that similar brain mechanisms or mental strategies were being used for all of the components. One would then design one or more tests that would perfectly measure those abilities—tests on which nothing other than those abilities would enhance or impede test-takers' performance. Then, if one were motivated to search for individual or group differences in mathematical abilities, one would know how to go about it. Furthermore, in that case, once one had administered the correct tests and obtained the results, one would know exactly what the data meant, in the sense that one would not have to wonder whether they reflected expertise in computation, in reasoning of some kind, or in both. And, of course, the same argument applies to spatial and verbal abilities.

Problems in Specific Studies

Perhaps the most widely-publicized research concerning sex differences in mathematics has been the work reported by Benbow and Stanley (1980, 1983), which was described in Chapter 2 of this volume. The headlines about their research in the popular media suggested strongly that boys were better than girls at mathematics and that this difference might well be biologically based (see Caplan & Caplan, 1994, pp. 38–39). We think it is worth looking at the research reported in Benbow and Stanley's publications in some detail, because its flaws are typical of those in studies of sex differences in mathematics.

First of all, Benbow and Stanley reported that they were comparing "mathematical reasoning ability" in the two sexes, but they did not define what they meant by that expression. This makes the next question all the more intriguing: What measure did they use to tap whatever it was that they meant by "mathematical reasoning ability"? In fact, they used the mathematics part of the Scholastic Aptitude Test (SAT-M). Nevertheless, an individual's performance on the SAT-M can be affected by a wide range of factors other than whatever Benbow and Stanley could possibly have meant by "mathematical reasoning ability."

For instance, in the SAT-M the respondents have to select answers to multiple-choice mathematics questions. Now, suppose that a student gets the wrong answer to a geometry problem. This could be

- because the student has poor geometrical ability
- because the student has simply not had enough experience in applying a specific geometrical method
- because the student did not know which geometrical method to use
- because the student had trouble doing the numerical calculation part of a question (as in "If one angle of a triangle is 28°, what is the sum of the other two angles?").

Furthermore, a student who has trouble with such a calculation might have trouble due to

- having a distractible personality
- experiencing hallucinations
- being sleepy
- if she is a girl, believing that she is unlikely to get this answer right, because, after all, "girls can't do mathematics"
- if he is a boy, believing that he is expected to get this answer right, because, after all, "boys are good at mathematics"
- anxiety about test-taking in general
- anxiety about that particular test or at that particular moment.

Of course, anxiety could be caused by something as unmathematical as family problems. In fact, in interviews in the Benbow and Stanley study (see Kolata, 1980), many respondents said that they did not want to take accelerated mathematics classes, for fear that their peers would consider them "different," a factor that could clearly have considerable impact on their performance on the SAT-M and other mathematics tests (so that they might think that a high score would be embarrassing to show their friends and family). Consequently, the SAT-M is clearly not a pure and simple test of whatever mathematical reasoning might be. Furthermore, one would expect that a test of mathematical reasoning would at least be a good predictor of how well a student performs in college mathematics courses, and yet the SAT-M does not predict such performance very well (Fox & Cohn, 1980; Slack & Porter, 1980).

Another problem with the work of Benbow and Stanley is that they seem to have assumed that all of the students in their sample had had the same amount of mathematics education because they were all students in grade 7 (aged 12–13) in the United States. However, it is known that, even when girls and boys are in the same classes, they can receive quite different amounts of instruction (Eccles & Jacobs, 1987). According to Leinhardt, Seewald, and Engel (1979), by grade 7 boys may have received as much as 36 hours more mathematics instruction from their teachers than have girls. In addition, boys are more likely to be expected and encouraged to play mathematically related games than are girls (Astin, 1974; Fox & Cohn, 1980; Leinhardt et al., 1979). Thus, boys would have had more practice in mathematics than girls by the time they took the SAT-M. As a result, boys' skill level and their comfort with the tasks that they were asked to perform would be expected to have been enhanced.

A further problem arose when the findings of Benbow and Stanley were discussed as though they proved something about males in general compared with females in general. Their research had included only highly selected students from grade 7: They were only included in the study if they had scored within the top 2–5% on one of several mathematics tests and had accepted the invitation to participate in the study. Of course, students with less self-confidence about their mathematical abilities might well have been more likely to decline this invitation. There is all the difference in the world between finding sex differences in mathematical abilities and finding sex differences on one particular test of certain mathematical abilities when only certain, highly selected students are tested.

Problems with Reviews of the Literature

The pervasiveness, in society in general and in the field of education in particular, of the belief that males are superior to females in terms of their mathematical abilities often leads those who set out to summarize the research literature to exaggerate the magnitude and to overlook the inconsistency of sex differences, and simply to conclude that males are superior to females in this respect (e.g., Pallas & Alexander, 1983). However, with respect to mathematical abilities, just as with respect to spatial and verbal abilities, sex differences simply do not appear in many studies; and, when they do appear, they may be present only on certain tests, or only at certain ages, or for members of some populations but not others (e.g., Hogrebe, 1987).

In addition, even when sex differences in mathematical, spatial, or verbal performance do appear, they are very small and account for only a tiny percentage of the variance in performance, as Hyde (1981) elegantly demonstrated. If a difference in mathematical performance of similar magnitude were found to depend upon eye color or the presence or absence of freckles on one's arms, say, then it would be readily recognized that the role of eye color or of freckles was so trivial as hardly to warrant serious attention.

Problems with the Construction of Theories

Theories are models or explanations that people propose to explain the observations they have made or other kinds of data they have collected. At an international symposium held in Stockholm in 1986, Benbow offered a theory to explain the findings of the study that she had conducted with Stanley (see Benbow & Benbow, 1987). In view of its definitional and methodological limitations, any findings from that study need to be taken with many grains of salt. Indeed, we would maintain that it was so deeply flawed that it was difficult to draw firm conclusions from their results at all, and certainly not that males were better than females at mathematics. Nevertheless, in common with many 19th-century researchers, Benbow proposed a theory to explain males' alleged superiority. As we have written elsewhere: "Once data have been gathered to test a theory, the theory often comes to seem to be true, even if the data do not support the theory particularly well" (Caplan & Caplan, 1994, p. 43).

Beyond these considerations, Benbow's proposed theory is particularly problematic for two main reasons. The first is that she claimed that sex differences in hormones led to males' greater proficiency in mathematics, even though in their study they had not measured the participants' hormone levels. The other reason that this theory is problematic is that, of all kinds of theories, those which implicate biological causes are politically the most conservative and the most dangerous for the group that is assumed to be inferior. Once we believe that women are inferior and that there is a biological cause for this, it would indeed seem relatively pointless to operate on egalitarian principles. For instance, even efforts to enhance the performance of females on mathematical tasks would be founded on the assumption that they could never really reach males' superior level of functioning. This would, of course, be an invalid conclusion even if the cause were found to be biologically based. Nevertheless, this is the way that many people react to such results. Thus, it is dangerous to propose publicly and confidently a biological theory that is yet unfounded; and, further, even if a biological explanation were well-grounded, it would be vital to present it accurately and to explore its precise implications, in the knowledge that, with or without justification, other people will readily jump to use such statements as though they supported the status quo.

DO MALES HAVE BETTER SPATIAL ABILITIES THAN FEMALES?

Definitional Problems

The construct of *spatial abilities* is even harder to define with precision than is that of mathematical abilities, for at least the latter might, in principle, be defined as "all of the abilities that are needed to succeed in school mathematics courses." Compared with spatial abilities, there has existed a relatively well-defined realm of activities in schools and universities that are considered to be mathematical. In the case of spatial abilities, however, there has been no such clear-cut realm. Most people would say that academic subjects such as some portions of geography (for instance, map reading), large portions of architecture, auto repair, clothes making, some engineering courses, and many visual arts courses surely require a contribution from whatever "spatial abilities" refers to. However, defining that term has proved very problematic for researchers. One could define it by trying to produce a comprehensive list of all of its components, or one could try to find a more abstract definition that included a description covering the various components that most people would consider to be spatial abilities. The one thing that seems pretty clear is that there is not just one spatial ability.

A vast array of abilities has been encompassed by the definitions of spatial abilities provided by different researchers and theorists. They include:

- map reading
- figuring out where in a room a sound originated
- doing jigsaw puzzles
- finding a shape that is embedded in a complex visual display

- imagining how a three-dimensional assembly of blocks would look if turned through a certain number of degrees
- recalling the sequence of a series of shapes that one has seen when no longer allowed to see them but only to touch them
- matching one shape to another
- figuring out how a sequence of gears will move

and so on (see, e.g., Cooper & Shepard, 1973; French, 1951; Guilford, 1947; Harris, 1978; Harshman, Hampson, & Berenbaum, 1983; Lips, Myers, & Colwill, 1978; Maccoby & Jacklin, 1974, pp. 91–98; Thurstone, 1950).

In trying to come up with more abstract definitions rather than mere lists of skills, one theorist will propose a definition, and another will propose one that includes only part of the one offered by the first but that adds some new element (e.g., Harris, 1978; Lips et al., 1978). Some theorists suggest that some kind of visualization of a rearrangement of objects in space is a necessary part of a good definition of the term, but that requirement means leaving out some of the tasks listed above that are generally thought to be "spatial." In fact, in the process of trying to write these paragraphs, we found ourselves in the following dilemma that can arise when one tries to define any construct whatsoever:

- If we choose an abstract definition, then should we not exclude from a list of skills that fit that definition anything that is inconsistent with it?
- But, if we then think of a skill that really feels like it belongs in the list of "spatial abilities" but then find that it doesn't fit the abstract definition that we have chosen, what do we do? Do we alter the abstract definition, or do we declare that this particular skill is not, after all, spatial?

The development of such techniques as factor analysis can sometimes be helpful in this sort of endeavor. For instance, we could, in principle, administer a large number of skill tests to a large number of people, see which ones clustered together, and then use common sense to determine whether one or more of the clusters that emerged seemed spatial. Next, we would try to find a description or a definition that fitted all of those tests. However, there are problems with this approach. In reality, we cannot administer tests of all possible skills, and so we have to choose to eliminate some; but there is always the danger that we will eliminate some that "really do" tap whatever spatial abilities turn out to be, or that we will end up choosing a definition of "spatial abilities" into which an eliminated test would actually have fitted.

Furthermore, this approach depends heavily upon what we have referred to as common sense for deciding whether a specific cluster is spatial or not. This in itself may prove to be quite clear and unarguable, but it is more likely that there will be some doubt as to which particular kind of common sense reasoning we should use. One type of common sense might have to do with postulated brain organization (in other words, based upon which kinds of tasks used the same brain mechanisms), while another might have to do with socially grouped tasks (in other words, based upon which kinds of tasks were generally performed by an individual at the same time or for the same purpose). These alternative interpretations could radically affect the clusters that the researcher identifies. So, in a sense, here we are back to our previous problem of people simply not being able to agree upon a single definition or approach.

All these difficulties have led to a great deal of confusion and have certainly not led to consensus about the definition of the term "spatial abilities" within the research literature. For instance, in an oft-cited review chapter, Harris (1978) commented:

> Spatial ability has been variously defined: "to move, turn, twist, or rotate an object or objects and to recognize a new appearance or position after the prescribed manipulation has been performed" (Guilford, 1947); "to recognize the identity of an object when it is seen from different angles" (Thurstone, 1950); "to think about those spatial relations in which the body orientation of the observer is an essential part of the problem" (Thurstone, 1950); "to perceive spatial patterns accurately and to compare them with each other" (French, 1951). Each characterization implies mental imagery, but of a distinctly kinetic rather than a static kind. (p. 405)

However, according to the definition given by Lips et al. (1978), "Spatial abilities are those that enable a person to locate an object in space, mentally rearrange objects, recognize shapes, and so on" (p. 156). Two of these three features do not involve the mental rearrangement or rotation that was at the core of the definitions listed by Harris. As we discuss in the following section, these definitional problems can lead to intense confusion and uncertainty when we seek to review the evidence and theories in the literature.

Problems in Specific Studies

The vastness of the array of studies of so-called spatial abilities makes it impossible to discuss their problems comprehensively, but we give some examples here. First of all, though, as we have discussed elsewhere (Caplan & Caplan, 1994, p. 32), it is important to emphasize that, even when sex differences in spatial abilities are found, they are very small and unreliable, and the distributions of scores that are obtained by males and females overlap considerably. This is quite striking in view of the intensely sex-differential socialization to which children are subjected in terms of the development of their spatial abilities.

As Caplan et al. (1985) pointed out, the results of studies are often overgeneralized. For example, Wittig (1979) discussed a study by Baughman and Dahlstrom (1968) that is commonly cited as showing that males perform better on spatial abilities tasks than do females. However, although this pattern was obtained in the case of 437 White children, in the same study no sex difference was obtained in the case of 642 Black children.

Caplan et al. (1985) referred to the lack of definitional consensus that we discussed earlier as another problem with specific studies: It is difficult to determine precisely what has been measured in experiments and with what other abilities it might be confounded. In some studies, tests are used that turn out to be influenced more by clearly nonspatial factors than by supposedly "spatial" factors. For instance, as John Richardson mentioned in Chapter 1, Sherman (1978, pp. 25–26) suggested that scores on the Rod and Frame Test, which has been considered a good test of spatial ability, might be affected by assertiveness and by fear or uneasiness, because it is often administered to women by male experimenters in a darkened room. Given the large proportion of women who have been victims of sexual or other forms of physical aggression by men (e.g., Russell, 1986, 1990), it is certainly plausible that for such women the testing situation rather than the task would hamper their performance.

In addition, an abstract rod and frame are used in this test, and that has often yielded a male superiority in maintaining one's sense of physical orientation as the rod and frame are moved. However, according to Naditch (1976), when the rod was replaced by a human figure, and when participants were told that this was a test of empathy or the ability to understand how others feel, females actually performed better than males. Naditch's study was not published, but in a more recent study by Sharps, Welton, and Price (1993) the sex difference in a test of mental rotation disappeared when the test instructions were changed so as to deemphasize the spatial nature of the task.

Richardson (1994) obtained more complex results with a very different task. In what he described as a spatial test, students were shown upright and inverted male figures, and they were asked to say in which hand (right or left) the figure was holding a black disk. He used the same task but with female figures and with the information that this was a test of how one thinks about and relates to other people. In the case of introductory undergraduate students, men performed better than women on both tasks, but among advanced undergraduates or postgraduates there was no sex difference on the former task. The explanation that Richardson offered for this was that "prior experience is an important determinant of gender differences in spatial ability" (p.440).

However, it is hard to know how to interpret Richardson's findings, as these were so different from both those of Naditch and those of Sharps et al. The task he used was quite different from theirs, and his students were all psychology students, so that even the introductory students may have been aware of the task's very spatial nature, no matter what he told them he was testing. Nevertheless, Richardson noted that the magnitude of the sex difference that appeared in another part of his study indicated that, in recent years, there had been a decrease in the magnitude of a sex difference when it was found, which certainly goes counter to a biological explanation of any alleged or obtained sex differences.

Another problem with specific studies of spatial abilities is that, not only has the testing situation often been more comfortable for males, but also the particular skills that have been tested in such studies have, on balance, tended to be those that are stereotypically male, so that male participants are more likely to feel comfortable performing the tasks and are also more likely to have had practice in carrying them out:

> If tests of spatial ability included the ability to judge how much flour is in a cup, or how to use a dress pattern in sewing, the results might look quite different. Spatial abilities may very well be based on stereotypically male abilities. The wonder is that in spite of this, the few differences found between females' and males' spatial abilities are small and unreliable. (Caplan & Caplan, 1994, p. 34)

Problems with Reviews of the Literature

The definitional problems mentioned earlier cause enormous confusion when one tries to review the literature concerning sex differences in spatial abilities. This is because one researcher will use a particular test to measure "spatial abilities" and find a male superiority, whereas another researcher will use a different test to measure "spatial abilities" and find no sex difference. At best, this makes it virtually impossible to compare studies with each other. How does one compare studies in which the actual or operational definitions (or both) vary from study to study?

Often, when assessing sex differences in some ability or behavior, reviewers use what has been called a "box score" approach (Caplan, 1979), adding together the results of two or more studies, so that the result appears to be that there is a male superiority. (For instance, if the male:female mean scores are 200:175 in one study and 150:150 in a second study, these are added to make 350:325, yielding an apparent overall male superiority.) This leads to the erroneous conclusion that males are better than females on spatial tasks, which means that the "no difference" results are lost. If both of the studies have been carefully designed and executed, how can one justify essentially ignoring the no-difference one?

In fact, if one thinks about it, what is happening is that the latter result is merely reducing the apparent overall difference. This does not make sense statistically, unless both studies were carried out in exactly the same way, with subjects drawn in exactly the same way from exactly the same population. If both studies are valid, then at the very least we need to conclude that in some spatial abilities there is no sex difference. It is also possible that the first study was well designed but that the tests used in it do not really tap what most people would consider to be spatial skills. If either of these is the case, then the box score approach leads to a misrepresentation of the truth. What is more appropriate is a search for "boundary conditions": That is, one needs to investigate whether some characteristic of the test or testing conditions of the subject population in the first study was more likely to yield a sex difference than those in the second study. An obvious instance would be if the test items in the first study tended to be about diagrams of plays on a football field or of automobile gears, rather than about clothing patterns for sewing or plans for arrangements of furniture. If the test items in the second study were more likely to be of a kind to which members of the two sexes had received equivalent amounts of exposure, it would be no surprise that no difference had appeared. In this situation, simply adding the results together masks important information about the real abilities of women and men.

Related to this issue is a consequence of methodological errors in particular studies. Even if all researchers used the same definition and the same tests of "spatial abilities," there may well be other errors and problems with the way the studies are designed, executed, or interpreted. If so, then before attempting any summary of research in this field, one needs to analyze all of these limitations, to eliminate studies that are flawed in major ways, and to establish which bits of the remaining studies are likely to yield valid information. Finally, one must undertake the admittedly arduous task of piecing together these fragments and figuring out the current state of the field on that basis. Few researchers seem to wish to do this, although all that we are really advocating is a critical, questioning review of the literature rather than a superficial summary.

Problems with the Construction of Theories

As we noted, theories have often been based on profoundly flawed studies, and it is disturbing that people are often so fascinated by theories that they become absorbed by their cleverness, by their intriguing twists and turns and implications, and they overlook the fact that those theories are based on research that leaves a lot to be desired. Especially when theories fit with the beliefs and aims of those who hold political, social, and economic power in the society in which the theories are proposed, the question of the truth or falsehood of those theories too often takes a back seat as the claims themselves are warmly welcomed into the fold of the élite. In the 20th century as in the 19th century, claims that alleged sex differences in brain physiology lead to alleged female inferiority in intellectual spheres have tended to be hospitably ushered into that fold (Bleier, 1988).

A good example of this is a claim by one respected writer about sex differences in spatial abilities: that females were spatially inferior due to a genetic factor. Harris (1978) asserted that spatial abilities were sex-linked in such a way that the test scores obtained by mothers and sons should be more similar to each other than those obtained by mothers and daughters, and that there should be no correlation between those obtained by fathers and sons. The actual data do not follow this pattern, but in a review article Harris claimed that the theory was true and even presented a chart purporting to illustrate this truth. However, examination of the numbers contained in that chart show that the correlations do not follow the pattern implied by the theory. If one looked only at the claims about the theory's correctness, one would never suspect that it fails to hold water.

A number of different theories have been proposed with regard to an alleged cerebral basis for sex differences in spatial abilities, as John Richardson pointed out in Chapter 1 of this volume. To begin with, these theories conflict with each other, so they cannot all be true. Theorists such as Levy (1972) suggested that the spatial abilities localized in only one hemisphere of the brain were the superior ones, but others such as Buffery and Gray (1972) claimed that those based in both hemispheres were superior, whereas McGuinness (1980) asserted that "*both* hemispheres appear to operate in all tasks" (p.244). Indeed, neuropsychological research always provides at least a few studies that can be used to support any theory, and those who have eagerly sought to prove a male superiority in spatial abilities have frequently availed themselves of selected studies in that field to support their theories.

DO FEMALES HAVE BETTER VERBAL ABILITIES
THAN MALES?

Definitional Problems

The construct of *verbal abilities* has been defined and operationalized in as many different ways as that of spatial abilities. However, in Western cultures, at least, people are more likely to assume that they know what is meant by the former than by the latter. As we have written elsewhere, "When we hear someone say, 'That student is verbally skilled,' we tend to believe we know what that means. But unless everyone has in mind the same, precise definition or the same list of tests that measure 'verbal abilities,' then in fact we do *not* all agree about its meaning" (Caplan & Caplan, 1994, p. 91).

Researchers have rarely even attempted to define the term. Instead, they have simply used some test or studied some kind of behavior, reported the results, and drawn a conclusion concerning sex differences in verbal abilities. It is worth inspecting the following list of just some of the abilities measured in recent decades that have been presented as "verbal abilities," in order to get a sense of just how vast and varied the range of such abilities is purported to be:

> vocabulary size; speed of reading; reading comprehension; ability to express an idea in the fewest possible words; ability to make a number of different words from a group of letters; frequency of initiating conversations; ability to memorize lists of unrelated words quickly; ability to read, write, understand, or speak a foreign language; understanding of analogies; creative writing; fluency; age when speaking first word or first sentence; age when making first sound with the throat, tongue, or lips; skill at playing such word games as "Hangman"; amount of spontaneous production of sounds by infants, while awake or asleep; toddlers' talk to other children; toddlers' making of play noises; children's talking to themselves while performing tasks; children's requests for information from their mothers; children's following of instructions; children's mimicry of nonsense or meaningful words; use of incomplete sentences; adults' use of "ahs" (when speaking); ability to learn a code; color-naming skill; choice of pictures after hearing descriptive sentences; skill at doing anagrams; use of plural noun formations; length of sentences; errors in similes; free associations; and descriptions of abstract pictures and pictures of faces.

(Many of these come from reviews and tables in Maccoby & Jacklin, 1974, pp. 75–87; others come from Ho, 1987; Pepin, Beaulieu, Matte, & Leroux, 1985; Waber, 1977; Wilkie & Eisdorfer, 1977.)

No one has measured all of the above abilities. In any case, it is clear that, just as with mathematical and spatial abilities, a person's performance on many of the tests that are said to tap these abilities can be enhanced or impeded by a host of factors that no one would consider to be essentially verbal. As with other kinds of abilities, there has never been a consensus of what verbal abilities are. Are infants' productions of sounds with the throat and tongue verbal abilities or not? Is the use of incomplete sentences an indicator of a speaker's verbal ability or of the speaker's level of anxiety, confusion, or pressure of speech? None of these definitional problems would matter as much if all of the above tests yielded the same result or at least the same pattern of results, but that is not the case. Females do not produce consistently higher scores on all of the tests that have been called "verbal."

Problems in Specific Studies

Specific problems concerning the way in which data are interpreted arise frequently in research into verbal abilities. An investigator might do a fine job of counting the number of incomplete sentences that are spoken by elementary-school girls in comparison with elementary-school boys, or of seeing how many vocabulary words they can read and define, for instance, but the error lies in concluding that, if one finds a sex difference on such measures as these, then that proves that girls are verbally superior to boys. Until and unless agreement is miraculously reached about what "verbal abilities" are and how they can be defined, and until and unless they are fully and accurately tested by counts of incomplete sentences or knowledge of vocabulary, it is simply wrong to draw such conclusions.

Another frequent error in individual studies is intimately related to both definitional and theoretical issues: This is a dilemma involving the question of the ages of participants. Suppose that one had definitively proven that Test V was the perfect measure of "verbal abilities" (that term having miraculously been perfectly defined). If one administered Test V to a group of preschool children and found a female superiority, what would that tell us about sex differences in verbal abilities? Would it tell us that there *was* such a sex difference? In one sense, of course, it would. Recall, however, from the beginning of this chapter our concern about people's readiness to infer from an extant sex difference that that difference was biologically based and, therefore, inevitable. Thus, in another sense, we could not infer from the study we have described that there was a female verbal superiority but only that, by preschool, either an innate sex difference had persisted or a sex difference had developed, perhaps because parents speak more to their infant and toddler daughters than they do to their infant and toddler sons.

To avoid that uncertainty, one would obviously have to test younger children, before sex differences in socialization could possibly have had a chance to take effect. In reality, this is impossible, however, because the sexes are treated so differently from birth. The next obstacle is the problem of what to test. One cannot count infants' incomplete sentences or vocabulary, since they do not yet speak in words, and by the time that they do, they will have had well over a year of socialization. Ideally, then, one would test the known precursors of verbal abilities. However, these are at present unknown. Some researchers have counted frequency of vocalization (the production of sounds with the throat, for instance) in infants, but that has not been shown to predict what in older children and adults one would be more likely to call verbal abilities.

Problems with Reviews of the Literature

The main point to make about reviews of the literature on sex differences in verbal abilities is that, as with reviews of mathematical and spatial abilities, rarely is it noted that

- sex differences are by no means systematically and invariably found
- sex differences do not exist at all ages
- the sex differences that are found tend to account for very little of the variance in individual performance.

And what is the right way to deal with the fact that, within some studies, males have scored higher on some tests or subtests that were described as "verbal," while females scored higher on other tests or subtests that were also described as "verbal" (Maccoby & Jacklin, 1974, pp. 77, 83–84)? One could say that one sex was better in one subset of verbal abilities and that the other sex was better in another subset of verbal abilities, but that would make it seem as though a clear, coherent construct of verbal abilities had been proven to exist, thus implying that it was reasonable to talk about subsets of the construct rather than to talk about what might in reality be quite different sets of skills.

As with the other two major categories of cognitive ability, when one wishes to review the literature with regard to verbal abilities, how does one pull together the data from studies in which such varied measures have been used, as well as such a wide range of ages of participants? It seems to make little sense to treat a study of infants' vocalization as being as important as a study of college students' vocabulary, but how should one decide which was the more important and what were the relative degrees of their importance? One primary criterion ought to be the quality of each study, including how reliable and valid the measures were, how large and varied a sample of participants was included, how appropriate were the statistics that were used, and so on. But even when one has taken all such factors into consideration, how does one decide how to weight each study? Does one develop a scale of "goodness" of studies and rate each one accordingly, with all of the biases and the problems that this would introduce? But if one does not do that, are there any alternatives other than giving them equal weighting or allowing chaos to reign?

A second criterion for assigning the relative degrees of importance to various studies should by all rights be the degree to which a study is correlated with the construct of verbal abilities. But until researchers and theorists can arrive at a consensus about a good, useful, operational definition of that construct, one cannot even begin to search for such correlations. Finally, given the current state of the art of defining these kinds of constructs, even if one could find a number of high-quality studies, we must ask:

> How can we compare a study, for instance, of the foreign language skills of 230 undergraduates from Hong Kong (Ho, 1987) to one of the ability of 56 preteen and teenage children to play the spelling game of Hangman (Pepin et al., 1985) to one of the ability of 64 people between the ages of 60 and 79 years to memorize lists of unrelated words (Wilkie & Eisdorfer, 1977)? (Caplan & Caplan, 1994, p. 93)

Problems with the Construction of Theories

The major problem in coming up with any theory to explain sex differences in verbal ability is that, as mentioned above, it is not clear that there is any significant difference in the average ability range that cannot be accounted for by differential socialization. Thus, the quest for a theory of sex differences in verbal abilities has sometimes become a quest for a theory to explain the allegedly greater prevalence of extreme reading and language problems in males than in females (Kinsbourne & Caplan, 1979). Nevertheless, an important recent study by Shaywitz, Shaywitz, Fletcher, and Escobar (1990) showed that, contrary to popular belief, males do not have more extreme verbal kinds of disabilities than females: Those in boys are simply diagnosed more often than those in girls.

WHY ARE SCHOLARS AND THE GENERAL PUBLIC SO INTERESTED IN FINDING SEX DIFFERENCES IN COGNITION?

Like 19th-century British and North American society (where so much of the early research about sex differences in human cognition was conceived and executed), contemporary British and North American society is deeply sexist. Although, in recent years, some social movements have made it less socially acceptable within some circles to make sexist, racist, and other oppressive remarks in certain forms, the prejudice has not disappeared but has only in many cases come to be expressed in more veiled or subtle ways.

Thus, for example, it is no longer socially acceptable in some settings to state that "Women are less intelligent than men," but it remains socially acceptable, especially when cloaked in scientific language, to state that "Women are less spatially skilled than men" or that "Women's performance on Test X is inferior to that of men."

Whenever and wherever there is an inequitable distribution of power, those powerful individuals and groups who wish to maintain their share of the power will find scapegoats. Scapegoats allow the powerful to blame anything that goes wrong upon someone other than themselves, as a way of justifying their clinging to power's reins (Caplan, 1989): "This problem isn't *my* fault: It's those women who are causing all the trouble, so don't take any of my power away from me!" In a sexist society, there is always the danger of anything being used to demean and oppress women: That is the essence of sexism and of patriarchy. It should not then be at all surprising that vast sums of research money and enormous amounts of researchers' and theorists' time and energy are poured into the intense, often obsessive search for sex differences.

Wine, Moses, and Smye (1980) have described a fascinating pattern in the history of research into sex differences: When the sexes have been compared on a given trait or kind of behavior and males have been found to display more of the relevant quality, it has been given a positive or even high-status label, such as "assertiveness." In contrast, those traits and behavior that have been found more frequently in females have been given negative, low-status labels, such as "dependency." What is particularly important about the study carried out by Wine et al. is that they showed that information produced by research has often been distorted by labels, so that, for example, research that actually showed that men interrupt and talk rudely more than women was mislabelled as exhibiting "men's superior assertiveness," but women's greater interpersonal skills were mislabelled as "women's dependency or immaturity." In this context, we might well ask why verbal abilities were described as higher in females than in males. After all, surely a sexist society that wished to remain sexist would aim to find a way to conceal *any* female superiority.

There appear to be two reasons why apparent evidence of women's superior verbal ability was not covered up. One was the sheer volume of studies that revealed a female superiority: The more studies there are, the harder it is to cover them up. However, the second reason is unsurprising in view of the work by Wine et al. (1980). It is that the superiority was, in a sense, hastily acknowledged in the rush to demean verbal abilities themselves. In the 19th century, "In relation to the . . . finding of women's ability to read faster, Lombroso and Ferrero . . . pointed out that [t]his finding should not come as the shock to the scientific community that it apparently did. They pointed out that women had a greater rapidity of perception but what accompanies such a trait is also a trait for 'lying' that is 'almost pathological' " (Gildiner, 1977, p. 82). This may seem quaint, but in our own time it is generally assumed that women talk more than men. However, Spender (1980; Cline & Spender, 1987) has shown dramatically that this is not true: Indeed, in mixed-sex groups women spoke less than one third of the time, while in groups in which women spoke as much as one third of the time people of both sexes believed that the women did most of the talking.

CONCLUSIONS

We hope that this chapter has illustrated the truly shoddy nature of the research that has been used to justify keeping women out of powerful, influential, and often well-paid positions on the grounds that they lack the intellectual capacity to carry out the duties that these positions require. Kimball (1981) described the way in which, when our culture believes that a situation has been found that is harmful to males, it pours money, time, and energy into helping boys and men, but it does not do the same when girls and women are thought to be harmed. The example that she gave concerned children's education and learning disabilities. She pointed out that boys had been reported to have far more reading disabilities than girls, whereas girls had been reported to have more trouble with mathematics than boys (though even these long-believed claims have been shown to be wrong and to result from the way that sexist biases have shaped the design and execution of research on learning disabilities: see Caplan, 1992). Where, she asked, did the vast majority of money and staff for remediation go? The answer: into reading disabilities.

Although it is perhaps true that reading is a more essential skill, in that it is required for more aspects of living and functioning than is mathematics, the disproportion goes far beyond that difference. It seems that, within the education system, when boys have trouble, they are given help and attention (Kinsbourne & Caplan, 1979); however, when girls have trouble, they are streamed out of the area of their trouble, as when they are encouraged not to take advanced mathematics and science courses (see Chapter 2, this volume). This pattern has profound implications for children's future lives and work, because the courses that children choose to take at school directly affect their options for higher education and employment. It is therefore not surprising to discover that the disproportion of men in such fields as engineering, science (especially the "hard" sciences), the piloting and navigation of aircraft and ships, and architecture goes far beyond what the occasional, tiny, undependable sex differences in performance on cognitive tests would warrant.

What is striking is the way that those who carry the banner of the myth of females' inferior intelligence have continued to march forward, even when it meant stepping over and ignoring significant contradictory findings and major methodological biases in order to do so. It is not difficult to imagine that, had the banner somehow borne the claim that females were superior to males in intelligence, we as a culture would have been quick to point out how sexist the research was, how poorly it had been executed, and how irresponsibly it had been interpreted. As yet, because of the definitional problems and methodological errors we have covered in this chapter, we cannot make any claim about the existence of sex differences in intelligence or cognition. We can only confidently conclude that there was a sex difference in the way that a particular group of people scored on a test or battery of tests that someone had decided to call tests of intelligence or a specific cognitive ability.

It is quite impossible to overestimate the devastating effects that mistaken beliefs and gross exaggerations of girls' and women's cognitive limitations have had on their lives. Both the individuals who suffer and the society that places such obstacles in the path of people who want to become what they are capable of becoming lose immeasurably in richness, energy, and creativity. Nevertheless, well-conducted research into sex differences can be important. We need to answer a number of questions:

- What kind of sex differences exist?
- To what extent do these sex differences exist?
- What are the causes of these sex differences?
- What are the social implications of these sex differences?
- Can the scales be balanced?
- Do we want to balance the scales?

When we are able to answer these questions, then we can act constructively to set right the injustices that are currently entrenched in our society.

NOTE

1. Many people who have been called "people of color," "members of minority groups," or "non-Whites" have expressed their dislike of those terms. Nayyar Javed drew our attention to the term *racialized,* which reflects the fact that the division of people into races is a sociopolitical act that is wrongly assumed to be scientifically justified.

REFERENCES

Astin, H. (1974). Sex differences in mathematical and scientific precocity. In J. Stanley, D. Keating, & L. Fox (Eds.), *Mathematical talent: Discovery, descriptions, and development* (pp. 70–86). Baltimore, MD: Johns Hopkins University Press.

Baughman, E. E., & Dahlstrom, W. G. (1968). *Negro and white children: A psychological study in the rural south.* New York: Academic Press.

Benbow, C. P., & Benbow, R. M. (1987). Extreme mathematical talent: A hormonally induced ability? In D. Ottoson (Ed.), *Duality and unity of the brain: Unified functioning and specialisation of the hemispheres* (pp. 147–157). London: Macmillan.

Benbow, C. P., & Stanley, J. (1980). Sex differences in mathematical ability: Fact or artifact? *Science, 210,* 1262–1264.

Benbow, C. P., & Stanley, J. (1983). Sex differences in mathematical reasoning: More facts. *Science, 222,* 1029–1031.

Bleier, R. (1988). *Science* and the construction of meanings in the neurosciences. In S. V. Rosser (Ed.), *Feminism within the science and health care professions: Overcoming resistance* (pp. 91–104). Oxford, U.K.: Pergamon.

Buffery, A., & Gray, J. (1972). Sex differences in the development of spatial and linguistic skills. In C. Ounsted & D. Taylor (Eds.), *Gender differences: Their ontogeny and significance* (pp. 123–158). Edinburgh: Churchill Livingstone.

Caplan, P. J. (1979). Beyond the box score: A boundary condition for sex differences in aggression and achievement striving. In B. A. Maher (Ed.), *Progress in experimental personality research* (Vol. 9, pp. 41–87). New York: Academic Press.

Caplan, P. J. (1989). *Don't blame mother: Mending the mother-daughter relationship.* New York: Harper & Row.

Caplan, P. J. (1992). Gender issues in the diagnosis of mental disorder. *Women and Therapy, 12,* 71–82.

Caplan, P. J. (1995). *They say you're crazy: How the world's most powerful psychiatrists decide who's normal.* Reading, MA: Addison-Wesley.

Caplan, P. J., & Caplan, J. B. (1994). *Thinking critically about research on sex and gender.* New York: HarperCollins.

Caplan, P. J., MacPherson, G. M., & Tobin, P. G. (1985). Do sex-related differences in spatial abilities exist? A multilevel critique with new data. *American Psychologist, 40,* 786–799.

Cline, S., & Spender, D. (1987). *Reflecting men at twice their natural size.* New York: Seaver.

Cooper, L. A., & Shepard, R. N. (1973). Chronometric studies of the rotation of mental images. In W. G. Chase (Ed.), *Visual information processing* (pp. 75–176). New York: Academic Press.

Eccles, J. S., & Jacobs, J. E. (1987). Social forces shape math attitudes and performance. In M. R. Walsh (Ed.), *The psychology of women: Ongoing debates* (pp. 341–354). New Haven, CT: Yale University Press.

Fox, L., & Cohn, S. (1980). Sex differences in the development of precocious mathematical talent. In L. Fox, A. Brody, & D. Tobin (Eds.), *Women and the mathematical mystique* (pp. 94–112). Baltimore, MD: Johns Hopkins University Press.

French, J. W. (1951). *The description of aptitude and achievement tests in terms of rotated factors (Psychometric Monographs,* No. 5). Chicago: University of Chicago Press.

Gardner, H. (1983). *Frames of mind: The theory of multiple intelligences.* New York: Basic Books.

Gardner, H. (1993). *Multiple intelligences: The theory in practice.* New York: Basic Books.

Gildiner, C. (1977). *Science as a political weapon: A study of the nineteenth century sex differences literature.* Unpublished manuscript, York University, Department of Psychology, Ontario. Available from the author at 386 Huron St., Ste. 200, Toronto, Ontario M5S 2G6, Canada.

Guilford, J. P. (1947). *Printed classification tests* (Army Air Forces Aviation Psychology Research Program Report No. 5). Washington, DC: U.S. Government Printing Office.

Harris, L. J. (1978). Sex differences in spatial ability: Possible environmental, genetic, and neurological factors. In M. Kinsbourne (Ed.), *Asymmetrical function of the brain* (pp. 405–522). New York: Cambridge University Press.

Harshman, R. A., Hampson, E., & Berenbaum, S. A. (1983). Individual differences in cognitive abilities and brain organization: Part I. Sex and handedness differences in ability. *Canadian Journal of Psychology, 37,* 144–192.

Ho, D. Y. F. (1987). Prediction of foreign language skills: A canonical and part canonical correlation study. *Contemporary Educational Psychology, 12,* 119–130.

Hogrebe, M. C. (1987). Gender differences in mathematics. *American Psychologist, 42,* 265–266.

Hyde, J. S. (1981). How large are cognitive gender differences? A meta-analysis using ω^2 and *d. American Psychologist, 36,* 892–901.

Kimball, M. M. (1981). Women and science: A critique of biological theories. *International Journal of Women's Studies, 4,* 318–337.

Kinsbourne, M., & Caplan, P. J. (1979). *Children's learning and attention problems.* Boston: Little, Brown.

Kolata, G. B. (1980). Math and sex: Are girls born with less ability? *Science, 210,* 1234–1235.

Leinhardt, G., Seewald, A., & Engel, M. (1979). Learning what's taught: Sex differences in instruction. *Journal of Educational Psychology, 71,* 432–439.

Levy, J. (1972). Lateral specialization of the human brain: Behavioral manifestations and possible evolutionary basis. In J. A. Kiger, Jr. (Ed.), *The Biology of behavior* (pp. 159–180). Corvallis, OR: Oregon State University Press.

Lips, H., Myers, A., & Colwill, N. (1978). Sex differences in ability: Do men and women have different strengths and weaknesses? In H. Lips & N. Colwill (Eds.), *Psychology of sex differences* (pp. 145–173). Englewood Cliffs, NJ: Prentice-Hall.

Maccoby, E. E., & Jacklin, C. N. (1974). *The psychology of sex differences.* Stanford, CA: Stanford University Press.

McGuinness, D. (1980). Strategies, demands, and lateralized sex differences. *Behavioral and Brain Sciences, 3,* 244.

Mobius, P. J. (1901). The physiological mental weakness of women (A. McCorn, Trans.). *Alienist and Neurologist, 22,* 624–642.

Naditch, S. F. (1976). *Sex differences in field dependence: The role of social influence.* Paper presented at the annual convention of the American Psychological Association, Washington, DC.

Pallas, A. M., & Alexander, K. L. (1983). Sex differences in quantitative SAT performance: New evidence on the differential coursework hypothesis. *American Educational Research Journal, 20,* 165–182.

Pepin, M., Beaulieu, R., Matte, R., & Leroux, Y. (1985). Microcomputer games and sex-related differences: Spatial, verbal, and mathematical abilities. *Psychological Reports, 56,* 783–786.

Richardson, J. T. E. (1994). Gender differences in mental rotation. *Perceptual and Motor Skills, 78,* 435–448.

Romanes, G. J. (1887). Mental differences between men and women. *Nineteenth Century, 21,* 654–672.

Russell, D. E. H. (1986). *The secret trauma: Incest in the lives of girls and women.* New York: Basic Books.

Russell, D. E. H. (1990). *Rape in marriage.* Bloomington, IN: Indiana University Press.

Sattler, J. M. (1982). *Assessment of children's intelligence and special abilities* (2nd ed.). Boston: Allyn & Bacon.

Sharps, M. J., Welton, A. L., & Price, J. L. (1993). Gender and task in the determination of spatial cognitive performance. *Psychology of Women Quarterly, 17,* 71–83.

Shaywitz, S. E., Shaywitz, B. A., Fletcher, J. M., & Escobar, M. D. (1990). Prevalence of reading disability in boys and girls: Results of the Connecticut Longitudinal Study. *Journal of the American Medical Association, 264,* 998–1002.

Sherman, J. A. (1978). *Sex-related cognitive differences: An essay on theory and evidence.* Springfield, IL: Thomas.

Slack, W., & Porter, D. (1980). Training, validity, and the issue of aptitude: A reply to Jackson. *Harvard Educational Review, 50,* 392–401.

Spender, D. (1980). *Man made language.* London: Routledge & Kegan Paul.

Thurstone, L. L. (1950). *Some primary abilities in visual thinking* (Report No. 59). Chicago: University of Chicago, Psychometric Laboratory.

Waber, D. P. (1977). Sex differences in mental abilities, hemispheric lateralization, and rate of physical growth at adolescence. *Developmental Psychology, 13,* 29–38.

Wilkie, F. L., & Eisdorfer, C. (1977). Sex, verbal ability, and pacing differences in serial learning. *Journal of Gerontology, 32,* 63–67.

Wine, J. D., Moses, B., & Smye, M. D. (1980). Female superiority in sex difference competence comparisons: A review of the literature. In C. Stark-Adamec (Ed.), *Sex roles: Origins, influences, and implications for women* (pp. 148–163). Montreal: Eden.

Wittig, M. A. (1979). Genetic influences on sex-related differences in intellectual performance: Theoretical and methodological issues. In M. A. Wittig & A. C. Petersen, *Sex-related differences in cognitive functioning* (pp. 21–65). New York: Academic Press.

CHAPTER 4

The Meanings of Difference

Cognition in Social and Cultural Context

Mary Crawford and Roger Chaffin

Should social scientists study sex differences? The question is a matter of considerable debate (Kitzinger, 1994; see also Chapter 3, this volume). Some researchers feel that scientific data can be used to dispel myths and stereotypes about women (for example, Halpern, 1994; Hyde, 1994) and to offer corrections to both feminist and antifeminist dogma (Eagly, 1994, 1995). Other researchers see the study of sex differences as a necessary corrective to decades of research that has uncritically assumed that studies carried out on men apply equally to both sexes (McHugh, Koeske, & Frieze, 1986). Others maintain that the hope of such "truths" is naïve, because "sex differences" have no genuine existence outside particular social frameworks. These critics maintain that, rather than being a neutral and objective tool for uncovering the fundamental natures of women and men, science is a social enterprise that is embedded in relationships of power. Differences that are "documented" have invariably been used to legitimate and defend existing differences in power (see Hare-Mustin & Marecek, 1994; Hollway, 1994). Nevertheless, sex difference is still a dominant framework for research and theory on gender and cognition.

We, ourselves, have not remained neutral in this debate (see Crawford, 1989, 1995; Crawford & Chaffin, 1986; Crawford, Chaffin, & Fitton, 1996; Crawford & Marecek, 1989). The epistemological starting points of different researchers affect the kinds of question that they believe to be interesting and important, and our own epistemological stance has developed over many years of thinking and writing about women and gender. We see the sex-

difference framework as having particular, demonstrable, negative consequences, and we have increasingly come to believe that we should be asking
different, more profound questions (cf. Kitzinger, 1994). In this chapter, we
describe these consequences of a sex-difference approach, before shifting
the focus to a new perspective that conceives of gender as a social system
that organizes relations of status and power. The gender system works at
three levels to produce and maintain itself: *sociocultural, interactional,* and
individual. The sex-difference approach focuses exclusively on the individual level and, by obscuring the other levels of the system, contributes to the
maintenance of the system itself. Instead, we use the gender-system framework to explain how situation and context give rise to "sex differences in
ability."

GENDER AS DIFFERENCE

Gender as a Media Event

Research on sex differences in cognitive abilities has proceeded on the assumption that, if the variables under study were defined clearly enough and
measured accurately enough, such differences could be stated as fact and
their meaning understood. However, the differences are fluctuating and variable. Often, highly publicized sex differences (such as those in spatial and
mathematical abilities) turn out to be limited to particular subgroups or not
replicable in further studies (see Chapter 3, this volume). They have a "now
you see them, now you don't" quality that seems inconsistent with the notion
that they represent fundamentals of human nature (Crawford, 1995, Unger,
1992; Unger & Crawford, 1996). Even if a reliable sex difference is identified using clearly defined measures, its meaning is not socially neutral.
Rather, the meaning of a sex difference is the product of social negotiation:
In other words, the meaning of the difference is culturally produced. And it
is produced in the context of a pre-existing system of meanings in which
sex difference is both polarized (men and women are "opposite" sexes) and
hierarchically ordered (women are "inferior").

Even if one accepts the search for sex differences as a worthwhile project
and the sex differences obtained in research as veridical, their meaning remains elusive and ideologically influenced. Consider the highly publicized
difference in mathematics performance upon standardized tests (Hyde, Fennema, & Lamon, 1990a). On average, White men do slightly better than
White women on standardized tests of mathematical ability. However, in
African Americans and Asian Americans, the difference is smaller. Age is an

important variable, too: Girls outperform boys until adolescence. When odd samples (such as specially selected mathematically precocious adolescents) are removed from the overall calculations, the difference shifts in the other direction: Girls very slightly outperform boys. Moreover, the differences appear in some mathematical skills, but not in others. Girls outperform boys on computational skills until high school when boys catch up. In problem solving, there are no differences until high school, when boys start to outperform girls. In the understanding of mathematical concepts, there are no sex differences at all.

This complex pattern of similarities and differences is scarcely a firm foundation on which to base conclusions about deep-seated, universal properties of human nature. Janet Shibley Hyde and her colleagues (Hyde et al., 1990a; see also Chapter 2, this volume) have provided a compelling illustration of how the meaning of such differences is often distorted as the result of treating them as absolute and interpreting them separately from their social context. The popular media dichotomize the sexes, reporting differences as a dualism. Headlines and cover stories emphasize that "girls can't do mathematics," announce that "estrogen destroys spatial ability," and trumpet the supposed "innate superiority" of boys. For instance, Eccles and Jacobs (1986) collected the following examples from *Time, Newsweek,* and other news sources:

> "The Gender Factor in Math: A New Study Says Males May Be Naturally Abler than Females"
>
> "Do Males Have a Math Gene?"
>
> "Male Superiority"
>
> "Boys Have Superior Math Ability, Study Says"

One would never suspect from such headlines that there was much more overlap than difference in the performance of boys and girls or that other factors apart from sex were related to test scores (see Beckwith, 1984; Hyde et al., 1990a; Unger & Crawford, 1996, pp. 85–92).

Gender as a Carrier Variable

One of the most persistent methodological problems in the study of sex differences is the difficulty of separating the effect of sex from the effects of all the other factors to which it is related in our society. The number of variables that interact with sex has been called the most pervasive problem in research on sex and gender (Jacklin, 1981). These interactions lead to confounding, in which the effects of two (or more) variables are mixed and it becomes impossible to decide which variable is causing observed effects. Because sex is a subject variable, research on sex differences is inherently correlational in nature, as John Richardson pointed out in Chapter 1. Sex is related to a great many differences in background and status, and so researchers cannot know whether their female and male samples are really comparable.

Suppose we are trying to determine whether women or men are better at a particular task. We need to compare women and men with similar prior experience, otherwise the differences that we find may be attributable to differences in their experience. For example, it seems likely that the differences in mathematical problem solving that appear in high school are related to the fact that in high school, for the first time, students are able to choose their courses, and boys tend to be more likely to choose courses in mathematics and science that develop this skill (see Chapter 2, this volume). Nevertheless, it is difficult to avoid confounding sex with experience, because our social world is so highly differentiated by sex: Food servers, secretaries, and bank tellers are more likely to be women; head waiters, office managers, and bank supervisors are more likely to be men.

One way of tackling this problem is to look for sex differences among schoolchildren and college students, whose experience is in some ways less differentiated by gender (see Chapter 3, this volume). This approach reduces, but does not entirely eliminate, differences in experience. Even when girls and boys are in the same class they are not necessarily sharing the same experience (see Sadker & Sadker, 1994). Girls and boys in a high-school mathematics class are not working in the same social context any more than they would be in a home economics or ballet class. The activities in question have different meanings for girls and boys, and girls and boys are treated differently by their teachers and their peers when they engage in them. We will argue that these meanings can affect the abilities that are exhibited and developed. In short, gender may often be simply a carrier variable or a proxy for a variety of sociocultural factors that are beyond experimental control.

Gender and Power

The sex-difference approach ignores the importance of power within social relations and the role of the sex-differences debate in maintaining power differences between men and women. Understandings of gender in the social sciences have been so thoroughly shaped by the idea of difference that it often seems that the only available alternative to maximizing difference is to seek to minimize it by focusing on evidence that women and men do not differ. Yet neither of these strategies confronts underlying issues to do with power, status, and domination (see Hare-Mustin & Marecek, 1988, 1990, 1994; Kitzinger, 1994).

Power has proved to be a very difficult concept for psychologists to incorporate into their theories (see Griscom, 1992; Yoder & Kahn, 1992). Although "power" is a word that we all use in everyday language, it is often left undefined and implicit in psychological research. The concept of social and political power is absent even in much of feminist research in psychology or, if it is mentioned, it is only in passing, as a kind of generic explanation of research results. "Power" is not investigated in its own right: The term is used as a rhetorical flourish rather than an explanatory concept. The concept is often used naïvely, as "something directly observable and measurable, a property possessed by discrete individuals, an internalized 'motive' which can be measured and then correlated with other variables" (Kitzinger, 1991, p. 112).

Generic Woman

The sex-difference approach treats "women" as a global category. However, women (and men) are located along other socially salient dimensions, too, such as race, (dis)ability, sexuality, class, and age. Foregrounding sex as the only or the most important difference moves these other dimensions to the background and contributes to the tendency to rely upon simplistic explanations for any observed differences.

Researchers into sex differences have often failed to consider the within-group diversity of women and men when they have chosen samples for study or offered interpretations of their findings (see Fine, 1985; Reid, 1993). It is a mistake to assume that women (or men) necessarily have very much in common with all others of their sex. A woman of wealth and privilege may have more in common with men of her own social class than with poor women. Women of "racialized" groups (see Chapter 3, note 1, this volume) share with men of those groups—and not with White women—the lived experience of racism. Lesbians share the experiences of social invisibility, heterosexism, and homophobia with gay men and bisexual people of both sexes, not with heterosexual women. The social positions of older and disabled women are not comparable with those of young, able-bodied women. When a research study concludes that women are different from men, it is important to ask: Which women—and which men—do we mean (Bohan, 1993; Crawford, 1995)?

Incorporating the diversity of people into research about cognitive abilities is a complex process. Feminist scholars realized early on that simply adding women to old male-centered paradigms was insufficient (see McIntosh, 1983; Spelman, 1988). In the same way, simply adding a sample of African American college students or a sample of older adults without reconceptualizing our questions and research methods is not sufficient to create an inclusive social science.

Essential Woman

The sex-difference approach is an *essentialist* approach: It views gender as a fundamental, essential part of the individual. According to Bohan (1993), essentialism conceptualizes gender as a set of properties residing in one's personality, self-concept, or traits. Gender is something women and men *have* or *are;* it is a noun. Claims that women as a group are less able than men in terms of their spatial or mathematical ability are based upon an essentialist stance. Such claims portray abilities as relatively uniform across situations and as determined by biology or socialization: Men and women differ in their abilities *because they are men and women.*

Essentialism does not necessarily imply biological determinism, nor even necessarily stress the biological underpinnings of gender-specific characteristics (although historically this has been the dominant form of essentialism with respect to gender). Rather, it is the location of such characteristics within the individual that defines essentialism and not the supposed origins (socialized or biological) of the characteristics. Essentialist models "portray gender in terms of fundamental attributes which are conceived as internal, persistent, and generally separate from the ongoing experience of interaction with the daily socio-political contexts of one's life" (Bohan, 1993, p. 7). These fundamental attributes (which comprise "masculinity" and "femininity") are believed to determine gendered roles and actions.

The distinction between the terms *sex* and *gender* was developed early in the contemporary wave of feminist research (Unger, 1979). It reflected a significant attempt to separate the biological (sex) from the social (gender) and thus to open ways to think about the role of situations and society in producing and maintaining gender differences (see Chapter 1, this volume). Nevertheless, the cultural force of essentialism is such that this distinction has not been maintained but has degenerated in confusion, inconsistency, and terminological squabbles (see Deaux, 1993; Gentile, 1993; Unger & Crawford, 1993). Instead of defining socially constructed modes of being and behaving, "gender" has collapsed into "sex": "The semantics of dualism spin a subtle but deadly web, one that entraps both concepts" (Putnam, 1982, p. 1).

The (re)conflation of sex and gender has now become ludicrous. "New" sex-difference studies virtually identical to those published two decades ago are now labelled studies of "gender differences." A lengthy report on National Public Radio discusses selective abortion based on the "gender" of the fetus. A psychological experimenter refers to the "gender" of the rats in her maze. As headlines concerning mathematics performance remind us (for example, "The Gender Factor in Math: A New Study Shows Males May Be Naturally Abler than Females"), such "gender differences" are just the old sex differences dressed up in a new label. They are still seen as residing fundamentally within the individual and as divorced from their social contexts, and they are as readily biologized as ever. Ironically, a feminist usage that was introduced to theorize the social construction of masculinity and femininity is nowadays enlisted to obscure it.

REFRAMING GENDER

Framing gender as difference has produced a body of empirical research, analysis, and popularization that has reflected categorical notions of gender and has recreated those oppositional categories. In addition, it has located the cause of social problems in girls and women themselves. It is difficult to criticize or change this paradigm from within. Calls for "nonsexist research" too often maintain the parameters of a science that treats sex as a subject variable, decontextualizes behavior, obscures issues of power, and provides the prevailing discourse with "evidence" of women's limitations.

If exhortations to move beyond models of difference are to be useful, they must include two important kinds of analysis. First, they must show particular, concrete, social consequences of the difference formulation. Second, they must reframe the issues in ways that are useful and congenial to researchers. In other words, critics have the responsibility to show what is wrong with the sex-difference approach and how to improve upon it (Crawford, 1995). We plan to accomplish these tasks in this chapter by placing the topic of difference within a framework in which gender is seen as a system for organizing relations of power and status.

The Gender System

We see the gender system as functioning at three levels: sociocultural, interactional, and individual (see Crawford, 1995; Crawford et al., 1996; Crawford & Unger, 1994; Unger & Crawford, 1996). At the sociocultural level, gender governs access to resources (for instance, in determining occupations that remain largely segregated and stratified by sex). At the interactional level, women and men (and girls and boys) are treated differently in ordinary everyday interactions, and they come to behave differently in return. At the individual level, women and men come to accept gender distinctions as part of the self-concept. They ascribe to themselves the traits, behaviors, and roles that are the norm for people of their sex within their culture. For example, girls lose confidence in their intellectual ability as they pass through the U.S. school system, although they earn higher grades than boys at every level (see Sadker & Sadker, 1994, chaps. 4 & 6). As a consequence, women and men engage in activities seen as appropriate for their sex, developing role-appropriate abilities and skills and providing some "objective" basis for their own and others' expectations. This is the level on which the sex-difference approach focuses. In so doing, it helps to create and to maintain the differences that are its subject matter. Thus, the gender system works, at each level, to sustain itself through complex cycles of self-fulfilling prophecies.

In our alternative to the sex-difference approach, gender is viewed as a social construct. On this view, gender is not an attribute of individuals but a way of making sense of transactions. Gender exists not in persons but in transactions; one might say that it is conceptualized as a verb, and not as a noun. Following West and Zimmerman (1987), feminist sociologists speak of "doing gender," and feminist psychologists are adopting this expression to designate how gender is a salient social and cognitive means through which information is filtered, selectively processed, and differentially acted upon to produce self-fulfilling prophecies about women and men (Crawford & Unger, 1994; Unger & Crawford, 1996). Gender-related processes influence behavior, thoughts, and feelings within individuals; they affect interactions among individuals; and they help to determine the structure of social institutions. When gender is regarded, not as an attribute of individuals, but as a system of meanings, the processes by which differences are created and power is allocated can be understood by considering how gender is played out at three different levels: societal, interpersonal, and individual.

All known societies recognize biological differentiation and use it as a basis for making social distinctions. Although there is considerable variability in the genetic, hormonal, and anatomical factors that form the basis for the label "male" or "female," and although these factors are not always consistent with one another within particular individuals, they are treated for social purposes as if they were dichotomous categories (Unger & Crawford, 1996). Gender is what culture makes out of the "raw material" of biological sex (which itself is already socially constructed), and the process of creating gendered human beings starts from birth. The newborn infant's vagina or penis represents sex (in middle-class Western society, if the genitals should be ambiguous, then medical science is recruited to eliminate this troublesome variability by surgical means). The pink or blue blanket that soon enfolds the baby represents gender. The blanket serves as a cue that this infant is to be treated as a boy or a girl, not as a generic human, from the very start.

Because gender is a governing ideology within which many other social roles are created, gender distinctions arise in every aspect of social life. Most broadly, the discourse of gender involves the construction of masculinity and femininity as polar opposites and the essentializing of the consequent differences. Feminist theorists within psychology have deconstructed the rhetoric of difference and deficiency that helps to maintain the gender system (see, e.g., Crawford, 1995; Kitzinger, 1987; Shields, 1975, 1982; Unger & Crawford, 1996; Weisstein, 1968).

The multileveled workings of the gender system can be illustrated by considering the vaunted difference in mathematical problem-solving ability between girls and boys. As Janet Shibley Hyde and Nita McKinley noted in Chapter 2, this difference first appears in high school (see also Hyde et al., 1990a). Part of the explanation for the difference is that in high school, for the first time, girls take fewer mathematics and science courses than boys (Chipman, Brush, & Wilson, 1985; Chipman & Thomas, 1985). However, the choice of which courses to take is, in turn, the result of perceived differences in ability.

Eccles (1989, 1994) and her coworkers have examined the tangled web of causal influences that result in these choices. The selection of mathematics and science courses is affected by students' expectations of success and the perceived value of these courses. These perceptions are, in turn, affected by structural factors that determine the opportunities and rewards available to women and men and the interactional processes through which these structural factors make themselves felt in day-to-day social communication. At a broader level, Hudson (1972, chap. 6) found that British schoolboys tended to see the sciences as intrinsically "hard" and "masculine," but that they tended to see the arts as intrinsically "soft" and "feminine." Thomas (1990) showed that similar perceptions were held by both male and female students at institutions of higher education. In other words, academic disciplines are themselves seen as gendered.

Perceptions of the value of taking mathematics and science courses reflect structural-level factors that provide different opportunities and rewards for women and men. In Eccles' (1994) model, factors that affect the perceived value of mathematics and science courses differentially for girls and boys include the following:

- *personal values* (girls value helping others more; boys value fame and fortune more);

- *goals for their lives* (girls value family more highly than occupation; boys value both equally);
- *definitions of these goals* (girls see potential for conflict between career and family goals, whereas boys see them as complementary);
- *definitions of success* (mothering may be seen as requiring a high level of involvement in children's lives, fathering as requiring commitment to career goals); and
- *single mindedness* (girls tend to be involved in and value several activities, whereas boys are more likely to pursue a single career goal to the exclusion of other goals).

The perceived value of taking a high-school mathematics or science course is therefore a product of the complex matrix of gendered social practices in which that choice is embedded.

The selection of mathematics and science courses is also affected by expectations for success in these courses that are, in turn, influenced by perceived abilities. Girls tend to have lower expectations for success in mathematics and science courses than boys do. Compared with boys, girls are more likely to underestimate their mathematical abilities and are less confident of success in science-related professions. These beliefs are, in turn, affected by interactions with other people who also have beliefs about the relationship between sex and relevant abilities. For example, parents attribute their daughters' success in mathematics to hard work and effort, and their sons' success to natural talent. They view mathematics as being more difficult for daughters than for sons, and they believe that mathematics (especially advanced mathematics) is more important for sons. Parents, then, provide an interpretative framework for their sons' and daughters' beliefs about their abilities (Eccles, 1989, 1994). Boys learn that they have natural talent in an important area; girls learn that hard work cannot wholly compensate for their lack of ability. In this manner, gender beliefs become reality as they are enacted in a multitude of daily interactions and choices.

The Social Structural Level: Gender as a System of Power Relations

In the broadest sense, gender is a classification system that shapes the relations among women and men. For example, virtually all societies label some tasks as "men's" work and others as "women's" work. Although there is a great deal of variability in the tasks that are assigned to each sex across societies, whatever is labeled "women's work" is usually seen as less important and desirable. Not only women's work but also women themselves are devalued. The gender system thus influences access to power and resources (Crawford & Marecek, 1989; Crawford & Unger, 1994; Sherif, 1982). It constrains the choices that women and men (and girls and boys) make regarding their daily activities, their relationships, and their careers (Burge & Culver, 1990; Eccles, 1994). Gender ideology is disseminated through the representation of gender stereotypes in the mass media, through patriarchal structures of family and religion, and through continued structuring of the workplace around gender inequality.

Men have more public power in most societies, controlling government, law, public discourse, and education. Historically, the gender system has been maintained at the structural level by laws that prevented women from voting, owning property, receiving education, and controlling their own bodies. In the United States and the United Kingdom, two waves of feminist political activity during the past 150 years have been directed to removing these overt structural underpinnings of female inferiority. Many legal barriers to women's equality have been removed (although the struggle over women's reproductive rights continues in both countries), but many of the social practices that these laws enabled remain in place. Schools and parents continue to prepare children for their "place in society," a place that is still largely different for women and for men (see Burge & Culver, 1990).

The scholarly and popular debate over sex differences has played an important role in maintaining the gender system (see Crawford & Unger, 1994; Tavris, 1992), just as the debate over racial differences in intelligence has maintained class and ethnicity as systems of social control (see Gould, 1981, 1994; Herrnstein & Murray, 1994). In these debates, particular ideologies of gender are represented and reproduced as "objective facts." In order to understand gender at the structural level, one must seek out and articulate alternative (suppressed) meanings. One might also analyze how those who hold positions of power within academic disciplines participate in the social construction of gender and the muting of these alternative perspectives through their rhetorical practices, their gate-keeping with respect to publication policies, and their theoretical biases. Far from being socially neutral, they are actively involved in the maintenance and reproduction of power relationships in ways that are not made explicit (Kitzinger, 1991; Sherif, 1979). Finally, understanding gendered social structures involves analyzing the representation of "scientific knowledge" in the mass media.

The Interpersonal Level: Gender as a Cue

Gender cues are used to tell us how to behave toward others in social interactions, although much of this sex-differential treatment occurs outside awareness. For example, observations in elementary-school classrooms show that, although teachers believe that they are treating boys and girls in a similar manner, boys receive more attention, both positive and negative, than girls do. Boys are yelled at and criticized more in front of their classmates. Indeed, in some classes a few boys are allowed to dominate class time by interacting constantly with the teacher, while most of the students remain silent (Eccles, 1989; Sadker & Sadker, 1994; Spender, 1982).

The behavior of men and boys is often evaluated more positively than the behavior of women and girls. Even when a woman and a man behave in identical ways, their behavior may be interpreted differently (see Barnes, 1990; Crawford, 1988; Porter & Geis, 1981; Wallston & O'Leary, 1981; Wiley & Eskilson, 1982; Yarkin, Town, & Wallston, 1982). In addition, sexual categorization is not simply a way of *seeing* differences, but also a way of *creating* differences. When men and women are treated differently in their ordinary daily interactions, they may come to behave differently in return. Thus, gender differences can be conceived as a self-fulfilling prophecy (cf. Deaux & Major, 1987; Rosenthal, 1966), a set of processes by which gender difference is created, the observed differences are conflated with sex, and belief in sex difference is confirmed.

In the latter part of this chapter, we provide many examples of the important role that is played by the physical and social context in determining gendered behavior. Here, we will provide one example of how cognitive performance is influenced by the expectations of others. In a classic experiment by Zanna and Pack (1975), female participants completed questionnaires that assessed their level of agreement with statements expressing traditional (e.g., "I am very sentimental") and nontraditional (e.g., "I am very career-oriented") views of the feminine gender role. Three weeks later, the participants were called back individually to read questionnaires that had supposedly been completed by men whom they would soon meet. Half of the women were to meet a highly desirable man (tall, Ivy-League senior, with no girlfriend, who wanted to meet new women) and the other half were to meet a less desirable man (short, non-Ivy-League freshman, with a girlfriend, who did not want to meet new women). After reading their "partner's" profile, the women received information about his image of the ideal woman. In one condition, the "partner" agreed with statements such as "The ideal woman would be very emotional/soft/passive," and he disagreed with statements such as "The ideal women would be very independent/competitive/dominant." In the other condition, the responses followed the opposite pattern.

The women then completed a questionnaire that would supposedly be shown to the man they had just read about. Included in the questionnaire were the same sex-role stereotypic items that they had completed earlier.

The women's final task was to complete as many of 50 four-letter anagrams as they could within 5 minutes. This task, they were told, was a behavioral measure of intellectual ability, and their score would be included in the information given to the man they would soon meet. The women who expected to meet a highly desirable man gave self-descriptions that were changed in the direction of the views about gender roles that were held by the man. Furthermore, if they expected to be paired with a desirable partner who held untraditional sex-role views, they performed significantly better on the anagram test than when the desirable partner held traditional views of women. (The women who expected to be paired with an undesirable partner showed no such effect on their responses.) In short, when presenting themselves to a desirable man whom they believed they would shortly meet, these women modified both their gender-role attitudes *and their apparent intellectual ability.* They were responding to gender-linked social influences that significantly affected their behavior and their cognitive performance: In other words, they were "doing gender."

"Doing gender" is not exclusively a female domain. Morier and Seroy (1994) repeated Zanna and Pack's (1975) study with male participants, and the pattern of responses mirrored those given by the women in the earlier study. Men who thought they were about to meet a desirable woman altered their gender-role attitudes so as to conform to their partner's perceived attitudes. The prospect of meeting an undesirable woman had no effect on the men's attitudes. (Unfortunately, Morier and Seroy did not replicate the anagram part of the study.) These studies show how social actors can create their own social reality. Their expressed attitudes and cognitive performance can be affected by a variety of considerations, including whether a task is congruent with masculinity or femininity, how the actors wish to present themselves, and the perceived costs of violating gender roles. At the interactional level, then, gender is continually enacted, negotiated, and recreated.

The Individual Level: Gender as Masculinity and Femininity

In the discourse of gender, particular traits, behaviors, and interests are associated with each sex and assumed to be appropriate for people of that sex. Gender is assumed to be dichotomous—a person can be classified as either "masculine" or "feminine," but not both—and to reside within the individual. Moreover, the masculine pole of this constructed dichotomy is the one that is more valued.

People develop their sense of self within prevailing discourses, of which the discourse of gender is one (see Shotter & Gergen, 1989). To a greater or lesser extent, women and men come to accept gender distinctions that are visible at the structural level and enacted at the interpersonal level as part of their self-concept. They become gender-typed, ascribing to themselves the traits, the behaviors, and the roles that are normative for people of their sex within their culture. Moreover, women internalize their own devaluation and subordination. Feminist theories of personality development (for instance, Miller, 1986) stress that so-called "feminine" characteristics such as passivity, excessive concern with pleasing others, lack of initiative, and dependency are psychological consequences of that subordination. Those members of subordinate social groups who adopt such characteristics are considered to be well-adjusted, even though the same characteristics would not be considered healthy in the case of adult men. Those who do not adopt such characteristics are controlled by psychiatric diagnosis, violence (or the threat of violence), and social ostracism.

Much of the psychology of women and gender has involved documenting the effects of internalized subordination. Laboratory and field research, as well as clinical experience, attest that, compared with boys and men, girls and women

- lack a sense of personal entitlement (Major, McFarlin, & Gagnon, 1984);
- pay themselves less for comparable work (Major & Deaux, 1982);
- are equally satisfied with their employment even though they are paid significantly less than men (Crosby, 1982);
- lose self-esteem and confidence in their academic ability as they progress through the educational system (Chipman & Wilson, 1985; Eccles et al., 1985; Sadker & Sadker, 1994); and
- are more likely to suffer from disturbances of body image, eating disorders, and depression (Hesse-Biber, 1989; McCaulay, Mintz, & Glenn, 1988; McGrath, Keita, Strickland, & Russo, 1990).

In short, gender differences are the result of a self-fulfilling prophecy (Unger & Crawford, 1996). Women are different from men, yet paradoxically this is not because they are women (Bohan, 1993). Each person behaves in gendered ways because they are placed in gendered social contexts. Women encounter different social contexts from those that men encounter. Women and men face different expectations and norms, even in what appear to be identical social situations. Therefore, if they try not to "do gender," they will encounter the social consequences of violating these norms and expectations.

In explaining observable differences in behavior, people often make what psychologists call the *fundamental attribution error* (Ross, 1977): that is, they overemphasize the internal, individual causes of behavior, and they underestimate the importance of the situation. Although psychologists' labelling of this tendency as "fundamental" suggests that it is a universal feature of human cognition, it is both culturally and historically specific (see Miller, 1984). Psychologists need to ask how errors of attribution are socially fostered, and how they contribute to the process of essentializing women's behavior.

Keeping Sight of the System

We have conceptualized gender as a system operating at three levels in order to provide a heuristic for examining gender effects upon cognitive performance. We hope that it will foster thinking across disciplinary boundaries. Gender at the social structural level has traditionally been the province of sociology, anthropology, and mass-communication studies, whereas gender at the interactional level has been encompassed by social psychology and interpersonal-communication studies, and gender at the individual level falls within cognitive, developmental, and personality psychology. Each researcher has to focus upon one particular level, but it is important to keep sight of the system as a whole. Moreover, we hope that conceptualizing gender as a social system will help researchers in this field to recognize that they have conceptual and methodological concerns in common with those attempting to understand other systems of social classification, such as those relating to age, "race," sexuality, and social class.

When gender is conceived as a social system rather than simply as an attribute of individuals, different questions emerge from those that were prompted by a sex-difference perspective. At the structural level, we can ask questions about gender as well as about "race," class, and age. For instance, how are girls and boys educated to take their different "places" in society? Moreover, we can examine how different academic disciplines construct and justify an individualistic understanding of gender. The texts of a discipline (such as research reports, public presentations, and their representations in the mass media), become our objects of analysis. At the interactional level, we can ask questions concerning how cognitive performance is influenced through situational cues that are linked to sex. Similar tasks and experiences may well have different meanings for women and men because their social positions differ. Finally, the individual can be viewed as reflecting the internalization of gender roles. Here, we can ask how people come to have beliefs about sex differences in cognition and about what constitutes "appropriate" abilities and tasks for women and men, how those beliefs are enacted in their self-presentation and in their choice of activities, and how engaging in gender-appropriate activities helps to develop specific abilities.

In the rest of this chapter, we look at the contribution of the interactional level to the gender system, because this has received rather less attention than the other two levels. The individual-difference perspective has resulted in the vast literature on sex differences that has been fairly comprehensively reviewed in the previous three chapters. Structural-level analyses of the gender system (Bem, 1993; Faludi, 1991; Hare-Mustin & Marecek, 1990; Lorber, 1993) compete with individualistic approaches in highly politicized, ongoing debates (Kitzinger, 1994). In these debates, the role of everyday social interaction in transmitting and creating the individual and group differences that we then label "gender differences in ability" has frequently been overlooked.

To demonstrate the importance of situations in shaping cognitive abilities, in the next section we look at research on *situated cognition,* which explores the ways in which the social and physical context of an activity affects the nature of the mental operations that people engage in and the mental abilities that they develop. The implications of this literature for sex differences in abilities have not been widely recognized. First, we review studies showing that mathematics performance is powerfully shaped by the specific situation in which mathematical abilities are brought to bear. We then consider the research evidence that experiences with mathematically related activities are very different for women and men. Finally, we turn to the literature on sex differences in spatial ability to argue that similar processes are at work there and that test performance may be affected by gendered expectations about ability.

MATHEMATICAL PERFORMANCE IN CONTEXT

Systemic effects upon mental abilities are not limited to those produced by the gender system. The literature on situated cognition suggests that abilities of everyday thinking are shaped by the immediate situations and cultural contexts in which they occur, to a much greater degree than most cognitive psychologists would expect (see Lave, 1988; Lave & Wenger, 1991; Light & Butterworth, 1993; Resnick, Levine, & Teasley, 1991; Rogoff, 1990; Rogoff & Lave, 1984; Suchman, 1987). Much of this work is carried out by anthropologists and ethnographers, and it explores interactions among the socio-structural, interpersonal, and individual levels of analysis. Our review is limited to studies of arithmetic skills.

Arithmetic in the Dairy

The arithmetic skills that people use in everyday settings are shaped a good deal more by the specific setting than by the invariant computational algorithms that are taught in schools. Scribner (1984) observed unskilled manual laborers (whose job title was that of "preloader") packing cases of milk products and juices for delivery to stores. The products were packed in cases of a standard size that could contain 4 gallons, 8 half-gallons, 16 quarts, 32 pints, or 48 half-pints. The preloaders' task was to repack the products into cases for delivery to stores so that each store got the number of containers of each size that it had requested. One store might order 18 gallons, 9 quarts, 17 pints, and 30 half-pints. These had to be packed into the standard-sized cases from the full and partly full cases in which they were stored. Experienced workers saved themselves a great deal of work by using partly full cases in order to minimize the number of containers they had to repack to complete an order. Preloaders were much more efficient at finding these optimal solutions than either students or office clerks from the same company, both groups whose arithmetic skills might have been expected to be superior to those of the preloaders.

When they were asked to think out loud, students and office workers revealed that they used computational strategies to solve the problems:

> I'm going to remove six quarts and put them in an empty case. Oh, that won't . . . . Oh, no, that's wrong. [Starts over again and returns units that she removed from the full case.] It was one case minus six, so there's two, four, six, eight, ten, sixteen. [Verifies that the case is full again by counting, pointing a finger as she counts.] So there should be ten in here. Two, four, six, eight, ten. [Counts her moves as she makes them keeping track.] One case minus six would be ten. (p. 26)

The preloaders, in contrast, did not use arithmetic but worked directly from the visual display. Scribner reported the description that was given by a preloader of how he had filled an order for half a case:

> PRELOADER: I walked over and I visualized. I knew the case I was looking at had ten out of it, and I only wanted eight, so I just added two to it. . . . [Later in an exchange with the interviewer on another order]. I was throwing myself off, counting the units. I don't never count when I'm making the order. I do it visual, a visual thing, you know.
>
> INTERVIEWER: OK, well, do it the way that you would do it, I mean, as far as that's concerned.
>
> PRELOADER: If I did it that way, you wouldn't understand it. See, that's why . . . this is what's throwing me off, doing it so slow. (p. 26)

Scribner found that the preloaders used a variety of different strategies to solve the problems that were presented by different configurations of cases and orders; in contrast, the students (and, to a lesser extent, the office work-ers, too) relied on a single counting strategy. In this study, one can see how everyday mental skills are shaped by the properties of the specific situation. Two aspects of the situation were central: One was the particular size and shape of the cases and the containers; the other was the preloaders' interest in minimizing the physical labor involved.

There are two lessons that can be drawn from this study. First, the quanti-tative skills used in this mundane setting were based upon specific physical properties of the items to be manipulated. The general-purpose algorithms that had been learned in school for arithmetic operations had been replaced by visually based representations that eliminated the need to recode the vi-sual displays into numerical information, reduced the need for arithmetic operations, allowed for much more rapid solutions, and led to more flexible problem-solving strategies. Second, the strategies that were used by the pre-loaders were not only adapted to the specific physical properties of the mate-rials to be handled, but they also promoted a goal that was specific to the work that they had to perform. Preloaders, but not students or office work-ers, minimized the physical labor that they had to expend by minimizing the number of containers to be moved.

Using Your Noodle in the Supermarket

Lave (1988) examined the everyday use of arithmetic by people shopping in the supermarket and reached conclusions that were similar to Scribner's. When shopping for groceries, people frequently encounter problems of the following sort: Which is the better buy, a 16-ounce package of noodles at $1.59 or a 10-ounce package at 97 cents? Lave's informants rarely solved "best-buy" problems through the use of arithmetic operations. Instead, they used a variety of strategies that allowed them to make the "best" selection on the dimension that they judged to be most relevant to their goals.

Like Scribner's dairy workers, Lave's informants were flexible with re-gard to the strategies that they adopted, depending upon whether the ratios in question involved prime numbers, whether the size of the package was convenient for storage for dividing into meal-sized portions, and so on. From the point of view of the shopper, a best-buy problem involves satisfying many constraints, such as the preferences and the appetites of the family members, the number of meals to be served, the availability of storage space, and the perishability of the product. These problems are complex and multidimensional, and the problem-solver is the final arbiter of what consti-tutes a problem and of what the "right" answer is. Lave's study demon-strated once again that the use of mental abilities within an everyday situation is finely tuned to the constraints of the situation and to the priorities of the problem-solver.

However, Lave went one step further and directly compared performance on best-buy problems in a supermarket with performance on arithmetic tasks that involved equivalent computational problems. The form of the problems was intended to allow the informants to estimate answers the way in which they appeared to have done in the supermarket. The participants performed almost flawlessly in the supermarket, but averaged only 70% on equivalent mathematical problems. Their duration of schooling and the duration since leaving school were related to their performance on arithmetic problems but were unrelated to their performance on best-buy problems. This result is another example of how the interpretation that a person gives to a task affects their ability to do it. Lave's description of her participants' anxieties about the arithmetic problems gives a vivid idea of the process by which this happens:

> This was supposed to be a relaxed, certainly not a test-like occasion, at home, with a staff person from the [research project] who had gotten to know the participants during the initial interview sessions. However, we were not successful in removing the evaluative sting from the occasion. Participants did not believe our claim that this was "not a test in the usual sense." They reacted to the request that we be allowed to observe their math procedures with comments of "ok, teacher," by clearing the work space, and by talking about not cheating. They spoke with self-deprecation about not having studied math for a long time. Common requests were phrased as, "May I rewrite problems?" and "Should I . . . ?" (p. 54)

Here, we can see the three levels of the social system interacting: individual, interactional, and social-structural. At an individual level, the informants were taking a test that might well have revealed them to be sadly deficient in elementary arithmetic skills. Both the informants and the interviewer were aware of this possibility and, on the interactional level, were trying to deal with the implications for the resulting loss of face on the part of the informant. Lave acknowledged that their attempts to deal with these expectations were at cross-purposes. This was because the expectations were shaped by sociocultural factors in a way that could not easily have been undone by the simple good intentions of the interviewer. The institution of school, the practices of the school classroom, and the participants' experiences of arithmetic exercises and tests had induced problem-solving strategies, negative self-evaluations, and student-teacher roles that neither participant could step out of. The participants were approaching these problems using inflexible computational algorithms that they had learned in mathematics class and had practiced only infrequently since then, instead of using the adaptive strategies that they had applied in the supermarket.

Non-Sense Making in the Mathematics Class

The question of how schools might produce this unfortunate divorce between mathematics in the classroom and mathematics in other realms has been the subject of much discussion (for instance, Brown, Collins, & Duguid, 1989; Bruer, 1993). What practices in the mathematics classroom are responsible for this schism between the classroom and the "real world"? Schoenfeld (1989) referred to the activities of the normal mathematics classroom as requiring a "suspension of sense-making," of which the bussing problem in the National Assessment of Educational Progress (NAEP) is a classic example:

> An army bus holds 36 soldiers. If 1,128 soldiers are being bussed to their training site, how many buses are needed? (NAEP, 1983, p. 316).

Of all the students who attempted this problem, approximately 70% carried out the appropriate arithmetic operation of dividing 36 into 1,128 and obtained the answer of 31 with a remainder of 12. However, of these only about a third gave the correct answer: 32 buses. One third gave the answer "31 remainder 12," and the remainder gave "31" as the answer.

Schoenfeld attributed this kind of "non-sense making" to the everyday activities and practices of the classroom. Students learn the skills that are appropriate to the activities in which they engage. These activities include a large number of work sheets containing problems for the students to solve. These problems are provided by the teacher, and the teacher has the right answers to them. The goal for both the students and the teacher is for the students to get the same answer as the teacher. While it might sound reasonable enough, this goal unfortunately eliminates sense making from the mathematics classroom. On this basis, it is not important for the students to understand the problem, the procedure, or the answer: The payoff is just for getting the right answer. Students learn what works. They also learn that mathematics problems are arbitrary, that the teacher is the arbiter of what the right answer is, and that mathematics problems are to be approached differently from problems in the real world.

One might wish to believe that this was a perverse overinterpretation of an isolated case. Unfortunately, the students who were given the NAEP problem were a national stratified sample: This problem is widespread. One might hope that some students would not be so literal and would look more deeply into the task that they were set. These behaviors are not, however, restricted to the unmotivated or to the less able. Schoenfeld (1989) described a similar failure of sense making on the part of able undergraduate students with strong mathematics backgrounds. We see this as constituting yet another demonstration of the sensitivity of cognitive abilities both to the specific situations in which they were acquired and to the specific situations in which they are tested.

Most of the research concerning cognitive abilities has been based on standard laboratory tasks. For example, these include the mental rotation task, in which the participant decides which abstract geometrical figures match a standard stimulus (Vandenberg & Kuse, 1978); and the Rod and Frame Test, in which the participant is seated in a darkened room and instructs the experimenter to adjust a luminous rod until it is at the true vertical (Witkin, Lewis, Hertzman, Machover, Meissner, & Wapner, 1954, pp. 25–27; see also Chapters 1 and 3, this volume). Many such tasks lack ecological (or "real world") validity because they examine behavior outside its normal social context (see Fine & Gordon, 1989; Neisser, 1976; Parlee, 1979). However, the research on situated cognition suggests that the context is critical: It determines what cognitive skills are acquired initially and then what skills are brought to bear on the task at the time of testing. As a result, performance on laboratory tasks may have little relevance to most jobs or everyday cognitive demands. If the importance of a task itself is unproven, then the importance of any gender-related difference in performance of that task is questionable. Hence, the belief that stripping behavior from its context results in greater objectivity of observation may well be an illusion. Instead, what might be happening is that the social context of the experiment or test is being substituted for the social context in which the relevant ability is normally displayed.

The work of Scribner, Lave, and Schoenfeld suggests that mathematical abilities are very finely tuned to the physical, social, and institutional contexts in which they are exhibited. The gender system results in girls and boys, men and women engaging in very different activities and being in very different social contexts, even when they are ostensibly engaged in the same activities. Taken together, these two observations would lead us to expect a large number of quite specific sex differences in performance in different situations, differences that reflect what women and men spend their time doing. Knowing about such differences may be of some value to educators, but they are not a source of information about any deep-seated, immutable differences between the abilities of women and men. Indeed, the "now you see them, now you don't" character of sex differences is exactly what one would expect if these differences were the result of particular gendered practices of society at large that led men and women to develop differential skills and strategies. In other words, this interpretation calls for sex differences to be regarded, not as immutable differences in cognitive ability, but as relatively long-term but reversible differences in cognitive skills or as ephemeral and situation-specific differences in cognitive strategies.

MATHEMATICS IN A GENDERED WORLD

We turn now to examine evidence that the situations in which mathematics is learned and used are different for men and women (see Crawford et al., 1996; Unger & Crawford, 1996). Girls start out liking mathematics and believing that girls are better at it than boys (Boswell, 1985). They perform better than boys on standardized tests and obtain better grades in mathematics as well as in other subjects. Yet, by the time that they are in secondary school, they score less well on advanced mathematics skills. The development of this difference cannot be attributed just to one or two isolated variables. Rather, there are many interacting factors that might be responsible. In the following sections we examine beliefs about mathematics being a male domain and the possibility of sex bias in standardized tests, which will illustrate influences at the cultural level. Gendered interaction in the classroom illustrates the interactional level. Girls' confidence in their mathematics abilities illustrates the individual level of gender effects.

Mathematics as a Male Domain

Consider for a moment the commonly held stereotype of a mathematician: a cerebral-looking, middle-aged man wearing glasses and an intense but absent-minded air—an Einstein, or perhaps just a "nerd." Now visualize a woman mathematician: The negative stereotypes that are applied include "unattractive," "masculine," "cold/distant," "unfeminine," "socially awkward," and "overly intellectual" (see Boswell, 1985). When Boswell (1979) asked both elementary and senior high-school students about their perceptions of people in mathematically related occupations such as science, engineering, and physics, they described men: men who were white-coated loners, isolated in laboratories, with no time for family or friends. Children learn very early that mathematics is a male domain. By the time they are 8 years old, they believe that adult women are generally inferior to adult men in mathematics (Boswell, 1985).

In the past, it was thought that the belief that "mathematics is for men" was held largely by girls and women, and that it deterred them from choosing mathematics courses and mathematics-related activities. However, a meta-analysis of mathematics attitudes found that men and boys hold this belief much more strongly than girls or women do (see Hyde, Fennema, Ryan, Frost, & Hopp, 1990b). This finding is interesting, because it suggests that gender-related influences upon choosing mathematics operate at the interactional and social-structural levels and not only at the individual level. In other words, the underrepresentation of girls and women in mathematics courses and careers cannot be explained by saying that they mistakenly believe that mathematics is for men, an individual "attitude problem." If both men and women share the belief, we need to look at its sources and its functions. The fact that it is held more strongly by men and boys suggests that there may be something in men's behavior toward the girls and women with whom they interact that tends to dampen the interest of girls and women in mathematics and science. Thus, once again, research findings can illustrate how conceiving of gender solely as an attribute of individuals can lead to simplistic analyses and recommendations. In order to understand gender, we must keep sight of the gender system.

The gender incongruence of mathematics for girls is heightened by the paucity of role models. Especially in secondary schools, the teachers of mathematics and science are predominantly men, and few young girls enjoy opportunities to offset negative influences through personal contact with women mathematicians and scientists. Nor do they learn about great women mathematicians such as Emmy Noether, who persisted in her research despite blatant sex discrimination and provided a mathematical basis for important aspects of the theory of relativity (see Crawford, 1981). Noether worked for years without a salary, and her lectures were listed under the name of a male colleague. Her story is far from unusual: Biology (Keller, 1983; Sayre, 1975), psychology (Scarborough & Furumoto, 1987), and other sciences reveal many cases of women who were denied access to resources and whose achievements against the odds are omitted from the histories of their professions. Yet, efforts to set the historical record straight are often resisted and disparaged as political correctness.

Sex Bias in Testing

The purpose of standardized tests such as the Scholastic Aptitude Test (SAT) is to predict performance in college. Yet, although women tend to produce lower scores on these tests, they achieve better grades than men in college. The tests thus underpredict the performance of women (Rosser, 1987; Stricker, Rock, & Burton, 1992). Testing activists have charged that a test that underpredicts the performance of more than half the people who take it should be considered a case of consumer fraud (Rosser, 1987, 1992). The consequences for women are serious. Nearly all of the four-year colleges and universities in the United States use test scores in their admissions decisions. Because women's college grades are higher than their test scores predict, some women are probably being rejected in favor of male applicants who will subsequently do less well in college.

Moreover, women lose out on millions of dollars in scholarships based on their test performance. More than 750 organizations use test scores in awarding scholarships. Only about one third of National Merit Scholarship finalists are women, and the proportion in other scholarship programs is similar (Sadker & Sadker, 1994, chap. 6). In New York State, students can win Regents Scholarships for college. If these scholarships were awarded on the basis of grades, women would win 55.5% of them; if SAT scores alone were used, men would win 56.5%. When, in 1990, New York State decided to change from using SAT scores alone to using both criteria, women won a majority of the awards for the first time in the program's 77-year history. Yet, men continue to win more than 60% of the more prestigious Empire State Scholarships, which require higher SAT scores (Verhovek, 1990).

Young women also lose out on opportunities to participate in special programs for the gifted. One example, the Study of Mathematically Precocious Youth at Johns Hopkins University, was discussed in Chapters 2 and 3. This program has consistently identified a greater number of talented boys than talented girls in a nationwide search for talented 12- and 13-year-olds (see Benbow, 1988; Benbow & Stanley, 1980). In addition, test scores affect both an individual's self-confidence and future academic aspirations (Rosser, 1992; Sadker & Sadker, 1994). For all of these reasons, sex bias in testing is an important issue.

Although standardized tests are supposed to be objective, they are devised by subjective human beings who share the values of society, and the content of the tests tends to reflect these values. In a review of the content of 74 psychological and educational tests, Selkow (1984) found that girls and women were underrepresented and confined to stereotyped roles. In mathematics tests, items tended to be set in contexts that were more familiar to boys, such as sports (Dwyer, 1979). When the results of these studies and others like them appeared, test publishers took action to remove the biases that had been uncovered, and they nowadays claim that their tests are fair or at least improved. There is no doubt that changes have been made in the way in which tests and test items are constructed. Nevertheless, the new items and types of item have had to be calibrated against performance on previous tests. Inevitably, change in the nature of standardized tests is a gradual process. Given the importance of the decisions that are made on the basis of testing in our society, continued research will be needed into the tests themselves and on how they produce similarities and differences among particular groups.

Critics have suggested that, although overtly biased items are now excluded, the new procedures still yield tests that reflect a bias toward male interests (Rosser, 1987, 1992; Sadker & Sadker, 1994, chap. 6). Part of the problem is the topics that are *not* defined as cognitive abilities by psychologists and test constructers. At least one testing specialist has maintained that standardized tests are deeply androcentric:

> Excluded are whole areas of human achievement that contribute to success in school and work. . . . Such characteristics and skills as intuition, motivation, self understanding, conscientiousness, creativity, cooperativeness, supportiveness of others, sensitivity, nurturance, ability to create a pleasant environment, and ability to communicate verbally and nonverbally are excluded from standardized tests. By accepting and reflecting the androcentric model of knowledge, standardized tests reinforce value judgments that consider this model of knowledge more valid and important than other ways of viewing the world. Content that is not tested is judged less valuable than that included on tests. (Teitelbaum, 1989, p. 330)

Gender Inequities in the Classroom

As we noted earlier, the single biggest influence upon mathematics performance is the number of mathematics courses previously taken (see Chipman & Thomas, 1985). The mathematics performance of girls and boys diverges only in high school, when girls begin taking fewer mathematics courses. When course-taking is controlled, the sex differences nearly disappear (Chipman et al., 1985). Nowadays, the sexes have become more equal in their selection of mathematics courses: Girls take courses in algebra and geometry nearly as often as boys, although they still tend to avoid courses in calculus (Sadker & Sadker, 1994).

Even when they are taking the same courses, however, boys and girls experience different worlds in the classroom. We noted earlier that there is evidence for differential treatment of boys and girls, and this extends to courses in mathematics. For example, one study of geometry classes in high school found that teachers of both sexes gave the male students more encouragement and less discouragement, checked their work more frequently, and spent more time with them (Becker, 1981). The effect of gender was compounded with that of race in determining which students received their teachers' attention: White boys received the most attention, followed by boys from minority groups and White girls, and girls from minority groups received the least attention of all. In addition, classroom interaction studies have shown that African American girls tend to become less active, assertive, and visible in class as they move through the elementary grades (Sadker & Sadker, 1994).

According to Sadker and Sadker (1994), girls are praised for their appearance, whereas boys are praised for their performance. In addition, girls experience sexual harassment from their peers and teachers far more often than boys do. Research on educational equity over the last 20 years has revealed such a dismal pattern of deeply ingrained sexism that Sadker and Sadker entitled their book, *Failing at Fairness: How America's Schools Cheat Girls.* In the voices of the young women whom they interviewed, both the sexism and its effects on bright girls are evident:

> "I have a teacher I respect so much because he is smart. When he asks a question he challenges my mind. I thought he would respect my intelligence, too, but he calls me the class 'model' and says things like, 'What music are you listening to? Is there a short circuit up there?' It's like he's trying to make me think I'm an airhead."

> "I had just learned I got into Stanford. Instead of congratulating me, several boys began to tease me. They said, 'In California, 90 percent of the girls are pretty. The other 10 percent go to Stanford.' They were just kidding around, but since I am not very attractive, the way they did it hurt."

> "It seems to me teachers treat girls in one of two ways. They either ignore them and choose to interact with boys, or they treat girls as sex objects by being especially nice to the ones they find attractive. I think this hurts all girls emotionally."

> "In my science class the teacher never calls on me, and I feel like I don't exist. The other night I had a dream that I vanished." (p. 135)

Gender inequity that can affect mathematics and science performance extends to educational experiences out of school. Boys are more likely than girls to participate in activities such as chess clubs, mathematics clubs, summer computer courses, and science camps. In short, boys live in a mathematically enriched environment that encourages achievement; girls live in a mathematically impoverished one that encourages self-doubt.

Low Confidence, Low Self-Expectations

Given the structural and situational variables described above, it is not surprising that girls' lower confidence about their abilities is a consistent finding in many studies (Chipman & Wilson, 1985), although meta-analysis shows that the difference is not large (Hyde et al., 1990b). Moreover, girls' confidence in their own abilities continues to be undermined. In 1992, the Mattel

Corporation introduced Teen Talk Barbie, the first talking Barbie since the 1970s. Among the words that they put in her mouth: "Math class is tough." Sadker and Sadker (1994) commented:

> The national flap over Barbie's "Math class is tough" faux pas is a symptom of the inroads females have forged in this formerly male preserve. The *Washington Post* dubbed the doll "Foot-in-Mouth Barbie," and the American Association of University Women warned that this was precisely the kind of role model girls did not need. Math teachers around the country registered their dismay. "We've been working so hard at closing the gender gap and fighting math anxiety for girls," an Illinois teacher told us. "This is the last thing we need." (p. 122)

By the time that they are in junior high school (at about 11 years of age), girls are losing their early confidence that they can do mathematics as well as or better than boys, and this change in attitude is independent of their actual performance. While their grades remain better than those achieved by boys, girls rate themselves lower than boys do in mathematical ability, they consider their mathematics courses to be harder, and they are less sure that they will succeed in future mathematics courses (Eccles et al., 1985). Confidence about mathematics and attitudes toward success in mathematics are more important in determining whether girls will choose to take preparatory mathematics courses at college than are their actual mathematics achievement scores (Sherman, 1983). In high-school girls of equal ability, those who are less confident are more likely to discontinue studying mathematics (Sherman, 1982). Moreover, female college students are less confident than their male counterparts that they can do well in computer courses, and this attitude affects their course enrollment (see Miura, 1987). By the time they are in college, doing well in mathematics is unrelated to feelings of overall competence among women, although not among men (Singer & Stake, 1986). For many young women, then, mathematics changes from a valued skill to something that is "just not me."

As we noted earlier, parents of girls probably play a part in these attitude changes by providing an interpretative framework for their sons' and daughters' beliefs about their abilities (Eccles, 1989). Boys learn to attribute their performance to ability, but girls learn to attribute their performance to hard work and luck. Once again, we see the three levels of the gender system at work. Enduring stereotypes, based in part upon the economic and occupational realities of gender at the structural level, influence parents' understanding of their children's performance and abilities. Parents play a key role in inducing self-attributions in their children that conform to these stereotypes. Their children then choose courses and invest effort in their classes in a way that results in the development of skills that conform to those stereotypes. This process is ongoing and self-perpetuating, fitting each person to the niche that their society makes available for them to fill.

Mathematical skills are deployed in different social worlds by women and by men. When this point is considered in conjunction with evidence of the degree to which mathematical skills are situation specific, then sex differences in the performance of mathematically related tasks are only to be expected. The other major area in which women consistently tend to do less well than men on certain kinds of test is that of spatial abilities (Halpern, 1992). Therefore, we now turn to examine the role of the gender system in the production of sex differences in spatial abilities.

SPATIAL PERFORMANCE IN CONTEXT

Sex differences in spatial ability are among the largest and most reliable of cognitive sex differences (although see Chapter 3, this volume). Men and boys tend to produce higher scores than women and girls on tests of spatial perception and on tests of mental rotation but not on tests of spatial visualization (Linn & Petersen, 1986; Voyer, Voyer, & Bryden, 1995). It is not uncommon to hear scientifically sophisticated people citing these sex differences in spatial ability as a reason or a justification for the fact that there are fewer women engineers, pilots, architects, mathematicians, and so on. When these differences are seen from the wider perspective of the gender system, explanations such as these appear much less compelling. Although the role of the gender system in producing and maintaining these differences has been analyzed much less extensively than in the case of sex differences in mathematical abilities, one can see a similar interrelationship between cultural practices, social expectations, and attributions of ability. In this section we briefly review research evidence for sex differences in spatial ability. Then, we consider some possible sources of these differences in the gender system.

Narrative reviews have generally come to the conclusion that there are gender-related differences in spatial ability, favoring males, that emerge during adolescence (Maccoby & Jacklin, 1974; McGhee, 1979; Meece, Parsons, Kaczala, Goff, & Futterman, 1982). Meta-analyses have supported this picture (Linn & Petersen, 1985, 1986; Voyer et al., 1995; see Chapter 2, this volume). However, this topic, perhaps more than any other area, illustrates the complexity of the issues in research on gender-related differences in cognition. To begin with, there is little agreement on the definition of the term "spatial ability" (see Chapter 3, this volume). Although some researchers see it as a unitary construct, others argue that it is composed of varying numbers of subskills (Halpern, 1992; Voyer et al., 1995), and still others argue that it is so ill-defined that it is useless as a psychological construct (Caplan, MacPherson, & Tobin, 1985). There are a number of tests that attempt to measure spatial ability, and it is not clear how these tests should be grouped or compared with each other. Some show sex differences, but others do not. On those tests that do show sex differences, the differences appear at different ages for different tests. The size of the difference seems to be decreasing over time on some tests, increasing on others, and has remained constant on yet others.

Two major meta-analyses of sex differences in spatial abilities have been conducted (see Linn & Petersen, 1985; Voyer et al., 1995). A major focus of both studies was to identify tasks that measured the same spatial subskill. To this end, various tests of spatial ability were classified on the basis of the homogeneity across different studies of the size of the sex difference that was obtained: Studies for which the effect size was homogeneous can be viewed as replications. Linn and Petersen (1985) classified tasks into three categories. In *spatial perception tasks,* the participant must locate the horizontal or vertical in a visual field in spite of distracting information. The most frequently studied examples are the Rod and Frame Test (Witkin et al., 1954, pp. 25–27) and the Water-Level Test (Piaget & Inhelder, 1948/1956). *Mental rotation tasks* involve the ability to imagine how a two- or three-dimensional figure would appear if rotated in space. Finally, *spatial visualization* tasks require complex analysis of the relationships between different spatial representations. Examples include the Embedded Figures Test, the Hidden Figures Test, and the Block Design subtest of the Wechsler Intelligence Scales.

Voyer et al.'s (1995) exhaustive review of the literature was based on a total of 286 studies, including those examined by Linn and Petersen. Nevertheless, Voyer et al. found that Linn and Petersen's classification did not divide the tasks into homogeneous classes. Instead, they found that it was necessary to treat each task separately: the Cards Rotation Test; the Mental Rotations Test (which is administered in booklet form); generic mental rotation tasks (which are administered using computers or slide presentations); the Spatial Relations subtests of the Primary Mental Abilities Test and the Differential Aptitude Test; the Rod and Frame Test; the Water-Level Test; the Paper Form Board; the different versions of the Embedded Figures Test; the Identical Blocks Test; Block Design; and Paper Folding.

Moreover, it turned out to be necessary to subdivide further six of these tasks. This meant that the same task was measuring different skills in different procedural conditions. For the Mental Rotations Test, sex differences were larger when the test was scored out of 20 rather than 40. (The former system of scoring penalizes guessing more heavily than the latter.) For the Identical Blocks Test and the Embedded Figures Tests, sex differences were larger with individual administration than with group administration. Voyer et al. suggested that the former procedure might tend to increase performance pressure. For the Water-Level Test, sex differences were larger when a strict criterion was used for correct responding. For the Rod and Frame Test and for Block Design, there were sex differences in adolescents, but not in adults or children.

When the tests were classified in this manner into 24 types of test procedure, Voyer et al.'s results reproduced the main features of Linn and Petersen's analysis. All of the sex differences were in the direction of men or boys performing better than women or girls did. Mental rotation tasks produced the largest and most consistent differences (which were significant in each of six different test procedures); spatial perception tasks produced smaller and less consistent differences (significant in four out of seven test procedures); and spatial visualization tasks produced the smallest and least consistent differences (significant in only three out of 11 test procedures).

These data imply three important points concerning sex differences in spatial ability. The first point is that spatial ability is not a unitary construct. Voyer et al. chose to regard their tests as measuring separate components of a general spatial ability, but their data do not compel this conclusion. Rather, it is an *assumption* that there is some psychological capacity that underlies what we think of as spatial ability. In addition, when the ability being measured is specific to each test, it is important that each test should have predictive validity: Do sex differences on the test correspond to differences in some real skill that people use in their everyday lives? If not, then there is no reason to pay any attention to sex differences or any other kind of differences on the measure. In fact, evidence of predictive validity is lacking in the vast majority of spatial tasks: It is simply assumed that mental rotation tests, the Rod and Frame Test, the Water-Level Test, and other tasks measure "real" abilities. Our concern about predictive validity is not merely an idle caution. A recent study by Hecht and Proffitt (1995) directly tested this assumption using the Water-Level Test: In an ironic reversal, people with expertise in relevant domains in the everyday world were found to perform less well on this test than people with little experience.

The second point is that the specificity of the tasks that generate sex differences throws doubt on the interpretation of differences as being caused by biological factors. It is hard to imagine a selection pressure that would select for mental rotation ability while not also selecting for spatial problem-solving ability. Instead, the specificity of the tasks that produce sex differences seems more likely to be explained in terms of experience. As we showed in the case of mathematical skills, cognitive skills and strategies tend to be very finely adapted to the situations in which they are used. It is plausible that some activities in which men engage more than women may lead to the development of specific cognitive skills that are tapped by tests of spatial perception and mental image rotation. In a later section, we review some of these differences in activity, and we describe other features of Voyer et al.'s analysis that support this interpretation.

The third point is that situational variables are very important in some of these tasks. For example, the need to partition mental rotation into tasks scored out of 20 and those scored out of 40 suggests that the sex difference in this task is, at least in part, due to differences in the strategic use of guessing by men and women. The need to partition the Identical Blocks and Embedded Figures tests according to whether they are administered individually or in groups suggests that the sex difference in these tasks is, at least in part, due to sex differences in reaction to the experimenter. Other tests of spatial ability may well be subject to similar contextual influences. The finding of homogeneous variance on a test is evidence, not that situational variables are unimportant, but simply that they were not manipulated in the studies surveyed. In a later section, we review studies that show that the manipulation of situational variables in a mental rotation task can result in the disappearance of sex differences.

These meta-analyses also illustrate the more general point, that the science of human abilities is part of the gender system and is shaped by that system. One sees this happening in these studies themselves. Before sex differences in spatial abilities can be usefully discussed, different abilities have to be identified. In these studies, the size of the sex difference was used as the criterion for identifying the different types of spatial ability, but this is not an obvious choice. Given the concerns of the authors, the choice was a sensible one, but, if the goal had been simply to understand the nature of spatial abilities, then some other basis for classification would almost certainly have been selected (cf. Carpenter & Just, 1986). As a result, our understanding of the component skills that make up spatial ability has been shaped by the gender system. This understanding becomes, in turn, a part of the system. We now turn to consider the sociocultural factors that might influence spatial abilities.

Effects of Gendered Expectations on Spatial Memory

As in the case of mathematical ability, there are good reasons to think that the sex differences found in spatial-perception and mental-rotation abilities result from the workings of the gender system. Here we first describe studies suggesting that some of the sex differences in spatial ability are due to gendered expectations about these abilities. We then go on to describe studies showing that girls and boys have very different experiences of activities that promote the development of spatial skills.

In the United States, people believe that large sex differences in spatial ability exist and that spatial skills are inherently "masculine." College students rate activities that involve spatial skills as being more masculine than other activities, and men say that men participate in these former activities more than women say that women do (Newcombe, Bandura & Taylor, 1983). Another study obtained a similar pattern of results in the case of beliefs about memory for different types of information (Crawford, Herrmann, Holdsworth, Randall, & Robbins, 1989). In the latter study, the participants were asked to rate how well women in general, men in general, and they themselves could remember various types of information, such as names, places, directions, shopping lists, and conversations. Men and women were in accord that men were better at finding previously visited places and directions (spatial tasks), and that women were better at remembering shopping lists and names (verbal tasks). However, ratings regarding their own abilities followed divergent patterns from ratings regarding women and men in general. This study demonstrates that men and women hold similar views about the ability of each sex to remember various types of information. The pattern of items that each sex was thought to remember better followed traditional sex-role expectations: men were perceived as being better at remembering spatial information such as places and directions, and women were believed to be better at remembering verbal or relational information such as names, faces, and conversations.

People's beliefs about cognitive abilities affect their performance on tests of those abilities. Simply changing the instructions or the name of a task can either elicit or eliminate sex differences in certain tasks. For example, Herrmann, Crawford, and Holdsworth (1992) asked female and male participants to perform two memory tasks, remembering a list of items and remembering a set of instructions. They manipulated the gender label of the two tasks while keeping their task requirements constant. The list was entitled either "Grocery store list" or "Hardware store list," and it contained items such as brush, hose, chips, nuts, and salt. In a similar manner, the instructions were labeled either "Making a shirt" or "Making a workbench," and these contained neutral phrases such as "Rearrange the pieces into different groups," "Get the necessary tools and implements," "Find the corresponding parts," and "Follow the diagram and directions."

Both in the list task and in the instructions task, men remembered the masculine gender-typed set better than women did, and women remembered the feminine gender-typed set better than men did. Additionally, men were more affected by gender-typing than women: They performed significantly worse on the feminine gender-typed tasks of remembering the grocery store list and the instructions for constructing a shirt, whereas women performed only marginally worse on the masculine gender-typed tasks of remembering the hardware store list and the instructions for constructing a workbench. One possible explanation for this is that masculinity is more narrowly defined than femininity and so allows for less flexibility in performance.

A similar effect of gender-based expectations on spatial memory was described by Sharps, Welton, and Price (1993, Expt. 1). They reported that a sex difference found in a spatial memory task involving a map-like representation was eliminated when an isomorphic but more concrete version of the task was used. Women and men were shown an array of common objects (for example, a paper clip, a light bulb, etc.) upon a large board. Their task was to remember which objects were located where. No reference was made to "spatial memory." For half of the participants, the board was divided into a number of different areas by three-dimensional contours in various shapes (such as a cube or a cylinder). The other half of the participants were presented with a more abstract representation in which the board was divided into different areas by a two-dimensional map in which the shapes seen by the first group were drawn in outline. The two displays were the same size and contained the same number of objects.

The data showed no main effect of sex, but there was an interaction between the effects of sex and of type of representation. Men performed equally well on both versions of the task, while women performed better on the three-dimensional version than on the two-dimensional ("map") version. Unfortunately, the experimenters did not collect any evidence to show that the map version of the task had been seen as involving map-reading skills or that the participants saw men as more likely to be better at this task than women. If it can be assumed that the two tasks did differ in terms of their gender connotations, then the results of this experiment provide further support for the suggestion that sex differences in spatial memory performance are, in part, a result of demand characteristics of the task, rather than a result of intrinsic differences in ability.

Effects of Gendered Expectations on Mental Image Rotation

Expectations based on the gendered nature of the task also seem to affect performance on tasks that involve the rotation of mental images. The evidence suggests that even sex differences in mental-rotation ability, the largest and most robust of the sex differences in spatial ability, are extremely sensitive to the specific task conditions. Sharps et al. (1993, Expt. 2) examined the effects of instructions on performance in the Mental Rotations Test devised by Vandenberg and Kuse (1978), which had produced significant sex differences in previous research (Linn & Petersen, 1985, 1986; Voyer et al., 1995). The standard instructions were replaced with a paragraph that either de-emphasized the spatial nature of the task or else emphasized its spatial nature. The former instructions stated: "The following is an evaluation of . . . your abilities to reason and solve problems." In contrast, the latter instructions stated: "The following is an evaluation of some of your spatial abilities, of your abilities to reason and solve problems regarding physical objects in space. Such abilities are involved in mechanical skills, and in navigation, map reading, and work with tools." Men significantly outperformed women when the instructions emphasized the spatial nature of the task. However, when the spatial nature of the task was de-emphasized, the sex difference was eliminated. That is, the sex difference in this study was related to the identification of the task as a test of spatial abilities rather than by the demands of the task itself.

Sharps, Price, and Williams (1994) employed the same instructional manipulation with another paper-and-pencil mental rotation test containing items differing in difficulty: three-dimensional (3-D) block figures of the kind that were used in the previous study, two-dimensional (2-D) block figures of the same type, simpler 2-D figures, and 3-D figures of everyday objects. They found no sex difference at all for the two easiest types of item (simpler 2-D figures and 3-D figures of everyday objects). For the most difficult type of item, 3-D block figures, the effect of instructions interacted with the effect of sex. Men performed better than women when the participants were told that the test involved spatial abilities, but there was no sex difference under nonspatial instructions. In a second experiment, the gender connotations of the instructions were manipulated more directly. The task consisted of the mental rotation of 3-D block figures and was presented as being predictive of a person's ability in either interior design or combat aircraft flying. As for the 3-D figures in the first experiment, there was an interaction between the effects of instructions and sex. Men given "masculine" instructions performed better than men or women in any other conditions. As in the first experiment and as in the memory task that we described earlier (Herrmann et al., 1992), men were more affected than women by the manipulation of gender connotations.

These results indicate that sex differences in at least some mental rotation tasks are the product of the subjects' gender-based expectations about their own performance. It is likely that men learn that they are "good at" spatial tasks, whereas women learn that they are "not good at" them. These beliefs lead to a self-fulfilling prophecy when faced with a task labeled "spatial." However, when the task is gender-neutralized, the performance of women and men is identical. This account of the effect is not, however, the whole story. It is unclear why instructions affected the participants' performance on the most difficult 3-D block figure task, but not on the easier figures. Possibly, the task must be of a sufficient level of difficulty for the effects of a gender-labeling manipulation to be apparent. This might be expected if the effects were motivational in nature. However, if sex differences in performance are the product of the same mechanism, it is hard to understand why the 2-D block figures did not show any effect of instructions, because these items were sufficiently difficult to produce a sex difference.

An absence of instructional effects for mental rotation of 2-D images has been replicated by Richardson (1994). He found no effect of gendered task labeling when the figure to be rotated was a 2-D mannequin whose hands were marked, one by a black disk, the other by a white disk. The mannequin was viewed from either the front or the back, and half of the time it was inverted through 180°. The task was to decide which hand was holding the black disk. The subjects were asked to respond to as many of the figures as possible in the 7 minutes allowed. The instructions directly manipulated the gender connotations of this task by describing it as a measure of "personal empathy" or of "spatial thinking." There was a sex difference for introductory social-science students, but no effect of instructions.

In summary, sex differences in mental rotation appear to be highly specific to the type of task and the gender expectations that it elicits. At this point, it is not clear how much of this sex difference in mental rotation performance can be ascribed to gender-based expectations that are situationally specific, or whether more permanent differences in skill are also involved. It is, nevertheless, clear that expectations about the gender typing of a cognitive task can affect the performance of both men and women. Beliefs about differences, together with a desire to appear appropriately masculine or feminine, seem to create ample opportunity for the operation of self-fulfilling prophecies.

In this section, we have discussed several studies which suggest that cognitive performance is sensitive to rather subtle aspects of the testing situation. We have suggested that these effects are characteristic of the way in which gender is continually reproduced and maintained by the gender system in everyday interaction. Sex is a salient social category, and distinctions that are based upon sex affect everything from the ability to remember who said what (Taylor, Fiske, Etcoff, & Ruderman, 1978) to how competent another person is perceived to be (Pugh & Wahrman, 1983).

Gendered Experience with Activities Involving Spatial Abilities

The gender system may also produce more enduring (although not necessarily permanent) sex differences in spatial ability by channeling experience and thus affecting the development of expertise. To take an everyday example, if an individual who believes that men are better at directions is talking to a man and a woman who are together at a party, he may choose to give directions to a new restaurant to the man. The man in this couple thus gets more practice in a task involving spatial visualization and spatial memory, and the woman gets the message that she is unlikely to do well at such a task. The meta-analysis that was presented by Voyer et al. (1995) provides three types of evidence to suggest that the gender system affects the ability of individuals to perform tasks involving spatial skills. We have already noted the specificity of the tasks on which sex differences are found, which implicates learned skills rather than biologically based mechanisms. The same conclusion is suggested by the finding that the size of some sex differences changes with age and has changed over time.

Voyer et al. found that the magnitude of the sex difference increased with age on the Mental Rotations Test and the Spatial Relations scales of the Primary Mental Abilities Test and the Differential Aptitude Test. In addition, they concluded that the evidence for sex differences in early childhood was not convincing for any of the tests that they had examined. This suggests that sex differences on these three tests (and possibly on others) are due at least in part to cumulative differences in experience. Voyer et al. also found that the size of the sex difference had changed over time on several tasks: Differences had decreased in the case of the Cards Rotation, Water-Level, Embedded Figures, and Identical Blocks tests and had increased in the case of the Mental Rotations Test. These changes strongly suggest that sex differences on these tasks are due, at least in part, to the operation of the gender system: Apparently, the gender system has changed over recent decades in ways that have affected sex differences on these tasks.

Voyer et al. themselves agreed with this latter interpretation for the decreases, but they suggested that the increase in the sex difference for mental rotation was indicative of basic biological differences. This conclusion would appear to be unfounded: Changes over the course of a few decades almost certainly reflect changes in the gender system rather than changes in biology. There is no reason to think that all the changes in the gender system that have occurred in recent decades have been in the direction of decreasing differences between the sexes. For example, the introduction of computers and the strongly sex-differentiated pattern of their use may well have been a source of new or increased sex differences in certain skills.

We now turn to the evidence that girls and boys are provided with different educational experiences. Boys and girls are encouraged to play with different toys and engage in different activities from a very early age. Many of the sex differences in children's activities appear likely to promote the development of spatial abilities in boys more than girls. Boys are given vehicles and building equipment, and they are encouraged to build models from diagrams, to construct forts and playhouses, and to take apart and reassemble objects. They are more likely to be provided with science-related toys such as microscopes and puzzles. These toys may help them to learn about manipulating movement and space more than the dolls and miniature housekeeping equipment that tend to be provided for girls.

Beliefs about the suitability of different toys for boys and girls have been remarkably resistant to change. In a study conducted by Miller (1987), a sample of White middle-class college students indicated that suitable toys for boys included Tinkertoys (kits for building things from wheels and rods), a doctor's kit, building blocks, a toolkit, and a model airplane. Toys that were considered suitable for girls included a tea set, a doll house, a toy supermarket, and a toy telephone. In addition to the gender typing of particular toys, a total of 24 toys were seen as appropriate for boys, whereas only 17 toys were seen as appropriate for girls. Only nine toys were seen as suitable for children of both sexes.

These gender distinctions have been related to later differences in spatial ability. One way to separate the effects of sex and gender is to examine behavior as a function of both sex and gender-role identification. This approach was used by Tracy (1987) in a review of research on the play patterns of children aged between 3 and 13. Tracy concluded that children who had a masculine gender orientation played with a wider variety of toys and also developed better spatial and mathematics skills than children who had a feminine gender orientation did. In one previous study involving preschool children, both girls and boys who preferred activities such as climbing, building with blocks, or playing with toy vehicles achieved higher scores on a test of spatial ability than did girls and boys who preferred to play with dolls or housekeeping toys (Serbin & Connor, 1979).

Other activities that might affect spatial skills distinguish play in boys and girls. The permissible play space is greater in the case of boys than girls: Girls are kept closer to home, while boys learn to navigate a neighborhood "territory" (see Bryant, 1985; Feiring & Lewis, 1987; Herman, Heins & Cohen, 1987). Similar results have been obtained across different cultures (Munroe & Munroe, 1971). Some sports have strong spatial-skills components. Computers are stereotyped as masculine. Boys dominate video arcades and school computer clubs, and both games and educational software tend to be designed with boys in mind (Kiesler, Sproull, & Eccles,

1985). High-school girls rarely enroll in classes involving mechanical drawing, analytical geometry, or workshop skills. Differential practice may also
come from map reading or tinkering with cars in one's spare time (Sherman,
1967). Of course, a relationship between practice and skill does not prove
that skill differences are caused by practice: It is possible that those with
more aptitude or greater skill simply choose those activities that allow them
to practice spatial skills because they are enjoyable.

There is a relationship between gender-typed social roles and spatial visualization. Nash (1975) assessed gender preference by asking sixth- and
ninth-grade boys and girls whether they preferred to be their own or the
other sex, and measured their performance on a spatial visualization task. A
male gender preference proved to be positively related to spatial performance: Boys who preferred to be boys produced higher scores than boys
who would prefer to be girls, and girls who would prefer to be boys produced higher scores than girls who preferred to be girls. There were in fact
few sixth-grade boys and no ninth-grade boys who preferred to be girls.
However, many girls, especially in the younger group, preferred to be boys.
Children of both sexes who preferred to be boys did not differ in spatial
performance. When asked to explain their preference for being a boy, the
children of both sexes referred to the desirability of male activities such as
sports and to the high value that is placed upon male roles in our society.
Nash's study indicates that masculine attributes and preferences are a better
predictor of spatial performance than sex itself—possibly because children
who prefer to be boys act like boys and get more practice in forms of play
that are related to spatial skills.

One recent study by Hecht and Proffitt (1995) not only demonstrated the
effect of experience on spatial ability, but can also be regarded as evidence
that sex differences might be interpreted in ways that maintain the gender
system in its present form. It would appear that the poorer performance of
women on Piaget and Inhelder's (1948/1956) Water-Level Test paradoxically
reflects a higher degree of real-life expertise in everyday problems that tend
to influence performance on this test. In this test, the participant is asked to
indicate the orientation of the surface of a liquid in a tilted container. Young
children indicate that the surface is horizontal with respect to the container
rather than with respect to the ground. In adults, women tend to make this
mistake more often than men, and the difference has typically been interpreted as reflecting women's deficient spatial skills.

Hecht and Proffitt found that men and women in jobs that required the
regular handling of fluids in containers made this mistake *more frequently*
than those who were less expert in this regard. For instance, bartenders and
waitresses made more errors than comparable groups of bus drivers and

homemakers. The authors suggested that expertise in handling liquids in containers produced a preference for an object-relative perspective that was most effective for those people who needed to avoid spilling liquids in situations with a narrow margin for error. On this basis, we would argue further that gender-linked activities might account for differences between women and men in their performance on the Water-Level Test. In most societies, women are more involved than men in the preparation of food and drink, and this gender-based division of labor might affect their performance on this test in the direction that was found by Hecht and Proffitt: That is, greater experience would lead to "poorer" performance.

This study illustrates the way in which the gender system operates to create gender differences. First, activities are classified by gender. Second, gender-linked interpretations are given to observed differences in performance. These interpretations see the performance of women as being inferior to that of men; indeed, the history of sex-differences research is full of examples (Shields, 1975; see also Chapters 1 and 3, this volume). Occasionally, such interpretations are later challenged by new findings which indicate that the presumed disadvantage is, in fact, an advantage, and this seems to have happened in the case of the sex difference on the Water-Level Test. If this difference follows the same course as other sex differences that turn out to give women the advantage, it will shortly be dropped from the canon of sex differences that are felt to merit serious attention, and it will be replaced by others whose interpretation is more consistent with the continued functioning of the gender system.

Effects of Training and Practice on Spatial Abilities

If spatial abilities are strongly affected by relevant experience, it is likely that training on relevant spatial tasks should improve performance. While hundreds of studies have documented the existence of gender-related differences, surprisingly few have investigated the role of training and practice. The study by Richardson (1994) that we described earlier found that the sex difference in mental rotation that was obtained in first-year university students disappeared in advanced undergraduates and in master's level students. Their courses of study had apparently equalized whatever differences in experience were responsible for the sex difference in ability that was obtained in the case of the first-year students.

This result suggests that effects of training upon spatial ability might generally be larger for women than for men. This possibility was examined in a meta-analysis by Baenninger & Newcombe (1989). They found that training did improve performance, and both general experience and specialized training were associated with better performance on spatial tests for both sexes. There was also a tendency for training effects to be larger for women than for men, but it was not significant. The authors suggested that sex differences in training effects would be expected only if males were near asymptote on the test, and that training effects would not, therefore, provide a critical test of this hypothesis. It is also possible that significant sex differences in training effects would appear if the type of task were included as a factor. Baenninger and Newcombe's study did not distinguish spatial tasks that show sex differences from those that do not. Training effects would be expected to be larger for women than for men only in the case of tasks that show an initial sex difference in favor of men (M. Baenninger, personal communication, March 1995).

One factor that might make a large contribution to the development of spatial abilities is exposure to opportunities to learn about computers. In a recent study by Mundy-Castle, Wilson, Sibanda, and Sibanda (1989) in the African country of Zimbabwe, Black and White children were provided with the computer-learning tool, LOGO. The use of pretests and posttests showed that these children obtained higher scores on the Arithmetic scale of the Wechsler Intelligence Scale for Children—Revised (WISC-R) than children who had not been exposed to computers. Clearly, the cognitive development of these 11- and 12-year-old children had been facilitated. In addition, however, Black girls showed large gains in their scores on the Block Design scale of the WISC-R, and this suggests that there was also a specific improvement in their spatial reasoning performance.

These studies clearly indicate the role of experience and practice in spatial skills. They suggest that those researchers who wish to test for gender-related differences in performance should, in principle, first match the male and female research participants in terms of relevant background experiences, and not simply match them in terms of age or grade in school. Otherwise, any observed "sex" difference may simply reflect the fact that sex is correlated with particular experiences (Hyde, 1981). Moreover, a culture's provision of differential experience is not of course haphazard, but is connected to structural and institutional aspects of gender. These studies also indicate that one way to develop young girls' cognitive abilities is to provide them with computers and "boys' toys." As Halpern (1992) commented: "We may be shortchanging the intellectual development of girls by providing them with only traditional sex stereotyped toys" (p. 215). To be effective, however, this strategy would also have to involve changing the gendered cultural meanings of those toys and activities.

CONCLUSIONS

In this chapter, we have argued that the most interesting questions in the area of gender and cognition are not about "sex differences in ability," but about how difference is produced and justified as part of a gendered social order. We conceptualize difference, not only as an attribute of individuals, but also as the socially constructed product of a system that organizes relations of power and status. We have described the operation of the gender system as functioning at three levels: the sociocultural, the interactional, and the individual. At the sociocultural level, gender is a social construct that governs relations among groups and determines access to resources. At the interactional level, gender is a salient social and cognitive category that provides a way of seeing differences and, as a result, a way of creating them. At the individual level, women and men come to accept gender distinctions as part of their self-concept and ascribe to themselves those traits, behaviors, and roles that are the norm for people of their sex in their culture. Thus, the gender system works at each level to sustain a social system of inequality.

We reviewed research on mathematical and spatial abilities in order to illustrate how gender-related effects upon cognitive performance are systemically produced. We focused particularly upon the interactional level, which has been neglected in research on cognitive abilities. Our examination of mathematical ability provides the first indication of the powerful role played by the immediate situation in shaping the cognitive skills deployed and developed. The work reported by Scribner, Lave, and Schoenfeld suggests that mathematical abilities are finely tuned to the physical, social, and institutional contexts in which they are used. We reviewed evidence that the situations in which mathematics is learned and used are, in fact, different for men and women. Mathematics is seen as a male domain: Girls have few female role models. In addition, tests of mathematical ability tend to underpredict women's performance. Moreover, teachers and parents have different expectations for girls and boys, and they react differently to their aspirations, successes, and failures.

We next examined sex differences in spatial ability. Meta-analytic studies indicate that there are sex differences on some tasks involving spatial abilities, but not on others. Some portion of the sex difference is attributable to the immediate testing situation, which is an effect of the interactional level. We examined studies that showed one way in which these interactional effects can be produced: Gendered expectations about the task can affect both spatial memory and mental-rotation performance. Another portion of the sex differences on spatial tasks is attributable to differences in the experiences of men and women, an effect arising at the sociocultural level. In meta-analyses, this was indicated by the absence of reliable sex differences in young children, an increase in the size of sex differences with age, and changes in the size of sex differences over time. We reviewed studies that locate the source of some of these sex differences in experience: Girls and boys have very different experiences in a variety of domains with tasks that appear to involve spatial skills.

We are all products of the gender system. This and other systems for classifying people have profoundly shaped the development of ability tests and the scientific understanding of the abilities that they measure. The use of sex differences as a criterion for identifying separate components of spatial ability in meta-analytic studies is one remarkable example of this. More generally, some abilities have been selected for measurement and hence endorsed as significant. Others, more strongly associated with feminine sensibilities, have not been afforded this stamp of approval. This point was originally made by Teitelbaum (1989) with respect to tests of mathematical and verbal ability, but it applies even more strongly to tests of spatial abilities. The relevance of tasks involving spatial skills to everyday activities is perhaps less obvious than that of tasks involving mathematical and verbal skills. Nevertheless, in at least one case, it turns out that poorer performance on a laboratory task that exhibits a reliable sex difference is associated with greater skill on the relevant real-world task (Hecht & Proffitt, 1995).

Our final point is that the social construction of "sex differences," including their justification through the research and rhetoric of science and their dissemination as "news" through the mass media, is an essential component of the gender system. Those individual differences that have received so much attention may be thought of as the residue of the gender system within individual identities and subjectivities. To study these sex differences in isolation from the social-structural and interactional factors that produce and maintain them is to participate uncritically in the reproduction of inequality within a gendered social order.

ACKNOWLEDGMENTS

Portions of this chapter have been adapted from the accounts contained in Crawford (1995) and Unger and Crawford (1996).

REFERENCES

Baenninger, M., & Newcombe, N. (1989). The role of experience in spatial test performance: A meta-analysis. *Sex Roles, 20,* 327–344.

Barnes, L. L. (1990). Gender bias in teachers' written comments. In S. L. Gabriel & I. Smithson (Eds.), *Gender in the classroom: Power and pedagogy* (pp. 140–159). Urbana, IL: University of Illinois Press.

Becker, J. R. (1981). Differential treatment of females and males in mathematics classes. *Journal for Research in Mathematics Education, 12,* 40–53.

Beckwith, B. (1984). How magazines cover sex differences research. *Science for the People, 16,* 18–23.

Bem, S. (1993). *The lenses of gender.* New Haven, CT: Yale University Press.

Benbow, C. P. (1988). Sex differences in mathematical reasoning ability in intellectually talented preadolescents: Their nature, effects, and possible causes. *Behavioral and Brain Sciences, 11,* 169–232.

Benbow, C. P., & Stanley, J. C. (1980). Sex differences in mathematics ability: Fact or artifact? *Science, 210,* 1262–1264.

Bohan, J. (1993). Regarding gender: Essentialism, constructionism and feminist psychology. *Psychology of Women Quarterly, 17,* 5–22.

Boswell, S. L. (1979). *Nice girls don't study mathematics: The perspective from elementary school.* Paper presented at the meeting of the American Educational Research Association, San Francisco, CA.

Boswell, S. L. (1985). The influence of sex-role stereotyping on women's attitudes and achievement in mathematics. In S. F. Chipman, L. R. Brush, & D. M. Wilson (Eds.), *Women and mathematics: Balancing the equation* (pp. 175–198). Hillsdale, NJ: Erlbaum.

Brown, J. S., Collins, A., & Duguid, P. (1989). Situated cognition and the culture of learning. In M. Yazdani & R. W. Lawler (Eds.), *Artificial intelligence and education* (Vol. 2, pp. 245–268). Norwood, NJ: Ablex.

Bruer, J. (1993). *Schools for thought: A science of learning in the classroom.* Cambridge, MA : MIT Press.

Bryant, B. K. (1985). The neighborhood walk: Sources of support in middle childhood. *Monographs of the Society for Research in Child Development, 50*(3), 1–116.

Burge, P. L., & Culver, S. M. (1990). Sexism, legislative power, and vocational education. In S. L. Gabriel & I. Smithson (Eds.), *Gender in the classroom: Power and pedagogy* (pp 160–175). Urbana, IL: University of Illinois Press.

Caplan, P., MacPherson, G. M., & Tobin, P. (1985). Do sex-related differences in spatial abilities exist? *American Psychologist, 40,* 786–799.

Carpenter, P. A., & Just, M. A. (1986). Spatial ability: An information processing approach to psychometrics. In R. J. Sternberg (Ed.), *Advances in the psychology of human intelligence* (Vol. 3, pp. 221–253). Hillsdale, NJ: Erlbaum.

Chipman, S. F., Brush, L. R., & Wilson, D. M. (Eds.). (1985). *Women and mathematics: Balancing the equation.* Hillsdale, NJ: Erlbaum.

Chipman, S. F., & Thomas, V. G. (1985). Women's participation in mathematics: Outlining the problem. In S. F. Chipman, L. R. Brush, & D. M. Wilson (Eds.), *Women and mathematics: Balancing the equation* (pp. 1–24). Hillsdale, NJ: Erlbaum.

Chipman, S. F., & Wilson, D. M. (1985). Understanding mathematics course enrollment and mathematics achievement: A synthesis of the research. In S. F. Chipman, L. R. Brush, & D. M. Wilson (Eds.), *Women and mathematics: Balancing the equation* (pp. 275–328). Hillsdale, NJ: Erlbaum.

Crawford, M. (1981, August). Emmy Noether: She did Einstein's math. Ms., pp. 86–89.

Crawford, M. (1988). Gender, age, and the social evaluation of assertion. *Behavior Modification, 12,* 549–564.

Crawford, M. (1989). Agreeing to differ: Feminist epistemologies and women's ways of knowing. In M. Crawford & M. Gentry (Eds.), *Gender and thought* (pp. 128–145). New York: Springer-Verlag.

Crawford, M. (1995). *Talking difference.* London: Sage.

Crawford, M., & Chaffin, R. (1986). The reader's construction of meaning: Cognitive research on gender and comprehension. In E. Flynn & P. Schweickart (Eds.), *Gender and reading: Essays on readers, texts, and contexts* (pp. 3–30). Baltimore, MD: Johns Hopkins University Press.

Crawford, M., Chaffin, R., & Fitton, L. (1996). Cognition in social context. *Learning and Individual Differences, 1,* 341–362.

Crawford, M., Herrmann, D. J., Holdsworth, M. J., Randall, E. P., & Robbins, D. (1989). Gender and beliefs about memory. *British Journal of Psychology, 80,* 391–401.

Crawford, M., & Marecek, J. (1989). Psychology reconstructs the female. *Psychology of Women Quarterly, 13,* 147–166.

Crawford, M., & Unger, R. K. (1994). Gender issues in psychology. In A. M. Colman (Ed.), *Companion encyclopedia of psychology* (Vol. 2, pp. 1007–1027). New York: Routledge.

Crosby, F. (1982). *Relative deprivation and working women.* New York: Oxford University Press.

Deaux, K. (1993). Commentary: Sorry, wrong number—A reply to Gentile's call. *Psychological Science, 4,* 125–126.

Deaux, K., & Major, B. (1987). Putting gender into context: An interactive model of gender-related behavior. *Psychological Review, 94,* 369–389.

Dwyer, C. A. (1979). The role of tests and their construction in producing apparent sex related differences. In M. A. Wittig and A. C. Petersen (Eds.), *Sex-related differences in cognitive functioning: Developmental issues* (pp. 335–353). New York: Academic Press.

Eagly, A. H. (1994). On comparing women and men. *Feminism and Psychology, 4,* 513–522.

Eagly, A. H. (1995). The science and politics of comparing women and men. *American Psychologist, 50,* 145–158.

Eccles, J. (1989). Bringing young women to math and science. In M. Crawford & M. Gentry (Eds.), *Gender and thought: Psychological perspectives* (pp. 36–58). New York: Springer-Verlag.

Eccles, J. (1994). Understanding women's educational and occupational choices: Applying the Eccles et al. models of achievement-related choices. *Psychology of Women Quarterly, 18,* 585–610.

Eccles, J. S., Adler, T. F., Futterman, R., Goff, S. B., Kaczala, C. M., Meece, J. L., & Midgley, C. (1985). Self-perceptions, socializing influences, and the decision to enroll in mathematics. In S. F. Chipman, L. R. Brush, & D. M. Wilson (Eds.), *Women and mathematics: Balancing the equation* (pp. 95–122). Hillsdale, NJ: Erlbaum.

Eccles, J., & Jacobs, J. (1986). Social forces shape math attitudes and performance. *Signs: Journal of Women in Culture and Society, 11,* 367–389.

Faludi, S. (1991). *Backlash: The undeclared war against American women.* New York: Doubleday.

Feiring, C., & Lewis, M. (1987). The child's social network: Sex differences from three to six years. *Sex Roles, 17,* 621–636.

Fine, M. (1985). Reflections on a feminist psychology of women: Paradoxes and prospects. *Psychology of Women Quarterly, 9,* 167–183.

Fine, M., & Gordon, S. M. (1989). Feminist transformations of/despite psychology. In M. Crawford & M. Gentry (Eds.), *Gender and thought: Psychological perspectives* (pp. 146–174). New York: Springer-Verlag.

Gentile, D. (1993). Just what are sex and gender, anyway? A call for a new terminological standard. *Psychological Science, 4,* 120–122.

Gould, S. J. (1981). *The mismeasure of man.* New York: Norton.

Gould, S. J. (1994). Curveball: Review of *The Bell Curve. New Yorker, 71,* 139–149.

Griscom, J. (1992). Women and power: Definition, dualism, and difference. *Psychology of Women Quarterly, 16,* 389–414.

Halpern, D. F. (1992). *Sex differences in cognitive abilities* (2nd ed.). Hillsdale, NJ: Erlbaum.

Halpern, D. F. (1994). Stereotypes, science, censorship, and the study of sex differences. *Feminism and Psychology, 4,* 523–530.

Hare-Mustin, R., & Marecek, J. (1988). The meaning of difference: Gender theory, postmodernism, and psychology. *American Psychologist, 43,* 455–464.

Hare-Mustin, R., & Marecek, J. (Eds.). (1990). *Making a difference: Psychology and the construction of gender.* New Haven, CT: Yale University Press.

Hare-Mustin, R., & Marecek, J. (1994). Asking the right questions: Feminist psychology and sex differences. *Feminism and Psychology, 4,* 531–537.

Hecht, H., & Proffitt, D. R. (1995). The price of expertise: Effects of experience on the water-level task. *Psychological Science, 6,* 90–95.

Herman, J. F., Heins, J. A., & Cohen, D. S. (1987). Children's spatial knowledge of their neighborhood environment. *Journal of Applied Developmental Psychology, 8,* 1–15.

Herrmann, D. J., Crawford, M., & Holdsworth, M. (1992). Gender-linked differences in everyday memory performance. *British Journal of Psychology, 83,* 221–231.

Herrnstein, R. J., & Murray, C. A. (1994). *The bell curve: Intelligence and class structure in American life.* New York: Free Press.

Hesse-Biber, S. (1989). Eating patterns and disorders in a college population: Are college women's eating problems a new phenomenon? *Sex Roles, 20,* 71–89.

Hollway, W. (1994). Beyond sex differences: A project for feminist psychology. *Feminism and Psychology, 4,* 538–546.

Hudson, L. (1972). *The Cult of the Fact.* London: Cape.

Hyde, J. S. (1981). How large are cognitive gender differences? A meta-analysis using ω^2 and *d. American Psychologist, 36,* 892–901.

Hyde, J. (1994). Should psychologists study gender differences? Yes, with some guidelines. *Feminism and Psychology, 4,* 507–512.

Hyde, J., Fennema, E., & Lamon, S. J. (1990a). Gender differences in mathematics performance: A meta-analysis. *Psychological Bulletin, 107,* 139–155.

Hyde, J., Fennema, E., Ryan, M., Frost, L., & Hopp, C. (1990b). Gender comparisons of mathematics attitudes and affect: A meta-analysis. *Psychology of Women Quarterly, 14,* 299–324.

Jacklin, C. (1981). Methodological issues in the study of sex-related differences. *Developmental Review, 1,* 266–273.

Keller, E. F. (1983). *A feeling for the organism: The life and work of Barbara McClintock.* San Francisco, CA: Freeman.

Kiesler, S., Sproull, L., & Eccles, J. (1985). Pool halls, chips, and war games: Women in the culture of computing. *Psychology of Women Quarterly, 2,* 451–562.

Kitzinger, C. (1987). *The social construction of lesbianism.* London: Sage.

Kitzinger, C. (1991). Feminism, psychology, and the paradox of power. *Feminism and Psychology, 1,* 111–129.

Kitzinger, C. (Ed.). (1994). Should psychologists study sex differences? *Feminism and Psychology, 4,* 501–546.

Lave, J. (1988). *Cognition in practice.* Hillsdale, NJ: Erlbaum.

Lave, J., & Wenger, E. (1991). *Situated learning: Legitimate peripheral participation.* New York: Cambridge University Press.

Light, P., & Butterworth, G. (Eds.). (1993). *Context and cognition: Ways of learning and knowing.* Hillsdale, NJ: Erlbaum.

Linn, M. C., & Petersen, A. C. (1985). Emergence and characterization of sex difference in spatial ability: A meta-analysis. *Child Development, 56,* 1479–1498.

Linn, M. C., & Petersen, A. C. (1986). A meta-analysis of gender differences in spatial abilities: Implications for mathematics and science achievement. In J. S. Hyde & M. C. Linn (Eds.), *The Psychology of gender: Advances through meta-analysis* (pp. 67–101). Baltimore, MD: Johns Hopkins University Press.

Lorber, J. (1993). *Paradoxes of gender.* New Haven, CT: Yale University Press.

Maccoby, E. E., & Jacklin, C. N. (1974). *The psychology of sex differences.* Stanford, CA: Stanford University Press.

Major, B., & Deaux, K. (1982). Individual differences in justice behavior. In J. Greenberg & R. Cohen (Eds.), *Equity and justice in social behavior* (pp. 43–76). New York: Academic Press.

Major, B., McFarlin, D. B., & Gagnon, D. (1984). Overworked and underpaid: On the nature of gender differences in personal entitlement. *Journal of Personality and Social Psychology, 47,* 1399–1412.

McCaulay, M., Mintz, L., & Glenn, A. (1988). Body image, self-esteem and depression-proneness: Closing the gender gap. *Sex Roles, 18,* 381–391.

McGhee, P. (1979). The role of laughter and humor in growing up female. In C. B. Kopp (Ed.), *Becoming female: Perspectives on development* (pp. 183–206). New York: Plenum Press.

McGrath, E., Keita, G., Strickland, B., & Russo, N. (1990). *Women and depression: Risk factors and treatment issues.* Washington, DC: American Psychological Association.

McHugh, M. D., Koeske, R. D., & Frieze, I. H. (1986). Issues to consider in conducting nonsexist psychological research: A guide for researchers. *American Psychologist, 41,* 879–890.

McIntosh, P. (1983). *Interactive phases of curricular revision: A feminist perspective.* Wellesley, MA: Wellesley College, Center for Research on Women.

Meece, J. L., Parsons, J. E., Kaczala, C. M., Goff, S. B., & Futterman, R. (1982). Sex differences in math achievement: Toward a model of academic choice. *Psychological Bulletin, 91,* 324–348.

Miller, C. L. (1987). Qualitative differences among gender-stereotyped toys: Implications for cognitive and social development in girls and boys. *Sex Roles, 16,* 473–488.

Miller, J. B. (1986). *Toward a new psychology of women* (rev. ed.). Boston, MA: Beacon Press.

Miller, J. G. (1984). Culture and the development of everyday social explanation. *Journal of Personality and Social Psychology, 46,* 961–978.

Miura, I. (1987). The relationship of computer self-efficacy expectations to computer interest and course enrollment in college. *Sex Roles, 16,* 303–312.

Morier, D., & Seroy, C. (1994). The effect of interpersonal expectancies on men's self presentation of gender role attitudes to women. *Sex Roles, 31,* 493–504.

Mundy-Castle, A., Wilson, D., Sibanda, P., & Sibanda, J. (1989). Cognitive effects of LOGO among Black and White Zimbabwean girls and boys. *International Journal of Psychology, 24,* 539–546.

Munroe, R. L., & Munroe, R. H. (1971). Effect of environmental experience on spatial ability in an East African society. *Journal of Social Psychology, 83,* 15–22.

Nash, S. (1975). The relationship among sex-role stereotyping, sex-role preference, and the sex difference in spatial visualization. *Sex Roles, 1,* 15–32.

National Assessment of Educational Progress. (1983). *The third national mathematics assessment: Results, trends and issues.* Denver, CO: Education Commission of the States.

Neisser, U. (1976). *Cognition and reality.* San Francisco, CA: Freeman.

Newcombe, N., Bandura, M., & Taylor, D. G. (1983). Sex differences in spatial ability and spatial activities. *Sex Roles, 9,* 377–386.

Parlee, M. B. (1979). Psychology and women. *Signs: Journal of Women in Culture and Society, 5,* 121–133.

Piaget, J., & Inhelder, B. (1956). *The child's conception of space* (F. J. Langdon & J. L. Lunzer, Trans.). London: Routledge & Kegan Paul. (Original work published 1948)

Porter, N., & Geis, F. (1981). Women and nonverbal leadership cues: When seeing is not believing. In C. Mayo & N. Henley (Eds.), *Gender and nonverbal behavior* (pp. 39–61). New York: Springer-Verlag.

Pugh, M. D., & Wahrman, R. (1983). Neutralizing sexism in mixed-sex groups: Do women have to be better than men? *American Journal of Sociology, 88,* 746–762.

Putnam, L. (1982). In search of gender: A critique of communication and sex-roles research. *Women's Studies in Communication, 5,* 1–9.

Reid, P. T. (1993). Poor women in psychological research: Shut up and shut out. *Psychology of Women Quarterly, 17,* 133–150.

Resnick, L. B., Levine, J. M., & Teasley, S. D. (Eds.). (1991). *Perspectives on socially shared cognition.* Washington, DC: American Psychological Association.

Richardson, J. T. E. (1994). Gender differences in mental rotation. *Perceptual and Motor Skills, 78,* 435–448.

Rogoff, B. (1990). *Apprenticeship in thinking: Cognitive development in social context.* New York: Oxford University Press.

Rogoff, B., & Lave, J. (Eds.). (1984). *Everyday cognition.* Cambridge, MA: Harvard University Press.

Rosenthal, R. (1966). *Experimenter effects in behavioral research.* New York: Appleton-Century-Crofts.

Ross, L. (1977). The intuitive psychologist and his shortcomings: Distortions in the attribution process. In L. Berkowitz (Ed.), *Advances in experimental social psychology* (Vol. 10, pp. 174–221). New York: Academic Press.

Rosser, P. (1987). *Sex bias in college admissions tests: Why women lose out.* Cambridge, MA: National Center for Fair and Open Testing.

Rosser, P. (1992). *The SAT gender gap: ETS responds: A research update.* Washington, DC: Center for Women Policy Studies.

Sadker, M., & Sadker, D. (1994). *Failing at fairness: How America's schools cheat girls.* New York: Scribner's.

Sayre, A. (1975). *Rosalind Franklin and DNA: A vivid view of what it is like to be a gifted woman in an especially male profession.* New York: Norton.

Scarborough, E., & Furumoto, L. (1987). *Untold lives: The first generation of American women psychologists.* New York: Columbia University Press.

Schoenfeld, A. (1989). Explorations of students' mathematical beliefs and behavior. *Journal for Research in Mathematics Education, 20,* 338–355.

Scribner, S. (1984). Studying working intelligence. In B. Rogoff & J. Lave (Eds.), *Everyday cognition* (pp. 9–40). Cambridge, MA: Harvard University Press.

Selkow, P. (1984). *Assessing sex bias in testing: A review of the issues and evaluations of 74 psychological and educational tests.* Westport, CT: Greenwood.

Serbin, L. A., & Connor, J. M. (1979). Sex-typing of children's play preferences and patterns of cognitive performance. *Journal of Genetic Psychology, 134,* 315–316.

Sharps, M., Price, J., & Williams, J. (1994). Spatial cognition and gender: Instructional and stimulus influences on mental image rotation performance. *Psychology of Women Quarterly, 18,* 413–426.

Sharps, M., Welton, A., & Price, J. (1993). Gender and task in the determination of spatial cognitive performance. *Psychology of Women Quarterly, 17,* 71–83.

Sherif, C. W. (1979). Bias in psychology. In J. A. Sherman & E. T. Beck (Eds.), *The prism of sex: Essays in the sociology of knowledge* (pp. 93–133). Madison, WI: University of Wisconsin Press.

Sherif, C. W. (1982). Needed concepts in the study of gender identity. *Psychology of Women Quarterly, 6,* 375–398.

Sherman, J. A. (1967). Problem of sex differences in spatial perception and aspects of intellectual functioning. *Psychological Review, 74,* 290–299.

Sherman, J. A. (1982). Continuing in mathematics: A longitudinal study of the attitudes of high school girls. *Psychology of Women Quarterly, 7,* 132–140.

Sherman, J. A. (1983). Factors predicting girls' and boys' enrollment in college preparatory mathematics. *Psychology of Women Quarterly, 7,* 272–281.

Shields, S. A. (1975). Functionalism, Darwinism, and the psychology of women: A study in social myth. *American Psychologist, 30,* 739–754.

Shields, S. A. (1982). The variability hypothesis: The history of a biological model of sex differences in intelligence. *Signs: Journal of Women in Culture and Society, 7,* 769–797.

Shotter, J., & Gergen, K. J. (Eds.). (1989). *Texts of identity.* London: Sage.

Singer, J. M., & Stake, J. E. (1986). Mathematics and self-esteem: Implications for women's career choices. *Psychology of Women Quarterly, 10,* 339–351.

Spelman, E. V. (1988). *Inessential women: Problems of exclusion in feminist thought.* Boston: Beacon.

Spender, D. (1982). *Invisible women: The schooling scandal.* London: Writers' and Readers' Publishing.

Stricker, L., Rock, D., & Burton, N. (1992). *Sex differences in SAT predictions of college grades.* New York: The College Board.

Suchman, L. A. (1987). *Plans and situated actions.* New York: Cambridge University Press.

Tavris, C. (1992). *The mismeasure of women.* New York: Simon & Schuster.

Taylor, S. E., Fiske, S. T., Etcoff, N. L., & Ruderman, A. J. (1978). Categorical and contextual bases of person memory and stereotyping. *Journal of Personality and Social Psychology, 36,* 778–783.

Teitelbaum, P. (1989). Feminist theory and standardized testing. In A. M. Jaggar & S. R. Bordo (Eds.), *Gender/body/knowledge: Feminist reconstructions of being and knowing* (pp. 324–335). New Brunswick, NJ: Rutgers University Press.

Thomas, K. (1990). *Gender and subject in higher education.* Buckingham, U.K.: SRHE & Open University Press.

Tracy, D. M. (1987). Toys, spatial ability, and science and mathematics achievement: Are they related? *Sex Roles, 17,* 115–138.

Unger, R. K. (1979). Toward a redefinition of sex and gender. *American Psychologist, 34,* 1085–1094.

Unger, R. (1992). Will the real sex difference please stand up? *Feminism and Psychology, 2,* 231–238.

Unger, R., & Crawford, M. (1993). Commentary: Sex and gender—The troubled relationship between terms and concepts. *Psychological Science, 4,* 122–124.

Unger, R., & Crawford, M. (1996). *Women and gender: A feminist psychology* (2nd ed.). New York: McGraw-Hill.

Vandenberg, S. G., & Kuse, A. R. (1978). Mental rotations, a group test of three-dimensional spatial visualization. *Perceptual and Motor Skills, 47,* 599–604.

Verhovek, S. H. (1990, March 4). Girls win 51.3% in Regents Series. *New York Times,* p. 23.

Voyer, D., Voyer, S., & Bryden, M. P. (1995). Magnitude of sex differences in spatial abilities: A meta-analysis and consideration of critical variables. *Psychological Bulletin, 117,* 250–270.

Wallston, B., & O'Leary, V. (1981). Sex makes a difference: Differential perceptions of women and men. In L. Wheeler (Ed.), *Review of personality and social psychology* (Vol. 2, pp. 9–41). Beverly Hills, CA: Sage.

Weisstein, N. (1968). *Kinder, Kirche, Kuche as scientific law: Psychology constructs the female.* Boston: New England Free Press.

West, C., & Zimmerman, D. H. (1987). Doing gender. *Gender and Society, 1,* 125–151.

Wiley, M., & Eskilson, A. (1982). Coping in the corporation: Sex role constraints. *Journal of Applied Social Psychology, 12,* 1–11.

Witkin, H. A., Lewis, H. B., Hertzman, M., Machover, K., Meissner, P. B., & Wapner, S. (1954). *Personality through perception: An experimental and clinical study.* New York: Harper & Brothers.

Yarkin, K., Town, J., & Wallston, B. (1982). Blacks and women must try harder: Stimulus persons' race and sex and attributions of causality. *Personality and Social Psychology Bulletin, 8,* 21–24.

Yoder, J., & Kahn, A. (1992). Toward a feminist understanding of women and power. *Psychology of Women Quarterly, 16,* 381–388.

Zanna, M., & Pack, S. (1975). On the self-fulfilling nature of apparent sex differences in behavior. *Journal of Experimental Social Psychology, 11,* 583–591.

CHAPTER 5

Conclusions from the Study of Gender Differences in Cognition

John T. E. Richardson

This volume has been concerned with the hypothesis that there are gender differences in cognition. In principle, this might encompass differences of any sort between men and women or between boys and girls with regard to their intellectual functioning, experience, and behavior. Historically, however, this notion has usually been taken to refer to the possibility of gender differences in intellectual abilities, including specific abilities (such as verbal, spatial, and mathematical abilities) and "intelligence," construed as a generic form of ability. The hypothesis that there are gender differences in cognition has therefore been evaluated by comparing the performance of men and women or boys and girls on objectively scorable tests. This interpretation has been reflected in each of the substantive contributions to this volume by Janet Shibley Hyde and Nita McKinley, by Paula Caplan and Jeremy Caplan, and by Mary Crawford and Roger Chaffin.

The overall findings were well summarized by Hyde and McKinley in Chapter 2:

- There are essentially no consistent gender differences in measures of verbal ability, with the sole exception that women tend to perform better than men do on tests of speech production.
- Men tend to perform better than women do on some measures of spatial ability, but the magnitude of the gender difference varies markedly with the demands of each specific test.
- There are essentially no consistent gender differences in measures of mathematical ability, with the sole exception that beginning in high school men tend to perform better than women do on tests of mathematical problem solving.

• Differences between men and women on measures of science achievement are small, and their magnitude varies as a function of the specific area of science being tested.

Nevertheless, the authors of all three contributions have stressed the considerable variability in the research findings and the heterogeneity of the gender differences that have been obtained within the domains of verbal ability, spatial ability, and mathematical ability.

Relatively little attention seems to have been given to the issue of possible interrelationships and overlap among these domains. For example, the mental processes and representations that are used to parse and encode mathematical statements, equations, and formulas may be parasitic on those that are employed in order to comprehend verbal text. Certainly, there is evidence that mental arithmetic depends upon the system of working memory that supports the short-term retention of verbal information (see Lemaire, Abdi, & Fayol, 1996). Accordingly, one would expect gender differences in verbal ability to have some bearing on gender differences in mathematical ability. As a different example, Casey, Pezaris, and Nuttall (1992) found a gender difference in mathematical ability that became nonsignificant if mental-rotation performance was statistically controlled. This indicates that some gender differences in mathematical ability that are obtained may result from confounded gender differences in spatial ability. (Moreover, science achievement presumably depends upon all three kinds of ability.)

The synopsis that I have given above needs to be contextualized by noting that it represents a reasonable summary of the evidence produced by investigations carried out in Western countries (and especially the United States) during the last 30 years of the 20th century. In fact, Hyde and McKinley pointed out that the magnitude of some gender differences in cognitive performance appears to have been decreasing during the course of the last few decades. This phenomenon was originally noted by Jacklin and Maccoby (1972), and it was confirmed by Rosenthal and Rubin (1982). Hyde and McKinley themselves suggested that changes of this sort could, in principle, be attributed to a wide variety of factors, but they are typically ascribed to sociocultural factors rather than to biological mechanisms.

In Chapter 4, Crawford and Chaffin pointed out that on a sociocultural account of gender differences it was not to be expected that all such changes would inevitably be in the direction of the progressive disappearance of gender differences over the course of time. In the case of the Mental Rotations Test devised by Vandenberg and Kuse (1978), there has been essentially no change in the magnitude of the gender differences reported in the past 20 years (Masters & Sanders, 1993). However, Voyer, Voyer, and Bryden

(1995) observed that this comparison confounded the year of publication of each study and the age of the participants. They found that, when the age of the participants had been statistically controlled, there was a significant positive relationship between their year of birth and the magnitude of the gender difference on the Mental Rotations Test: That is, cohorts born more recently tended to produce larger differences. Nevertheless, this relationship may itself be confounded with differences in the nature and selectivity of the samples of participants, a problem that I discuss in more detail later on in this chapter. When these latter factors are controlled, even gender differences in mental rotation ability appear to be decreasing in magnitude (see Richardson, 1994).

In this concluding chapter, I want to discuss the kinds of analytic techniques that have led to the above conclusions concerning differences in the cognitive performance of men and women. I first of all describe the derivation of different measures of effect size and go on to consider the potential hazards in using meta-analytic techniques. I evaluate in turn the likelihood of biases occurring in the publication of research, in the sampling of participants, and in the sampling of test items, and I discuss the issue of the possible heterogeneity of research studies, especially with regard to their methodological quality. I consider the argument that the use of meta-analysis tends to constrain researchers in their choice of research questions, and that meta-analytic techniques constitute a "package" or technology that encourages a positivist, realist interpretation of gender differences in cognition. Nevertheless, I arrive at the conclusion that the ideas, arguments, and evidence contained in this volume lead to a rather different, constructionist interpretation, and that as a consequence future research into gender differences in human cognition will need to address a wider range of research questions using a wider range of research methodologies.

MEASURES OF EFFECT SIZE

Gender differences in objective performance are sometimes expressed using measures of effect size for two different reasons. First, they are aimed at enabling researchers to express the magnitude of any gender difference in terms that are independent of the specific methods and procedures that were employed. This in turn makes it possible to compare the outcomes of investigations that have used different methods and procedures and thus to integrate their results using techniques of meta-analysis. The various findings that have been obtained by the application of these techniques to research into gender differences in cognition were reviewed by Hyde and McKinley in Chapter 2, and they were also mentioned by Crawford and Chaffin in Chapter 4. There are, however, important issues that arise when using meta-analytic techniques, and I discuss these in the sections that follow this one.

Second, measures of effect size are thought to enable researchers to express the magnitude of any difference in terms that are independent of its level of statistical significance. Most psychologists appreciate the importance of distinguishing between statements describing the results of statistical tests and statements describing the importance or otherwise of the results in theoretical or practical terms. As Winer, Brown, and Michels (1991, p. 121) commented, a design that attains a sufficient level of statistical power can lead to the rejection of the null hypothesis even if the effects are trivial from a practical or theoretical point of view. However, in practice very few investigators bother to assess the magnitude of the effects that they obtain, and most confine themselves to reporting conventional test statistics such as t or F (Craig, Eison, & Metze, 1976; see also Chapter 3, this volume).

Two different approaches have been used to derive measures of effect size (Richardson, 1996). The first approach is based upon quantifying the proportion of the variance or variation in the dependent variable that is explained by the independent variable. This makes it possible to express the strength of the association between the two variables in terms of some kind of correlation coefficient (Winer et al., 1991, p. 121). Indeed, it is fairly well known that the linear correlation coefficient, Pearson r, has a straightforward interpretation as a measure of effect size, in that the quantity r^2 is equal to the proportion of the total variation in the dependent variable that can be predicted on the basis of its regression on the independent variable within the particular sample being studied (e.g., Hays, 1963, p. 505).

In an analogous manner, Pearson (1905) defined the *correlation ratio* in order to measure the strength of the association between a categorical independent variable (that is, a variable defined by two or more groups) and a continuous dependent variable. The square of the correlation ratio measures the proportion of the total variation in the dependent variable that can be associated with membership of the different groups defined by the independent variable for the particular samples being studied. This latter quantity is correctly described as the *differentiation ratio,* but some widely used texts confusingly refer to it as the "correlation ratio" (see, e.g., Hays, 1963, pp. 325, 547; Hedges & Olkin, 1985, pp. 101–102).

The second approach is largely confined to the measurement of effect size in research designs involving just two groups, and this is based upon the comparison of the relevant means. The absolute difference between the two means depends upon the specific procedure that was employed to obtain the raw data, but Cohen (1965) pointed out that a measure of effect size could be obtained by standardizing the difference between the two means by dividing it by the pooled within-group standard deviation. Hedges (1981) showed that the standardized mean difference obtained from a sample was a biased estimate of the standardized mean difference in the population from which the sample had been drawn. However, he showed that the former could be adjusted for sampling bias by being multiplied by a simple correction factor (see also Hedges & Olkin, 1985, pp. 76–85).

Studies of gender differences in cognition have in fact predominantly incorporated the standardized mean difference as a measure of effect size. The earliest example of this approach by Hyde (1981) had been carried out before the publication of the work by Hedges (1981), and her analysis used the uncorrected version of this index. Subsequently, however, researchers have usually corrected the standardized mean difference for sampling bias in accordance with the proposals made by Hedges (1981). Hedges and Becker (1986) commended the use of this statistic on several grounds: First, it is easy to understand and has a consistent interpretation across different research studies; second, it preserves information about the direction of the relevant effects; third, its sampling distribution is well understood; and, finally, it can be readily calculated from values of the statistics t and F that are reported in published research.

Wilcox (1987) pointed out that the standardized mean difference was based upon the pooled within-group standard deviation. He argued that if the assumption of homogeneity of variance were violated, then a unitless measure of effect size "would seem not to exist" (p. 47). In Chapter 2 in this volume, Hyde and McKinley discussed the hypothesis of greater male variability and concluded that there was in fact evidence in accord with this hypothesis for at least some specific cognitive tasks. Although they denied that this was a universal phenomenon, the assumption of homogeneity of variance in the performance of males and females does appear to be violated for some important cognitive abilities. In such a situation, Hedges and Olkin (1985, p. 78) remarked that the mean difference could be divided by the standard deviation of one of the two groups, and this is appropriate if one of the groups serves in some sense as a control (see Glass, 1976; Glass, McGaw, & Smith, 1981, pp. 29, 107). In research on gender differences, however, it would not be acceptable to privilege either males or females as constituting a baseline in this way.

META-ANALYTIC METHODS

Despite such difficulties, measures of effect size are widely used in the application of meta-analytic techniques, because these depend upon being able to convert the results of different studies into some common metric. Mullen

(1989) described meta-analysis as "a set of statistical procedures, and a general perspective, for the precise summary and integration of the results of previous research" (p. 14). Meta-analytic review is therefore intended to go beyond the traditional form of narrative literature review, which typically involves the piecemeal evaluation and informal integration of previous research studies in the relevant literature (see Glass, 1976).

The simplest form of meta-analysis is known as "vote counting" or the "box score" approach: Published studies are sorted according to whether their results were statistically significant and positive, statistically significant and negative, or nonsignificant, and the reviewer plumps for the majority outcome. Maccoby and Jacklin (1974) considered the hazards of such an approach in their compendious review of the literature on sex differences (pp. 355–356), but they implicitly invited their readers to adopt this approach by providing bare lists of the findings that had been obtained in different studies, and they adopted it themselves in arriving at their final conclusions. However, the uncritical use of vote counting gives rise to substantive problems (see Caplan, 1979; see also Chapter 3, this volume); and, as Hyde and McKinley pointed out in Chapter 2, it can be shown on purely statistical grounds that this approach may well yield conclusions that are seriously misleading (see Hedges & Olkin, 1985, pp. 48–52).

A more sophisticated approach is based upon combining the probability values or significance levels associated with different studies. This can be carried out in a number of different ways, but each aims to provide one overall estimate of the probability of obtaining the aggregated results if the null hypothesis is true (see Rosenthal, 1978). However, this approach is very limited in its practical scope, because it is not possible to make valid inferences regarding the consistency as opposed to the heterogeneity of the results that have been obtained across different studies based only upon their individual significance levels (see Hedges & Olkin, 1985, p. 4; Humphreys, 1980). Moreover, as Rosenthal (1978) himself acknowledged, the computation of an overall probability estimate says nothing about the size of the effect that is being examined.

Estimates of explained population variance have sometimes been used in meta-analytic research. However, their sampling properties are as yet poorly understood (see Richardson, 1996), and no detailed analysis seems to have been provided to explain how estimates obtained from a number of different studies might be combined. Not surprisingly, therefore, in her meta-analysis of research on gender differences in cognition, Hyde (1981) merely reported median values of the estimated squared correlation ratio from comparisons between the performance of males and females. The median values were 0.01 for verbal ability, 0.01 for quantitative ability, 0.043 for visual-spatial ability, and 0.025 for visual-analytic spatial ability (field articulation); in other words, these differences seemed to account for no more than 5% of the population variance.

Hedges and Olkin (1985, pp. 101, 103) argued that measures of effect size based upon explained variance were inappropriate for combining the results of different studies, because they were inherently nondirectional, and they therefore could take on similar values for conflicting patterns of results. They cited a hypothetical situation in which two identical studies yielded a difference between two treatment groups of one standard deviation in magnitude but in opposite directions. Estimates of explained variance would yield similar values in these two experiments, suggesting the erroneous conclusion that they had obtained broadly the same results.

This sort of objection does not seriously detract from the value of Hyde's (1981) meta-analysis, because all but one of the relevant effects were in the direction anticipated on the basis of previous research. The criticism is also overstated, since no one has ever claimed that estimates of explained variance are more than simply another part of the composite picture that a researcher builds in reporting data to indicate that one or more variables are helpful in understanding a particular behavior (Craig et al., 1976). They will not mislead if they are presented in the context of other measures of effect size, which was precisely the strategy adopted by Hyde herself. In the case of the example that was given by Hedges and Olkin, it is clearly accurate and informative to say that the independent variable had explained a similar amount of variance in the two studies.

Nevertheless, as Rosenthal (1984, p. 23) observed, most meta-analyses compare just two populations, and this is obviously true of meta-analyses of gender differences. In this situation, the correlation ratio is simply the point-biserial correlation coefficient, and the problem of combining different correlation coefficients has been discussed over more than the last 60 years. Hedges and Olkin (1985, chap. 11) described procedures for testing the homogeneity of correlation coefficients from several different studies, combining them to estimate a common correlation coefficient, or examining whether they could be predicted by either discrete or continuous independent variables. In principle, then, these methods could be applied to the study of gender differences.

To date, however, there seem to be only two studies that employed the point-biserial correlation coefficient as an index of effect size in order to compare cognitive performance among males and females. Plomin and Foch (1981) analyzed information that had been reported by Maccoby and Jacklin (1974, pp. 86–87, 90) from large-scale research into children's verbal and quantitative abilities. They obtained mean correlation coefficients of +0.10

in verbal ability and +0.20 in quantitative ability, in both cases reflecting better performance in girls. Nevertheless, Plomin and Foch pointed out that these figures corresponded to 1% and 4% of the total variance, respectively, and they concluded that "average differences between groups appear to be trivial compared with individual differences within groups" (p. 383). In contrast, Masters and Sanders (1993) carried out a meta-analysis of gender differences on the Mental Rotations Test and obtained a mean point-biserial correlation coefficient of +0.40, indicating that 16% of the variability in performance was accounted for by gender.

Hedges and Becker (1986) argued that the standardized mean difference (adjusted for sampling bias) was better suited to meta-analytic endeavors than estimates of explained variance, because it was a directional measure whose sampling properties were fairly well understood. Indeed, this index has been employed in the vast majority of meta-analytic studies of gender differences in cognition, and the findings of the most important examples are displayed in Table 5–1. Cohen (1965) proposed that "small," "medium," and "large" effects be operationalized as effects for which the difference between the population means was 0.25σ, 0.5σ, and σ, respectively, where "σ" refers to the pooled within-group standard deviation. Later, however (Cohen, 1969, pp. 22–24), he characterized them as effects for which the standardized mean difference was 0.2, 0.5, and 0.8, respectively. Critics have argued that there is "no wisdom whatsoever" in this practice (Glass et al., 1981, p. 104), but nowadays Cohen's guidelines are often mentioned when evaluating obtained effect sizes. On this basis, the majority of the estimates of effect size in Table 5–1 would be regarded as "small," as was indeed emphasized in each of the substantive contributions to this volume. The most obvious exception is the category described by Linn and Petersen (1985, 1986) as "mental rotation" tasks. Within this category, the Mental Rotations Test constructed by Vandenberg and Kuse (1978) would seem to be the only cognitive test that gives rise to effects that psychologists in general would consider to be "large" (Eagly, 1995).

Eagly (1995) argued that such figures were potentially misleading and tended to trivialize the results of research on gender differences because measures of effect size are typically not presented in most other areas of psychological research. She claimed that the magnitude and consistency of effect sizes in gender-differences research "show a range of values that is probably fairly typical of the range of values produced for many other areas of inquiry in psychology" (p. 154). However, by way of an example, Eagly had mentioned a survey of meta-analyses concerned with the efficacy of psychological, educational, and behavioral treatments (Lipsey & Wilson, 1993), and this had found an average mean effect size of 0.50. Hyde and

TABLE 5-1 Estimates of Effect Size in Meta-analytic Reviews

Domain	k^a	Estimated effect size[b]
Mathematical abilities[c]		
Computation	45	−0.14
Concepts	41	−0.03
Problem solving	48	+0.08
Mixed or unclassifiable	120	+0.19
Scholastic Aptitude Test	5	+0.40
Overall	259	+0.20
Spatial abilities[d]		
Mental rotation	29/78	+0.73/+0.56
Spatial perception	62/92	+0.44/+0.44
Spatial visualization	81/116	+0.13/+0.19
Overall	172/286	+0.45/+0.37
Verbal abilities[e]		
Vocabulary	40	−0.02
Analogies	5	+0.16
Reading comprehension	18	−0.03
Speech production	12	−0.33
Essay writing	5	−0.09
Scholastic Aptitude Test	4	+0.03
Anagrams	5	−0.22
General/mixed	25	−0.20
Other	5	−0.08
Overall	119	−0.11

[a]Number of sample effect sizes contributing to the estimate.

[b]A positive effect size reflects better performance in males than in females; a negative effect size reflects better performance in females than in males.

[c]Data from Hyde, Fennema, and Lamon (1990).

[d]In each pair of values, the first represents data from the review by Linn and Petersen (1985, 1986), and the second represents data from the review by Voyer, Voyer, and Bryden (1995).

[e] Data from Hyde and Linn (1988).

Plant (1995) demonstrated that the effect sizes obtained in meta-analyses concerned with gender differences were characteristically lower than this. It can therefore be inferred that aggregated gender differences in general are smaller than the aggregated effects of psychological treatments. This conclusion certainly applies, on Eagly's own account, to the vast majority of gender differences in performance on tests of cognitive abilities.

The application of meta-analytic techniques to particular measures of effect size is often claimed to have a number of advantages over the use of traditional narrative review (see Chapter 2, this volume). Mullen (1989, pp.

7–9) summarized these as differences with respect to *precision, objectivity,* and *replicability*. First, whereas there are no formal procedures for extracting evidence from previous research in a narrative review, meta-analysis employs a specific set of techniques to yield a precise estimate of the relevant effect size. Second, the criteria and standards used in a traditional narrative review are typically left unstated, whereas they have to be made totally explicit in a meta-analytic review. Third, it is entirely possible (indeed, quite common) for different narrative reviews of a given research domain to come to different conclusions, but the explicit nature of the procedures used in meta-analytic reviews means that they can be quite readily replicated.

PUBLICATION BIAS AND THE "FILE DRAWER PROBLEM"

There are nevertheless a number of problems that meta-analysis shares in common with traditional narrative review. Perhaps the most fundamental problem is the possibility of publication bias: the possibility that the particular studies that have been located in the published literature and included in the review do not constitute a random sample of the population of studies that have been conducted in the research domain. There is evidence that the publication policies of psychological journals are biased in favor of manuscripts that report significant findings (see, e.g., Mullen, 1989, p. 30). This means that research that gives rise to nonsignificant results is likely to remain unpublished, and in principle, therefore, those studies that are published may be a biased sample of all those that are actually carried out. This was characterized by Rosenthal (1979) as the *file drawer problem* (see also Rosenthal, 1976, p. 454). Of course, even unpublished studies can be retrieved through an efficiently conducted computerized search if they have somehow been put in the public domain, perhaps through technical reports or conference proceedings.

In Chapter 2, Hyde and McKinley acknowledged that research on gender differences might have been subject to publication bias in the past, but they suggested that recent developments had made it more likely nowadays that manuscripts reporting no gender differences would be accepted for publication. Unfortunately, there seems to be no evidence to support or refute either of these proposals. In a meta-analytic study of the relation between socioeconomic status and academic achievement, White (1982) found that the reported correlations tended to be largest in books, less in journal articles, and smallest in unpublished sources. Similarly, the survey by Lipsey and Wilson (1993) concerning meta-analytic reviews of the effectiveness of psychological, educational, and behavioral treatments found that effect sizes tended to be greater in published studies than in unpublished studies. Neither of these trends was subjected to statistical test, however. (Indeed, test procedures do not exist for situations where the units of analysis are meta-analytic statistics: Mullen, 1989, p. 2). Moreover, these results do not appear to represent a universal phenomenon (see Glass et al., 1981, pp. 66–67, 226–227; Rosenthal, 1984, pp. 42–45), and thus one cannot assume that researchers' file drawers are crammed with unpublished studies showing no gender difference in cognitive performance.

Publication is not of course an all-or-nothing matter. Psychological journals are widely believed to vary in terms of the stringency with which they assess submitted manuscripts, and so the extent of any bias in favor of manuscripts reporting significant findings may vary from one journal to another. Some investigations are published in other ways (as chapters in books or as institutional technical reports, for example), and the extent to which these are subject to a formal process of editorial review may be variable, unknown, or nonexistent. Nevertheless, it could be argued, in particular, that dissertations submitted in fulfilment of research degrees were less vulnerable to publication bias, because the students' examiners would have been rather more concerned with the inherent quality of their work than with the statistical significance or otherwise of their results.

Rosenthal (1976, pp. 456–461; Rosenthal & Rubin, 1978) found that the magnitude of interpersonal expectancy effects tended to be rather less in the case of dissertations than in the case of other forms of publication, but the difference was small and not statistically significant. Rosenthal went on to show that this pattern did not occur for dissertations that had incorporated special controls against intentional or unintentional errors (i.e., errors of cheating and recording, respectively). He concluded that the trend for dissertations to show smaller effects was chiefly due to the less careful execution of certain dissertations (see also Rosenthal, 1984, pp. 42–45). However, this conclusion may be less plausible in other areas of inquiry. Using other material, Glass et al. (1981, pp. 66–67, 226–227) also found a tendency for effect sizes to be less in dissertations than in other forms of publication, and they inferred that there was a selection bias on the part of those controlling access to prestigious journals.

One solution to the file drawer problem is to focus upon studies that were not originally conducted in order to compare performance in males and females but were carried out for some quite different reason (cf. Caplan, 1979). These might have been designed to test particular theoretical hypotheses that were not inherently related to sex or gender, or perhaps simply to obtain normative data from representative samples of the general population. An example of the latter is a study by Feingold (1988), who looked at gen-

der differences in four successive standardizations of the Differential Aptitude Tests and the Preliminary Scholastic Aptitude Test. As Hyde and Mc-
Kinley remarked in Chapter 2, the original publication of these data was not
contingent upon whether or not gender differences were present, and therefore Feingold's conclusions are unlikely to be contaminated by publication
bias.

Some purely technical solutions have been put forward to address this
problem. If a meta-analytic reviewer concludes that the size of an effect is
statistically significant (i.e., nonzero) by combining the probability levels
obtained in different studies, Rosenthal (1969; 1976, p. 454; 1979) showed
how one could derive the minimum number of unpublished studies with
nonsignificant results that would need to be located in order to overturn that
conclusion. This was characterized as a "fail-safe number" by Cooper
(1979). Rosenthal (1984, p. 110) suggested that an effect size should be
regarded as robust when the relevant fail-safe number exceeded ($5K + 10$),
where K was the total number of studies contributing to the meta-analysis.
Voyer et al. (1995) used this criterion to infer that there were reliable gender
differences on at least some specific tests of spatial abilities.

A different solution was recommended by Light and Pillemer (1984, pp.
63–69). This is based upon evaluating a graph showing sample size plotted
against effect size across the different studies contributing to a review. If
different studies involve repeated sampling from the same populations, then
the study outcomes will estimate a common population effect size, but those
based upon small samples will be more variable than those based upon large
samples. It follows that the distribution of study outcomes should take the
form of an inverted funnel (in other words, it will be unimodal, symmetric,
and leptokurtic). Panels (a) and (b) in Figure 5.1 illustrate this phenomenon
by showing the results of computer simulations based upon 955 samples
using population effect sizes of zero and 0.5, respectively. If the distribution
of study outcomes in a meta-analysis takes this form, one could conclude
that there was no evidence of publication bias and that the study outcomes
were homogeneous estimates of a single effect size.

Publication bias would result in a paucity of studies that yielded a small
effect size, particularly if they had been based on only relatively small samples. This is illustrated in panels (c) and (d) in Figure 5.1, which contain
only those study outcomes shown in panels (a) and (b) that are statistically
significant by a two-tailed test using $\alpha = 0.05$. If the true effect size is zero,
this results in a distribution that is bimodal (or, in other words, a "hollow
funnel"), as in panel (c). However, if the true effect size is nonzero, then
this results in a distribution of study outcomes that is asymmetric, as in
panel (d). As Light and Pillemer (1984) put it, there is a "bite" or chunk

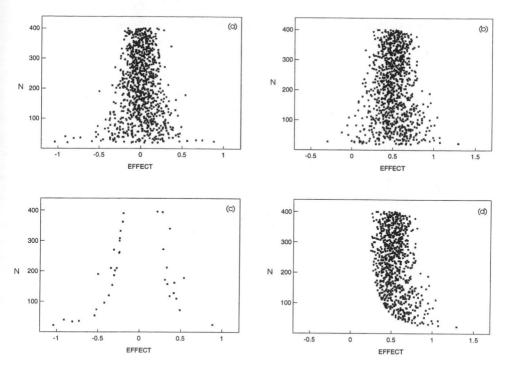

FIGURE 5.1. Results of computer simulations showing funnel distribution of effect sizes estimating a single population difference between means from two samples of equal size. The display is based upon five estimates for each possible sample size between 10 and 200 (and hence N takes all possible even values between 20 and 400). The true effect size is zero in panels (a) and (c) and $+0.5$ in panels (b) and (d). Panels (a) and (b) depict all 955 estimates to illustrate ideal funnel plots. Panels (c) and (d) contain only those effect sizes that are statistically significant at 5% by a two-tailed test to illustrate the potential effect of publication bias.

taken out of the display corresponding to effect sizes near zero obtained in studies using relatively small samples. Light and Pillemer presented an illustration of this using results from a review of the efficacy of educational programs aimed at surgical patients: Restriction of the analysis to published studies generated an asymmetric display, but the inclusion of dissertations (some of which had reported near-zero or negative effects) generated a broadly symmetric funnel plot.

This technique does not seem to have been previously applied to work on gender differences, but it is a straightforward matter to do so. Hyde and Linn (1988) presented a meta-analysis of gender differences in verbal ability, and panel (a) in Figure 5.2 shows a funnel plot for 121 measures of effect size listed in their Tables 1 and 2. With the exception of one outlier, the display is quite symmetrical around the (unweighted) mean of $+0.14$. The outlier is a study by Backman (1972) that used a total sample size of 2,925 and was reported to have obtained an effect size of $+1.43$. In fact, Becker and Hedges (1984) pointed out that the index of variation provided by Backman was a standard deviation of group means rather than of ungrouped observations; hence, the estimate of effect size may have been inflated and was not comparable to those obtained from the other studies.

Hyde, Fennema, and Lamon (1990) reported a meta-analysis of gender differences in mathematical ability, and panel (b) in Figure 5.2 shows a funnel plot for 255 measures of effect size listed in their Table 1. This display, too, is broadly symmetrical, but there is the suggestion of two different modes (one at zero, the other around $+0.40$), which suggests that the study outcomes were not homogeneous estimates of a single effect size. This heterogeneity was confirmed by Hyde et al. using formal statistical methods. However, the interesting point is that neither of the displays in Figure 5.2 shows any evidence of publication bias: Both funnel plots contain an appropriate distribution of effect sizes at values around zero.

Voyer et al. (1995) presented a meta-analysis of gender differences in spatial abilities. Following the results obtained in an earlier study by Linn and Petersen (1985), they initially classified the effect sizes into tests of mental rotation, tests of spatial perception, and tests of spatial visualization. Using this classification, Figure 5.3 shows funnel plots for the 172 measures of effect size used by Linn and Petersen (see Hyde & Linn, 1986, pp. 248–254) and the 190 additional measures of effect size that were listed by Voyer et al. Panel (a) shows a high degree of heterogeneity with regard to measures of mental rotation, which Voyer et al. themselves traced to both subject variables and procedural variables. Panels (b) and (c) show rather less heterogeneity with regard to measures of spatial perception and spatial visualization, and these displays are relatively symmetrical about the means of $+0.45$ and $+0.10$, respectively. Nevertheless, all three funnel plots in Figure 5.3 once again contain an appropriate distribution of effect sizes at values around zero, and none of these displays exhibits any evidence of publication bias.

A different sort of publication bias occurs when a study is accepted for publication but pertinent findings are omitted. If the participants' gender is considered to be irrelevant to the objectives of any particular investigation, it may be omitted from the research design, overlooked in the data analysis, eliminated from the written report, or dropped from any secondary accounts. For example, in reporting a number of experiments on mental rotation, Metzler and Shepard (1974) happened to mention informally that their male subjects had shown a faster rate of mental rotation than their female sub-

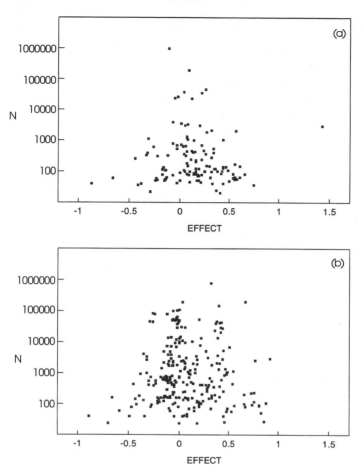

FIGURE 5.2. Funnel distributions of effect sizes for gender differences in (a) verbal ability, where a positive sign means that females produced higher scores than males (Hyde & Linn, 1988) and (b) mathematical ability, where a positive sign means that males produced higher scores than females (Hyde, Fennema, & Lamon, 1990). Sample size is plotted on a logarithmic scale.

jects. However, this finding was regarded as "relatively inconclusive" and omitted when their article was subsequently reprinted as a chapter in a text-book (see Shepard & Cooper, 1982, p. 342; cf. Cooper & Regan, 1982).

These considerations account for the situation that I described in Chapter 1, in which most publications ignore gender as an important social variable. I also mentioned that certain feminist writers had criticized this tendency as symptomatic of "gender insensitivity," whereas others had criticized the practice of routinely testing for gender differences with no coherent theoreti-

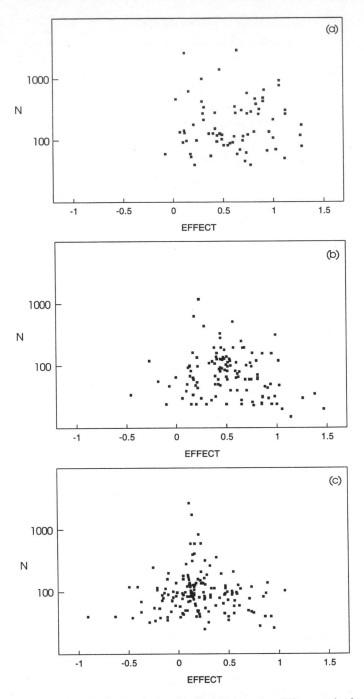

FIGURE 5.3. Funnel distributions of effect sizes for gender differences in three kinds of spatial ability: (a) mental rotation, (b) spatial perception, and (c) spatial visualization (Hyde & Linn, 1986, pp. 248–254; Voyer, Voyer, & Bryden, 1995). In each case, a positive effect size means that males produced higher scores than females. Sample size is plotted on a logarithmic scale.

cal justification for doing so. Nevertheless, it remains the case that a large number of published investigations in any particular field of research will have employed both male participants and female participants and consequently will be eligible (at least in theory) to be included in either a narrative review or a meta-analytic review.

In principle, the solution would be to try to obtain unpublished data from researchers who were active in the relevant field, and this strategy of "opening the drawers" was recommended as a general solution to the file drawer problem by Mullen (1989, pp. 33, 40). In practice, researchers may not be quite as helpful as Mullen indicated. In a personal communication (February 9, 1994), J. Eliot reported that he had written to 116 living researchers to request means and standard deviations by gender on tests of spatial ability. This had elicited four replies: Two of the respondents could provide no further data, while the other two were highly indignant: "Where do you get the gall to ask for data—implying that I am dishonest!"

BIAS IN SAMPLING PARTICIPANTS

Quite a different problem for both narrative reviews and meta-analytic reviews concerning gender differences is the possibility that the research studies that have actually been carried out and reported in the literature have involved samples of males and females that are systematically biased with regard to the particular dependent measure of interest. As I pointed out in Chapter 1, for the sake of convenience researchers often obtain their participants from within institutions that recruit, select, or otherwise accept candidates according to criteria that are biased toward one gender or the other. It follows that the results of their investigations may not provide unbiased estimates of differences in cognitive performance in the underlying populations.

In Chapter 2, Hyde and McKinley raised the issue of sampling bias in the context of the Study of Mathematically Precocious Youth. The samples involved in this study were explicitly biased, insofar as they were intended to be drawn from the upper 3% of the U.S. population with regard to mathematical ability. However, as Hyde and McKinley noted, they are also implicitly biased, insofar as the sampling process required schools to notify potential candidates of the program and the candidates themselves to volunteer to participate in a national administration of the Scholastic Aptitude Test (SAT). Hyde and McKinley suggested that gender might affect this recruitment process, although they considered that there was no direct evidence on this point.

In fact, Hyde and Linn (1988) had noted that there was sampling bias in the general administration of the SAT. First, they pointed out that it was only taken by selected samples of males and females (mainly those who are seeking admission to higher education), and that it was taken by fewer males than females. Second, they also pointed out that females taking the SAT were disadvantaged compared with males taking the SAT on the variables of parental income, father's education, and attendance at private schools. Finally, they added that there would be a disproportionate number of older women taking the SAT to satisfy entry requirements in returning to college who would be out of practice on timed tests such as the SAT. Such factors would imply that males taking the SAT are more highly selected in terms of their intellectual abilities to begin with, and this would tend to explain why gender differences favoring males arise on the verbal and mathematical portions of the SAT that are out of line with performance on psychometric tests (see Hyde et al., 1990; Hyde & Linn, 1988).

As I also pointed out in Chapter 1, the vast majority of research in psychology has been carried out using students in institutions of higher education and especially those taking courses in psychology. The analysis of gender differences in cognitive abilities does not have to be confined to such samples, however, because it is also possible to include normative data obtained from large representative samples with standard psychometric or educational tests. It is then an empirical matter whether effect sizes of similar magnitude will be obtained in the two kinds of study. In fact, it is possible to code the degree and the nature of the selectivity of the different samples in performing a meta-analysis. For example, Becker and Hedges (1984) used the following classification:

1: "unselected samples, including nationwide samples, school children not described as being in special programs or advanced courses, and most adult groups";
2: "samples of college students, school children enrolled in advanced or special courses (i.e., physics), and the like";
3: "highly select samples, including students from selective colleges and adults from the Terman study of 'geniuses' " (p. 586).

Becker and Hedges found that the absolute magnitude of gender differences in verbal ability, quantitative ability, visual-spatial ability, and field articulation all increased with the degree of selectivity of the samples. Employing an elaborated classification of sample selectivity, Hyde et al. (1990) confirmed that differences in mathematical ability favored males in direct proportion to the degree of sample selectivity and were essentially zero in general or relatively unselected samples. In contrast, Hyde and Linn (1988) examined verbal ability using a more extensive set of studies than Becker and Hedges had used, and they found that gender differences were roughly zero, regardless of sample selectivity.

However, controlling for the degree of selectivity of the sample as specified by the researcher will not take into account the possibility of self-selection on the part of the participants. Unless there is some kind of formal or legal obligation on the participants to undertake the testing procedure, the representativeness of the resulting sample will depend upon the willingness of the relevant individuals to take part in the study. At universities in the United States, for instance, participation in research projects being conducted by faculty members was often in the past a formal requirement on introductory psychology courses. This has recently come to be seen as an ethically rather dubious practice, and nowadays students are typically allowed a choice of ways in which to develop their awareness of research methods. Alternatively, researchers may choose to offer payments or some other inducement to volunteers to take part in their projects. In either case, there will be a sampling bias in the resulting data that will reflect the characteristics of those individuals who choose to participate in psychological research in return for the particular rewards on offer.

The authoritative review by Rosenthal and Rosnow (1969) on volunteer subjects found some evidence for the view that women were more likely to volunteer than men were if the task was presented in a generic or vague manner, whereas men were more likely to volunteer than women were if the task was presented as more specific or unusual. However, they cautioned that these trends might well interact with the gender of the researcher. They also concluded that volunteers tended to produce higher scores than nonvolunteers on tests of intelligence, and that in surveys of the general population volunteers were consistently of a higher educational level than nonvolunteers. Little is known about how these factors might interact to influence volunteering behavior, except that Rosenthal and Rosnow remarked that the tendency for volunteers to be more intelligent than nonvolunteers was more pronounced in the case of men than in the case of women.

Kruglanski (1973) argued that sampling bias resulting from the use of volunteers did not seriously undermine research aimed at demonstrating the effects of experimental treatments on a particular phenomenon, but that it was a fundamental problem in research that was aimed at estimating a given population parameter. Research on gender differences clearly falls within the latter category, because it attempts to estimate the direction and the magnitude of observable disparities between men and women. In fact, it is, in principle, quite possible that the use of volunteers is responsible for at least some gender differences in cognitive performance. For instance, studies using particular spatial tasks might involve a disproportionate number of intelligent men, whereas studies investigating general aptitude might involve a disproportionate number of women from within a wide range of abilities.

Moreover, other research has suggested that volunteers are more responsive to perceived demand characteristics than nonvolunteers are (Silverman, 1977, pp. 90–92), and Crawford and Chaffin pointed out in Chapter 4 that gender differences in performance are sometimes highly specific to the gendered expectations that they elicit.

Researchers have to beware of sampling bias in other contexts, too. In Chapter 2, Hyde and McKinley referred to statements in a textbook on gender differences in cognition (Halpern, 1992) to the effect that boys were more likely to show developmental disturbances of verbal functioning than girls were. Halpern stated in particular that "mild dyslexia is 5 times more likely to occur in males than in females, and severe dyslexia is 10 times more likely to appear in males than in females" (p. 65). Nevertheless, schools do not necessarily use the same criteria in order to identify boys and girls with learning difficulties (Vogel, 1990). In Chapter 3, Caplan and Caplan referred to a recent study by Shaywitz, Shaywitz, Fletcher, and Escobar (1990) that found no difference between boys and girls in the incidence of reading impairment, only in the likelihood that it would be diagnosed as such. It is worth examining the findings of this study in some detail.

Shaywitz et al. followed 445 children at 24 different schools through second and third grade and assessed them annually on measures covering the academic, cognitive, and behavioral domains. In each grade, these schools identified certain children as "reading disabled," rendering them eligible for special-education support under federal legislation. In second grade, 13.6% of the boys and 3.2% of the girls were identified by their school as reading disabled; in third grade, 10.0% of the boys and 4.2% of the girls were identified as reading disabled. In both cases, the gender difference was statistically significant. In agreement with previous reports, these results implied that the prevalence of reading disability based on school identification was two to five times higher in boys than in girls.

The researchers themselves identified children as "reading disabled" if their reading performance was 1.5 standard deviations or more below the level that would have been predicted on the basis of their Full Scale IQs. In second grade, 8.7% of the boys and 6.9% of the girls were identified by the researchers as reading disabled; in third grade, 9.0% of the boys and 6.0% of the girls were identified by the researchers as reading disabled. In neither case did the difference even approach statistical significance. Shaywitz et al. cited a number of previous reports that suggested that the gender ratio of boys to girls meeting research-based criteria for reading disability was between 1:1 and 1.5:1, which was in line with their own findings.

The results of the psychological assessment in third grade showed no overall difference between the boys and girls in either their IQs or their academic achievement, but the boys received significantly poorer ratings from their teachers across six different domains of classroom performance. Although Shaywitz et al. did not pursue their investigation of differences between boys and girls, a comparison of the two procedures for identifying reading disability showed that they could be differentiated with regard to teachers' ratings of classroom behavior. The majority of the 15 children who were identified as reading disabled by their school but who failed to meet the research criteria were judged to exhibit behavioral difficulties; in contrast, the majority of the 18 children who met the research criteria but who were not identified as reading disabled by their school were rated by their teachers as having no behavior problems.

Shaywitz et al. argued that decisions regarding individual children were influenced by teachers' perceptions of what constituted appropriate and inappropriate classroom behavior. Their findings indicate that some children (mainly boys) are identified by their schools as reading disabled on the basis of overactivity or other behavioral difficulties, rather than a genuine discrepancy between their ability and their reading achievement. Equally, other children (mainly girls) who satisfy research criteria for reading disability are not identified by their schools as reading disabled because their classroom behavior seems to be broadly appropriate. Indeed, teachers who work with such children claim that girls can often use better social skills to disguise their learning difficulties (Phillips, 1996).

Shaywitz et al. concluded that school-identified samples of children with reading disability were subject to a referral bias that would explain reports in the literature of an increased prevalence in boys. It follows that both narrative and meta-analytic reviews that seek to generalize from research studies based on school-identified cases are subject to sampling bias and might generate invalid conclusions. This would not explain the higher prevalence in boys of other developmental disorders where there is less scope for diagnostic error, such as temporal lobe epilepsy, cerebral palsy, and congenital hydrocephalus; this seems to be due to a more rapid development of girls during the first few years of life, which means that they proceed more quickly through those periods during which all children are vulnerable to the relevant diseases (Richardson, 1975a; Taylor, 1969; Taylor & Ounsted, 1972). However, the study by Shaywitz et al. serves to emphasize the need to maintain critical rigor and an attention to detail as assiduously when evaluating research on developmental disturbances of cognitive function as when evaluating the research concerned with normal cognitive abilities.

BIAS IN SAMPLING TEST ITEMS

A different sort of bias can arise in the sampling of particular items on which the participants in any study are to be tested. The idea that the test materials themselves can differentially favor males or females is an issue referred to in each of the three substantive contributions to this volume. Maccoby and Jacklin (1974, p. 68) noted that some tests, such as the Stanford Binet, had been constructed and standardized in such a way as to minimize differences between males and females in overall performance, whereas other tests, such as the Thurstone Primary Mental Abilities Test, had not. In the latter case, any differences that are obtained might be attributable to the weighting that is given to particular test items. In Chapter 3, Caplan and Caplan argued that this was essentially an intractable problem, since it was not, in principle, possible either (a) to incorporate the entire population of possible test items or (b) to make valid inferences from a mere sample of test items to that population.

This is, however, entirely analogous to the familiar problem of drawing valid inferences about an entire population on the basis of a sample drawn from that population. Most contemporary psychological research involves the application of classical forms of statistical inference to legitimate this process in the case of samples of participants, and the same methods can be applied to generalize from samples of test items. Most famously, in his article on what he called the "language-as-fixed-effect fallacy," Clark (1973) argued that it was essential to employ such techniques in the majority of psycholinguistic experiments. Clark described an approximate procedure that could be employed in determining whether the findings of a published study could be generalized beyond the particular sample of items that had actually been used. However, I put forward similar arguments and described more appropriate procedures to be used when working on raw data (Richardson, 1975b). It may be useful to spell out one version of these.

First, assume that there are p groups, each containing n participants and each receiving q items. The statistical model representing the score obtained by the kth participant in the ith group on the jth item takes the form (Winer et al., 1991, p. 510):

$$X_{ijk} = \mu + \alpha_i + \pi_{k(i)} + \beta_j + \alpha\beta_{ij} + \beta\pi_{jk(i)} + \epsilon_{m(ijk)}.$$

In this model,

$$\mu = \text{the grand mean of all potential observations}$$
$$\alpha_i = \text{the main effect for Group } i$$

$\pi_{k(i)}$ = the effect associated with Subject k in Group i

β_j = the main effect for Item j

$\alpha\beta_{ij}$ = the interaction between Group i and Item j

$\beta\pi_{jk(i)}$ = the interaction between Subject k in Group i and Item j

$\epsilon_{m(ijk)}$ = the experimental error associated with each observation.

Next, assume that both the Subjects factor and the Items factor are random factors, so that the levels included in the design are both random samples from an indefinitely large population of subjects and items, respectively. It can be shown that the expected values of the mean squares corresponding to different sources of variation are as described in Table 5–2 (see Winer et al., 1991, p. 510).

According to the standard procedures that most researchers will have learned and most statistical packages will carry out by default, the mean squares associated with the Groups term is compared with the mean squares for the Subjects within Groups term to yield a conventional F statistic:

$$F = \frac{\text{MS(Groups)}}{\text{MS(Subjects)}}$$

This is entirely appropriate when the Items factor is a fixed factor (that is, the items actually included exhaust the whole population in question). However, an inspection of Table 5–2 shows that, when the Items factor is a random factor, the expected value of the numerator in this fraction is the same as the expected value of the denominator only when the quantity $(n\sigma^2_{\alpha\beta} + qn\sigma^2_{\alpha})$ is zero. In other words, this statistic confounds the variability among the groups with the Groups by Items interaction, and in principle it can give rise to a statistically significant result even when there are no genuine differences among the groups at all (in other words, when $\sigma^2_{\alpha} =$

TABLE 5-2   Expected Values of Mean Squares for Experiments Generalizing across both Participants and Items

Effect	Degrees of freedom	Expected mean squares
Groups	$(p - 1)$	$\sigma^2_{\epsilon} + \sigma^2_{\beta\pi} + n\sigma^2_{\alpha\beta} + q\sigma^2_{\pi} + qn\sigma^2_{\alpha}$
Subjects	$p \cdot (n - 1)$	$\sigma^2_{\epsilon} + \sigma^2_{\beta\pi} + q\sigma^2_{\pi}$
Items	$(q - 1)$	$\sigma^2_{\epsilon} + \sigma^2_{\beta\pi} + pn\sigma^2_{\beta}$
Items × Groups	$(p - 1) \cdot (q - 1)$	$\sigma^2_{\epsilon} + \sigma^2_{\beta\pi} + n\sigma^2_{\alpha\beta}$
Items × Subjects	$p \cdot (n - 1) \cdot (q - 1)$	$\sigma^2_{\epsilon} + \sigma^2_{\beta\pi}$
Error	—	σ^2_{ϵ}

0). Such a result can thus always be attributed to the inclusion of particular test items, as Caplan and Caplan correctly observed. This is akin to one version of Clark's (1973) "language-as-fixed-effect fallacy."

In this kind of experimental design, there is no conventional F ratio that satisfies the structural requirements for a test on the Groups effect in terms of the expected values of the constituent mean squares. However, consider the following expression:

$$\text{quasi } F = \frac{\text{MS(Groups)} + \text{MS(Items} \times \text{Subjects)}}{\text{MS(Subjects)} + \text{MS(Groups} \times \text{Items)}}.$$

Effectively, the variance among the groups is being compared both with the variance among the participants within the groups and also with the Groups by Items interaction. An inspection of Table 5–2 shows that the expected value of the numerator of this fraction is equal to the expected value of the denominator only when $\sigma_\alpha^2 = 0$, and thus it provides an appropriate test of the null hypothesis that there is no difference among the groups. The statistic is known as a quasi F ratio, and under the null hypothesis it is approximated by the F distribution, although a special procedure is needed to determine the degrees of freedom (see Winer et al., 1991, pp. 375–376).

Determining the tail probability of this quasi F ratio provides the probability of results as extreme as those that were actually obtained on the assumption that there is no difference among the p groups. This then solves the problem posed by Caplan and Caplan of determining whether to accept an obtained gender difference in performance in the face of sampling variability in both the participants and test items. It does not, of course, rule out the possibility that the finding of such a difference (or the lack of such a difference) is an artifact that arises from *systematic* bias in the sampling of either participants or test items, but this problem arises whether or not one is seeking to generalize beyond the particular test items actually employed, and it can only be solved by the critical evaluation of the sampling procedure in each particular case.

There is a technical problem in the case of meta-analysis, insofar as measures of effect size normally involve standardizing differences between the relevant groups against the variance among the participants within the groups. As the first two lines of Table 5–2 indicate, this confounds the effect of groups with the Groups by Items interaction, which is tantamount to treating the Items term as a fixed factor rather than a random factor. Meta-analyses carried out upon different studies using precisely the same test consisting of precisely the same items (e.g., Voyer et al., 1995) are therefore open to the criticism that their results may well be specific to the particular items included in the test. However, researchers applying meta-analysis to studies using different tests with different test items (or even parallel forms of the same test) can claim to offer conclusions that do generalize beyond the specific items used in any particular study.

QUALITY CONTROL IN META-ANALYTIC RESEARCH

A different problem that needs to be addressed in meta-analytic reviews is the potential heterogeneity of research studies. Apart from the fact that the research that is relevant to a particular issue (such as whether there exist gender differences in cognition) will have been disseminated in a wide variety of forms, it will also have been conducted by a wide variety of researchers using a wide variety of techniques for a wide variety of purposes. As McGuire et al. (1985) commented:

> The average effect size may amalgamate statistical findings based on quite different interpretations of the theoretical hypothesis as well as on different operationalizations of the construct under study. It may reflect manipulations of noncomparable independent variables and their effects on noncomparable dependent measures. Moreover, the studies from which the summary data are derived may differ considerably in the extent to which they possess adequate internal and external validity. (p. 1)

This point is often expressed by saying that meta-analytic researchers can be guilty of "mixing apples and oranges" (Glass et al., 1981, pp. 218–220; see also Chapter 3, this volume).

Even if this particular criticism can be rebutted, one would not wish to allow any rotten apples or oranges into the meta-analytic basket. The best examples of narrative review include a critical evaluation of each of the studies under consideration. In focusing on the outcomes of different studies and especially in seeking to encompass all relevant studies, there is a danger that a meta-analyst will ignore details of research design and will overlook even very serious shortcomings in particular investigations. As a result, the conclusions will be influenced by design flaws as well as by any genuine effects. Ultimately, the meta-analyst might be engaged in the purely empty exercise of seeking to integrate the results of a sloppy and ill-conceived domain of research: As Eysenck (1978) characterized this, "garbage in—garbage out" (p. 517). Some of the contributors to the present volume might have some sympathy with this dictum as applied to the study of gender differences in cognition, but I think that all would agree that it was potentially dangerous to aggregate together studies of poor quality with studies of good quality (see also Mullen, 1989, p. 62).

In principle, it is possible to address the "garbage in—garbage out" issue and the "apples and oranges" problem either a priori or a posteriori (Cooper, 1984, pp. 65–66). First, one could refine the selection criteria for the meta-analysis so as to focus the study upon effect sizes in apples rather than in oranges, or upon effect sizes in sound fruit rather than in rotten fruit. As Mullen (1989, p. 125) remarked, this is clearly a more appropriate strategy when reviewing a body of research that encompasses a wide range of poorly constructed operationalizations of the constructs in question. On the basis of the arguments that were put forward in Chapters 3 and 4 in this volume, this criticism would certainly seem to apply to the constructs of "mathematical ability," "spatial ability," and "verbal ability."

The second strategy is to include all possible candidates within the meta-analytic investigation but to examine the degree of their variability with regard to measures of effect size. For instance, Becker and Hedges (1984) found that homogeneity of effect sizes could be achieved in studies of quantitative ability, visual-spatial ability, and field articulation by simply controlling the publication date of each study and the selectivity of the relevant sample. However, this was a relatively insensitive test, since the total number of studies in each case was quite small. This kind of approach is more appropriate in situations in which the researcher can unambiguously identify different operationalizations of the construct. An example is the meta-analysis that was carried out by Voyer et al. (1995), which identified significant heterogeneity among the alternative estimates of effect size that could be associated with variability between different spatial tests and between different ways of administering the same test.

In summary, then, one of other of these two strategies—refining the selection criteria or testing for heterogeneity of effect sizes—usually addresses the "apples and oranges" issue in meta-analytic reviews. With regard to the issue of quality control, the former strategy would lead the meta-analyst to select those studies that survived some criterion of peer review or those studies that could be shown to meet particular criteria of quality (Lepper, 1995). For instance, Voyer et al. (1995) included only published studies, and this led them to eliminate a number of unpublished studies that had been included in previous reviews by Maccoby and Jacklin (1974) and by Linn and Petersen (1985). The danger with this approach is that it incorporates an explicit publication bias into the review process and potentially discards a large amount of important data (Glass, 1976).

On the latter strategy, the decision to include studies of doubtful quality could be justified by demonstrating that the obtained estimates of effect size were homogeneous across the total set of studies available in the research literature, regardless of their apparent quality (see Hedges, 1982). Homogeneity was ultimately achieved in the study by Voyer et al. (1995), but only at the level of particular tests or test procedures. A more rigorous test was envisaged by Glass (1976), who suggested that "it is an empirical question whether relatively poorly designed studies give results significantly at variance with those of the best designed studies" (p. 4). In other words, one can evaluate whether effect sizes vary with some criterion of research quality, and a number of criteria of research quality have been put forward that can be used as moderator variables in meta-analytic reviews (see, e.g., Cooper, 1984, pp. 66–71).

As Hall (1980) pointed out, measures of effect size are analogous to a signal-to-noise ratio in psychophysical research, in that they indicate the magnitude of a difference relative to uncontrolled variation. Hence, effect size would be expected to be greater in better controlled studies. However, the available evidence suggests that there is no straightforward relationship between measures of effect size and the quality of research (Glass et al., 1981, pp. 221–226; Lipsey & Wilson, 1993). One issue noted by Lepper (1995) is that comparisons between studies of allegedly good and poor quality have sometimes lacked sufficient statistical power to detect differences in their outcomes. Another problem is that this relationship has only been studied in certain limited research domains involving formal experimental manipulations, and there seems to be no evidence at all with regard to studies of gender differences in cognition. Of course, Hall's analogy is only valid if there is a genuine "signal" in the first place. If there is really no gender difference in a particular cognitive ability, then this should be apparent in better controlled studies, whereas poorly executed research may often give rise to spurious significant "effects."

A basic difficulty with both the a priori and a posteriori strategies for assuring methodological quality in meta-analytic research is that they assume that researchers can provide a valid and reliable assessment of the quality of each study without regard to the effect size or to the level of statistical significance that was attained. The evidence in fact suggests that even experienced reviewers attain only what could most optimistically be called a moderate level of agreement on the quality of research studies (see Mullen, 1989, p. 62). For instance, McGuire et al. (1985) found that neither advanced-level graduate students studying research methodology nor researchers with a national reputation for their expertise in the relevant area achieved statistically significant interrater agreement in evaluating published research studies. In practice, then, the issue of assessing and assuring quality in meta-analytic research is not a straightforward one.

ASKING THE RIGHT QUESTIONS

Nevertheless, Linn and Petersen (1986) made the far more subtle point that "the research perspectives in a field influence what researchers study and constrain the possible outcomes from meta-analysis" (p. 69). As Hyde and McKinley noted in Chapter 2, biases can affect both meta-analyses and narrative reviews through the behaviors and measures that reviewers choose to include and also through the biases of researchers in the relevant field. Certainly, statistical techniques of whatever sophistication will not compensate for the preoccupations of other investigators. These operate at a number of different levels:

- in the choice of research questions
- in the choice of instruments and apparatus
- in the choice of participants and the means of recruiting them
- in the choice of contexts in which to conduct the research
- in the choice of publications for disseminating the findings.

As Mullen (1989, p. 12) noted, the particular studies that are included in meta-analyses have implications for the generality of the results that are obtained. Indeed, meta-analytic reviews actually tend to legitimate the preoccupations and biases of previous researchers, because they presuppose some commitment to established research questions and research methods.

Moreover, Lepper (1995) recently argued that meta-analysis committed the reviewer to the positivistic rhetoric that is traditionally associated with the design and analysis of laboratory-based experiments and, perhaps more crucially, to a realist interpretation of the relevant domain: "The fundamental premise on which meta-analysis is based is that studies that differ in their specific manipulations, procedures, and measures can be compared in terms of a single 'unbiased' and 'objective' index of effect size" (p. 412). It is true that in some meta-analytic research one can discern a conceptual and methodological "package" that reinforces a quite specific view of how research findings are most naturally to be expressed:

- the use of objectively scorable though relatively artificial tests to yield numerical measures of performance in selected tasks;
- the derivation of different indexes of effect size to transcend the particular methods, procedures, and measurements that were originally implicated in those tasks; and
- the application of meta-analytic techniques to obliterate any trace of specificity that might attach to an index of effect size obtained from a single empirical investigation.

The deliberate aim of this package is to generate global and thoroughly decontextualized measures that appear to possess an objective reality set completely apart from the mundane, particular, and richly contextualized episodes from which they were ultimately derived. In the present context, this realist interpretation is consonant with biological explanations of gender differences in cognitive performance.

However, the use of meta-analysis in psychological research is itself neutral between a positivist, realist approach or a social constructionist approach. For example, in Chapter 2, Hyde and McKinley noted that meta-analyses can incorporate moderator variables that code for properties of the test situation and so enable one to assess variations in effect sizes across different test situations. They then pointed out that meta-analyses of this sort had shown that the appearance and the magnitude of gender differences in performance on cognitive tasks were contingent on the particular testing procedure being employed. This implies that gender differences in cognition—as in many other aspects of behavior (see, for example, Eagly & Crowley, 1986)—are critically determined by contextual factors. This conclusion directly challenges the conventional positivist account that I outlined above. In short, then, the detailed findings of meta-analytic reviews concerning gender differences in cognition are more open to a social constructionist interpretation than to a realist one.

In Chapter 4, Crawford and Chaffin explored the broader implications of a thorough-going constructionist view of gender and gender differences. They criticized research into gender differences because it tends to conceptualize gender in terms of oppositional categories defined by means of a fundamental set of attributes located within the individual. As a consequence, it decontextualizes behavior, obscures issues of power, and helps to sustain social inequality. In contrast, Crawford and Chaffin characterized both gender and gender difference as constructs arising from a system that organizes relationships of power and status within society. On their argument, this system generates differences between men and women yet at the same time is socially constructed within the various discourses concerning those differences in science, the media, and everyday life.

Crawford and Chaffin observed that cognitive performance is sensitive to the specific situations in which the relevant abilities were originally acquired and to the specific situations in which they are used and tested. As they pointed out, the most recent meta-analytic reviews have shown that there is no single objective measure of gender difference in any cognitive domain. Rather, there exist reliable gender differences on some cognitive tasks but not on others. Indeed, the existence and the magnitude of these differences sometimes depend upon the exact testing and scoring procedures that are used. Crawford and Chaffin concluded that this throws doubt upon the interpretation of such differences as being due to biological factors. More fundamentally, as I mentioned above, in demonstrating the powerful influence of contextual factors, these recent meta-analytic reviews offer very little support to a realist interpretation of gender differences in cognition and are far more consistent with a social constructionist one.

These results suggest that one should focus upon the different skills and strategies that are adopted by individuals in everyday life as well as in formal testing situations. It has sometimes been suggested that gender differences in cognitive performance might reflect the dispositions of men and women to employ different cognitive strategies (e.g., Coltheart, Hull, & Slater, 1975; McGuinness, 1980). Traditionally, however, theorists have ignored basic information processes that might underlie gender differences in human cognition and have concerned themselves with global biological or sociological explanations. Crawford and Chaffin's analysis goes beyond this in trying to spell out the mental operations that might be involved, and it provides an account of gender differences in cognitive performance that is genuinely cognitive in nature (cf. Anderson, 1987).

Crawford and Chaffin observed that cognitive strategies are developed and implemented in response to specific tasks, goals, and contexts, and to that extent they depend upon the priorities of the individual. Therefore, gender differences in performance may reflect differences in the perceived demand characteristics of the task rather than any differences in ability. One consequence of this is that performance on either laboratory tasks or psychometric tests may have very little relevance to the cognitive demands of everyday situations. Crawford and Chaffin remarked that the predictive validity of cognitive tests was questionable because the social context of the laboratory experiment or the psychometric test was substituted for the social context in which the relevant ability was normally displayed.

Nevertheless, Crawford and Chaffin's account radically undermines the entire positivistic enterprise that attempts to reify observed differences between the cognitive performance of men and women as "objective" measures of effect size, because the latter overlooks the point that the "raw" data upon which it is grounded are essentially constituted in specific forms of social interaction between researchers and their participants. Of course, by the standards of everyday life, the interactions characteristic of most testing situations are artificial, if not downright bizarre. Nowadays, it is common for writers to pay lip-service to this idea by recognizing that experimental research might be of limited "ecological validity," and some have maintained that laboratory-based research reveals little or nothing about the real-life functions of cognitive processes (e.g., Yuille, 1986).

More radical critics have pointed to the power relationships that are inherent in the experimental situation and have put forward political and moral arguments regarding the effects of laboratory research upon both the participants and the researchers themselves (Heron, 1981). Rowan (1981) argued that both experimental and applied research exemplified the various forms of alienation that according to Marx would operate in any economic system where the workers (in this case, the participants) did not own the means of production. Ethical arguments aside, this need not matter if the researcher is concerned to test hypotheses about basic mechanisms involved in cognition. However, researchers investigating gender differences often claim to account for the behavior in men and women in everyday activities and thereby to illuminate the basic nature of maleness and femaleness.

As Crawford and Chaffin noted, the specificity of the cognitive tasks that generate gender differences tends to motivate theoretical accounts of those differences in terms of the differential life experience of boys and girls and of men and women: As they put it, men and women acquire and use cognitive skills in different social worlds. Crawford and Chaffin pointed to three sorts of evidence from meta-analytic reviews that provide support for this notion. First, the fact that gender differences in cognition are typically absent in young children; second, the fact that the size of such differences increases with age during childhood and adulthood; and, third, the fact that the gender differences on some kinds of task have apparently increased or decreased in their magnitude over the course of time.

In principle, the different life experiences of males and females can generate differences in their cognitive performance in two different ways:

- There are direct effects that result from their level of experience with different kinds of cognitive activity. Cognitive activities in which females engage more often than males (or vice versa) may lead to the development of particular cognitive skills. In this case, extended practice or training on appropriate tasks may lead to the modification or elimination of the gender differences in question.
- There are indirect effects that result from the cultural transmission of beliefs with respect to the relative abilities of men and women by parents, teachers, peers, and the media. These beliefs give rise to expectations concerning the individual's ability that tend to affect performance when a task is identified as one requiring the relevant cognitive abilities, thus constituting a self-fulfilling prophecy. In this case, disguising the nature of the task may lead to the modification or elimination of the gender differences in question.

Crawford and Chaffin argued that, in manipulating the relative levels of performance attained by male and female participants within particular cognitive tasks, both kinds of effect served to sustain the gender system. They concluded that, by endeavoring to study differences between males and females in isolation from the social-structural and interactional factors that produced and maintained them, psychologists participated uncritically in the reproduction of inequalities. Instead, "gender differences" should be conceived as the residue of the gender system in individual identities and subjectivities, and the purpose of psychological research should be to investigate how gender differences are produced, sustained, and justified as part of a gendered social order.

In order to achieve this, psychologists will need to address a wider range of research questions and to employ a wider range of methodologies. Crawford and Chaffin gave two examples of alternative methodologies that might be used in this context. One was the analysis of verbal protocols that result when participants are instructed to think aloud while carrying out a task (see Scribner, 1984). The other was an ethnographic approach based upon structured interviews intended to elicit informants' accounts of their perceptions and experiences regarding some particular domain of experience (see Lave, 1988; Sadker & Sadker, 1994). Although the first is typically associated with a realist epistemology, the second is most often associated with a constructionist epistemology according to which both the phenomena under investigation and the theoretical entities devised by the researcher are constituted in social practices (Henwood, 1996).

The use of qualitative methods represents a different tradition from the majority of research on gender differences in cognition (Eagly, 1995). Nevertheless, these research methods appear to be far more appropriate to investigating more deep-seated aspects of cognition, such as the personal meanings that are attached to cognitive tasks in daily life and individual differences in conceptions of knowledge and understanding. Indeed, there is an established literature based on the use of structured interviews in which men and women are claimed to differ characteristically (although not exclusively) with regard to their forms of intellectual development (e.g., Baxter Magolda, 1988, 1992; Belenky, Clinchy, Goldberger, & Tarule, 1986; Clinchy & Zimmerman, 1982). However, this research is prone to the same kinds of problem as quantitative research methods, especially in terms of a tendency to reify particular forms of cognition and to ignore the social context in which cognition actually takes place (see Crawford, 1989).

There are genuine differences of principle that separate quantitative and qualitative research methods, of course, just as there are differences of principle between different quantitative methods and between different qualitative methods. However, it is otiose to try to debate the relative merits of these two approaches without reference to the problems that they are to be used to address. In order to explore the nature of differences between women and men in cognition as well as in any other major domain of human experience, it will be necessary to employ a methodologically aware eclecticism in which the full range of options is carefully considered in each specific research context (see Hammersley, 1996). Regardless of the chosen method, what is crucial, according to Crawford and Chaffin, is that researchers should retain a clear view of the way in which these differences are constructed through the operation of the gender system.

CONCLUSIONS

On the basis of the ideas, arguments, and evidence contained in this book, it is now possible to put forward a fairly definitive statement concerning the nature and origins of gender differences in human cognition:

1. Gender differences in cognition have traditionally been construed in terms of differences between females and males in their intellectual abilities and consequently evaluated in terms of differences between females and males in their performance on objectively scorable tests.

2. The application of meta-analytic techniques has demonstrated reliable gender differences on some measures of speech production (where women tend to outperform men) and some measures of mental rotation, spatial perception, mathematical problem solving, and science achievement (where men tend to outperform women).

3. There is no evidence that such gender differences are contaminated by any bias in favor of the publication of research studies that report statistically significant findings or by biases in the sampling of test items.

4. There is however clear evidence that obtained gender differences are often contaminated by biases in the recruitment and selection of the research participants, and they tend to approach zero if researchers employ general or relatively unselected samples.

5. Meta-analytic techniques were originally developed to integrate the findings of a body of research into a global or "objective" measure of effect size, and to that extent they tend to foster an uncritical realist epistemology with regard to gender differences in cognition that is consonant with biological explanations of these differences.

6. However, meta-analytic reviews have provided three sorts of evidence that gender differences result instead from different experiences in males and females: Gender differences are typically absent in young children; their

magnitude typically increases with age; and, in some cases, their magnitude has apparently changed over recent decades.

7. More crucially, meta-analytic reviews have shown that the existence and the magnitude of these differences vary from one task to another, and sometimes depend upon the exact testing and scoring procedures that are used. This demonstrates that there is no single objective measure of gender difference in any domain or aspect of cognition.

8. On the contrary, "gender differences" are constituted in particular patterns of social interaction between researchers and participants, and they need to be understood as social constructs arising from a system that organizes relationships of power and status between men and women (and between boys and girls) within society at large.

9. Future psychological investigations will need to address a much wider range of research questions and to employ a judicious combination of quantitative and qualitative research methods in order to examine in detail how gender differences in cognition are generated, maintained, and articulated through the functioning of this gender system.

10. At the same time, it will be essential to ensure that investigations of gender differences in cognition play a positive role in addressing and remedying social injustices, and that they are not, as so often in the past, serving to reinforce and to perpetuate the differential relationships of power and status that exist in contemporary society.

REFERENCES

Anderson, N. S. (1987). Cognition, learning, and memory. In M. A. Baker (Ed.), *Sex differences in human performance* (pp. 37–54). Chichester, U.K.: Wiley.

Backman, M. E. (1972). Patterns of mental abilities: Ethnic, socioeconomic, and sex differences. *American Educational Research Journal, 9*, 1–12.

Baxter Magolda, M. B. (1988). Measuring gender differences in intellectual development: A comparison of assessment methods. *Journal of College Student Development, 29*, 528–537.

Baxter Magolda, M. B. (1992). *Knowing and reasoning in college: Gender-related patterns in students' intellectual development.* San Francisco: Jossey-Bass.

Becker, B. J., & Hedges, L. V. (1984). Meta-analysis of cognitive gender differences: A comment on an analysis by Rosenthal and Rubin. *Journal of Educational Psychology, 76*, 583–587.

Belenky, M. F., Clinchy, B. M., Goldberger, N. R., & Tarule, J. M. (1986). *Women's ways of knowing: The development of self, voice, and mind.* New York: Basic Books.

Caplan, P. J. (1979). Beyond the box score: A boundary condition for sex differences in aggression and achievement striving. In B. A. Maher (Ed.), *Progress in experimental personality research* (Vol. 9, pp. 41–87). New York: Academic Press.

Casey, M. B., Pezaris, E., & Nuttall, R. L. (1992). Spatial ability as a predictor of math achievement: The importance of sex and handedness patterns. *Neuropsychologia, 30,* 35–45.

Clark, H. H. (1973). The language-as-fixed-effect fallacy: A critique of language statistics in psychological research. *Journal of Verbal Learning and Verbal Behavior, 12,* 335–359.

Clinchy, B. M., & Zimmerman, C. (1982). Epistemology and agency in the development of undergraduate women. In P. Perun (Ed.), *The undergraduate woman: Issues in educational equity* (pp. 161–182). Lexington, MA: Heath.

Cohen, J. (1965). Some statistical issues in psychological research. In B. B. Wolman (Ed.), *Handbook of clinical psychology* (pp. 95–121). New York: McGraw-Hill.

Cohen, J. (1969). *Statistical power analysis for the behavioral sciences.* New York: Academic Press.

Coltheart, M., Hull, E., & Slater, D. (1975). Sex differences in imagery and reading. *Nature, 253,* 438–440.

Cooper, H. M. (1979). Statistically combining independent studies: A meta-analysis of sex differences in conformity research. *Journal of Personality and Social Psychology, 37,* 131–146.

Cooper, H. M. (1984). *The integrative research review: A systematic approach.* Beverly Hills, CA: Sage.

Cooper, L. A., & Regan, D. T. (1982). Attention, perception, and intelligence. In R. J. Sternberg (Ed.), *Handbook of human intelligence* (pp. 123–169). Cambridge, U.K.: Cambridge University Press.

Craig, J. R., Eison, C. L., & Metze, L. P. (1976). Significance tests and their interpretation: An example utilizing published research and ω^2. *Bulletin of the Psychonomic Society, 7,* 280–282.

Crawford, M. (1989). Agreeing to differ: Feminist epistemologies and women's ways of knowing. In M. Crawford & M. Gentry (Eds.), *Gender and thought: Psychological perspectives* (pp. 128–145). New York: Springer-Verlag.

Eagly, A. H. (1995). The science and politics of comparing women and men. *American Psychologist, 50,* 145–158.

Eagly, A. H., & Crowley, M. (1986). Gender and helping behavior: A meta-analytic review of the social psychological literature. *Psychological Bulletin, 100,* 283–308.

Eysenck, H. J. (1978). An exercise in mega-silliness. *American Psychologist, 33,* 517.

Feingold, A. (1988). Cognitive gender differences are disappearing. *American Psychologist, 43,* 95–103.

Glass, G. V. (1976). Primary, secondary, and meta-analysis of research. *Educational Researcher, 5*(10), 3–8.

Glass, G. V., McGaw, B., & Smith, M. L. (1981). *Meta-analysis in social research.* Beverly Hills, CA: Sage.

Hall, J. A. (1980). Gender differences in nonverbal communication skills. In R. Rosenthal (Ed.), *Quantitative assessment of research domains* (*New directions for methodology of social and behavioral science,* No. 5) (pp. 63–77). San Francisco, CA: Jossey-Bass.

Halpern, D. F. (1992). *Sex differences in cognitive abilities* (2nd ed.). Hillsdale, NJ: Erlbaum.

Hammersley, M. (1996). The relationship between qualitative and quantitative research: Paradigm loyalty versus methodological eclecticism. In J. T. E. Richardson (Ed.), *Handbook of qualitative research methods for psychology and the social sciences* (pp. 159–174). Leicester, U.K.: BPS Books.

Hays, W. L. (1963). *Statistics.* New York: Holt, Rinehart, & Winston.

Hedges, L. V. (1981). Distribution theory for Glass's estimator of effect size and related parameters. *Journal of Educational Statistics, 6,* 107–128.

Hedges, L. V. (1982). Fitting continuous models to effect size data. *Journal of Educational Statistics, 7,* 245–270.

Hedges, L. V., & Becker, B. J. (1986). Statistical methods in the meta-analysis of research on gender differences. In J. S. Hyde & M. C. Linn (Eds.), *The psychology of gender: Advances through meta-analysis* (pp. 14–50). Baltimore, MD: Johns Hopkins University Press.

Hedges, L. V., & Olkin, I. (1985). *Statistical methods for meta-analysis.* Orlando, FL: Academic Press.

Henwood, K. L. (1996). Qualitative inquiry: Perspectives, methods and psychology. In J. T. E. Richardson (Ed.), *Handbook of qualitative research methods for psychology and the social sciences* (pp. 25–40). Leicester, U.K.: BPS Books.

Heron, J. (1981). Philosophical basis for a new paradigm. In P. Reason & J. Rowan (Eds.), *Human inquiry: A sourcebook of new paradigm research* (pp. 19–35). Chichester, U.K.: Wiley.

Humphreys, L. G. (1980). The statistics of failure to replicate: A comment on Buriel's (1978) conclusions. *Journal of Educational Psychology, 72,* 71–75.

Hyde, J. S. (1981). How large are cognitive gender differences? A meta-analysis using ω^2 and d. *American Psychologist, 36,* 892–901.

Hyde, J. S., Fennema, E., & Lamon, S. J. (1990). Gender differences in mathematics performance: A meta-analysis. *Psychological Bulletin, 107,* 139–155.

Hyde, J. S., & Linn, M. C. (Eds.). (1986). *The psychology of gender: Advances through meta-analysis.* Baltimore, MD: Johns Hopkins University Press.

Hyde, J. S., & Linn, M. C. (1988). Gender differences in verbal ability: A meta-analysis. *Psychological Bulletin, 104,* 53–69.

Hyde, J. S., & Plant, E. A. (1995). Magnitude of psychological gender differences: Another side to the story. *American Psychologist, 50,* 159–161.

Jacklin, C. N., Maccoby, E. E. (1972). *Sex differences in intellectual abilities: A reassessment and a look at some new explanations.* Paper presented at the annual meeting of the American Educational Research Association, Chicago.

Kruglanski, A. W. (1973). Much ado about the "volunteer artifacts." *Journal of Personality and Social Psychology, 28,* 348–354.

Lave, J. (1988). *Cognition in practice.* Hillsdale, NJ: Erlbaum.

Lemaire, P., Abdi, H., & Fayol, M. (1996). The role of working memory resources in simple cognitive arithmetic. *European Journal of Cognitive Psychology, 8,* 73–103.

Lepper, M. R. (1995). Theory by the numbers? Some concerns about meta-analysis as a theoretical tool. *Applied Cognitive Psychology, 9,* 411–422.

Light, R. J., & Pillemer, D. B. (1984). *Summing up: The science of reviewing research.* Cambridge, MA: Harvard University Press.

Linn, M. C., & Petersen, A. C. (1985). Emergence and characterization of sex differences in spatial ability: A meta-analysis. *Child Development, 56,* 1479–1498.

Linn, M. C., & Petersen, A. C. (1986). A meta-analysis of gender differences in spatial ability: Implications for mathematics and science achievement. In J. S. Hyde & M. C. Linn (Eds.), *The psychology of gender: Advances through meta-analysis* (pp. 67–101). Baltimore, MD: Johns Hopkins University Press.

Lipsey, M. W., & Wilson, D. B. (1993). The efficacy of psychological, educational, and behavioral treatment: Confirmation from meta-analysis. *American Psychologist, 48,* 1181–1209.

Maccoby, E. E., & Jacklin, C. N. (1974). *The psychology of sex differences.* Stanford, CA: Stanford University Press.

Masters, M. S., & Sanders, B. (1993). Is the gender difference in mental rotation disappearing? *Behavior Genetics, 23,* 337–341.

McGuinness, D. (1980). Strategies, demands, and lateralized sex differences. *Behavioral and Brain Sciences, 3,* 244.

McGuire, J., Bates, G. W., Dretzke, B. J., McGivern, J. E., Rembold, K. L., Seabold, D. R., Turpin, B. M., & Levin, J. R. (1985). Methodological quality as a component of meta-analysis. *Educational Psychologist, 20,* 1–5.

Metzler, J., & Shepard, R. N. (1974). Transformational studies of the internal representation of three-dimensional objects. In R. L. Solso (Ed.), *Theories in cognitive psychology: The Loyola symposium* (pp. 147–201). Potomac, MD: Erlbaum.

Mullen, B. (1989). *Advanced BASIC meta-analysis.* Hillsdale, NJ: Erlbaum.

Pearson, K. (1905). *Mathematical contributions to the theory of evolution: XIV. On the general theory of skew correlation and non-linear regression* (Drapers' Company Research Memoirs, Biometric Series II). London: Dulau.

Phillips, P. (1996, March 12). From the sharp end. *Guardian Education,* p. 1.

Plomin, R., & Foch, T. T. (1981). Sex differences and individual differences. *Child Development, 52,* 383–385.

Richardson, J. T. E. (1975a). Differential rates of cerebral maturation between sexes. *Nature, 254,* 140.

Richardson, J. T. E. (1975b). Statistical analysis of experiments investigating stimulus attributes. *British Journal of Mathematical and Statistical Psychology, 1975, 28,* 235–236.

Richardson, J. T. E. (1994). Gender differences in mental rotation. *Perceptual and Motor Skills, 78,* 435–448.

Richardson, J. T. E. (1996). Measures of effect size. *Behavior Research Methods, Instruments, and Computers, 28,* 12–22.

Rosenthal, R. (1969). Interpersonal expectations: Effects of the experimenter's hypothesis. In R. Rosenthal & R. L. Rosnow (Eds.), *Artifact in behavioral research* (pp. 181–277). New York: Academic Press.

Rosenthal, R. (1976). *Experimenter effects in behavioral research* (enlarged ed.). New York: Irvington.

Rosenthal, R. (1978). Combining results of independent studies. *Psychological Bulletin, 85,* 185–193.

Rosenthal, R. (1979). The "file drawer problem" and tolerance for null results. *Psychological Bulletin, 86,* 638–640.

Rosenthal, R. (1984). *Meta-analytic procedures for social research.* Beverly Hills, CA: Sage.

Rosenthal, R., & Rosnow, R. L. (1969). The volunteer subject. In R. Rosenthal & R. L. Rosnow (Eds.), *Artifact in behavioral research* (pp. 59–118). New York: Academic Press.

Rosenthal, R., & Rubin, D. B. (1978). Interpersonal expectancy effects: The first 345 studies. *Brain and Behavioral Sciences, 3,* 377–386.

Rosenthal, R., & Rubin, D. B. (1982). Further meta-analytic procedures for assessing cognitive gender differences. *Journal of Educational Psychology, 74,* 708–712.

Rowan, J. (1981). A dialectical paradigm for research. In P. Reason & J. Rowan (Eds.), *Human inquiry: A sourcebook of new paradigm research* (pp. 93–112). Chichester, U.K.: Wiley.

Sadker, M., & Sadker, D. (1994). *Failing at fairness: How America's schools cheat girls.* New York: Scribner's.

Scribner, S. (1984). Studying working intelligence. In B. Rogoff & J. Lave (Eds.), *Everyday cognition* (pp. 9–40). Cambridge, MA: Harvard University Press.

Shaywitz, S. E., Shaywitz, B. A., Fletcher, J. M., & Escobar, M. D. (1990). Prevalence of reading disability in boys and girls: Results of the Connecticut Longitudinal Study. *Journal of the American Medical Association, 264,* 998–1002.

Shepard, R. N., & Cooper, L. A. (1982). *Mental images and their transformations.* Cambridge, MA: MIT Press.

Silverman, I. (1977). *The human subject in the psychological laboratory.* New York: Pergamon Press.

Taylor, D. C. (1969). Differential rates of cerebral maturation between sexes and between hemispheres: Evidence from epilepsy. *Lancet, 2,* 140–142.

Taylor, D. C., & Ounsted, C. (1972). The nature of gender differences explored through ontogenetic analyses of sex ratios in disease. In C. Ounsted & D. C. Taylor (Eds.), *Gender differences: Their ontogeny and significance* (pp. 215–240). Edinburgh: Churchill Livingstone.

Vandenberg, S. G., & Kuse, A. R. (1978). Mental rotations, a group test of three-dimensional spatial visualization. *Perceptual and Motor Skills, 47,* 599–604.

Vogel, S. A. (1990). Gender differences in intelligence, language, visual-motor abilities, and academic achievement in students with learning disabilities: A review of the literature. *Journal of Learning Disabilities, 23,* 44–52.

Voyer, D., Voyer, S., & Bryden, M. P. (1995). Magnitude of sex differences in spatial abilities: A meta-analysis and consideration of critical variables. *Psychological Bulletin, 117,* 250–270.

White, K. R. (1982). The relation between socioeconomic status and academic achievement. *Psychological Bulletin, 91,* 461–481.

Wilcox, R. R. (1987). New designs in analysis of variance. *Annual Review of Psychology, 38,* 29–60.

Winer, B. J., Brown, D. R., & Michels, K. M. (1991). *Statistical principles in experimental design* (3rd ed.). New York: McGraw-Hill.

Yuille, J. C. (1986). The futility of a purely experimental psychology of cognition: Imagery as a case study. In D. F. Marks (Ed.), *Theories of image formation* (pp. 197–224). New York: Brandon House.

Author Index

Subject Index